Dictionary of STATISTICS and METHODOLOGY

A Nontechnical Guide for the Social Sciences

W. PAUL VOGT

SAGE Publications
International Educational and Professional Publisher
Newbury Park London New Delhi

For information address:

SAGE Publications, Inc.
2455 Teller Road
Newbury Park, California 91320

SAGE Publications Ltd.
6 Bonhill Street
London EC2A 4PU
United Kingdom

SAGE Publications India Pvt. Ltd.
M-32 Market
Greater Kailash I
New Delhi 110 048 India

Printed in the United States of America

Library of Congress Cataloging-in-Publication Data

Vogt, W. Paul.
Dictionary of statistics and methodology: a nontechnical guide for the social sciences / W. Paul Vogt.
p. cm.
Includes bibliographical references.
ISBN 0-8039-5276-7.—ISBN 0-8039-5277-5 (pbk.)
1. Social sciences—Statistical methods—Dictionaries. 2. Social sciences—Methodology—Dictionaries. I. Title.
HA17.V64 1993
300′.1′5195—dc20 93-728

93 94 95 96 10 9 8 7 6 5 4 3 2 1

Sage Production Editor: Tara S. Mead

Contents

List of Illustrations

Preface

Almost all research studies contain technical terms that nonspecialists do not know and, a much greater problem, that they cannot easily look up. What is needed to lower the jargon barrier between readers and research is a handy reference work where students and others can find quick definitions of a wide variety of statistical and methodological terms. I've tried to satisfy that need in this dictionary.

Acknowledgments

As I worked on the book, I got a great deal of help. By telling me what they didn't understand, my students provided many insights about what to include. At all stages of the writing and editing, Elaine Rosenthal Vogt struggled hard to keep me accurate and insisted that I avoid the murky prose I've so often criticized in others. Three Sage reviewers—Lawrence Mohr, Virginia Clark, and Patricia Haden—provided many highly valuable suggestions and corrections. By her unflagging enthusiasm for the project, Sage's statistics editor, C. Deborah Laughton, helped keep my nose to the computer screen. All of these people deserve credit for what strengths the dictionary has; of course, I deserve the blame for its remaining weaknesses.

Introduction

This dictionary gives nontechnical definitions of statistical and methodological terms used in the social and behavioral sciences. Special attention is paid to terms that most often prevent educated general readers from understanding journal articles and books in sociology, psychology, and political science—and in applied fields that build on those disciplines, such as education, policy studies, and administrative science. The dictionary provides definitions that will enable readers to get through a difficult article or passage. But it does not, for the most part, directly explain how to do research or how to compute the statistics briefly described.

The emphasis throughout is thus much more on concepts than calculations. Because the concepts are often complicated, readers may find that a definition makes sense only after it has been illustrated by an example. That is why the examples are sometimes longer than the definitions.

Quite a few terms are included that might not meet some strict definitions of "methodological" or "statistical"—for instance, "learning curve," "opportunity costs," "SPSS," and "zero-sum game." But they, and several others like them, are defined because they meet the main criteria for inclusion: They pop up fairly often, in more than one discipline, and many people are unsure about what they mean.

Verbal definitions are used to the exclusion of algebraic definitions, even when mathematical symbols and formulas would be more efficient—at least for users already well familiar with statistics and social science methods. The general approach has been to treat the early stages of learning statistics more like studying a language than like learning a branch of mathematics.

When learning any language, beginners will sometimes be frustrated because they have to look up words in the definition of the term they just looked up. By writing the definitions in ordinary English whenever possible, I have tried to keep this unavoidable annoyance to a minimum. But it *is* unavoidable, and it is harder to avoid in a dictionary of technical terms than in a dictionary of a natural language—and there is no escape when defining advanced concepts that are built upon several more basic concepts. This is why many of the terms in this dictionary use other methodological or statistical terms in their definitions. Those terms, also defined in the dictionary, are indicated by an asterisk (*).

As in any language, in statistics and methodology, more than one word may be used to express the same idea. In such cases, I have defined fully what I believe to be the more common term and briefly defined and cross-referenced the others. But I have not tried to stipulate the "proper" labels for concepts that appear under more than one name; nor have I specified the "correct" use of terms that are used in different ways. In short, I have attempted to be inclusive and descriptive, not exclusive and prescriptive. The goal throughout has been to provide a comprehensive dictionary of terms that will increase access to works in the social and behavioral sciences.

How to Use This Dictionary

1. Entries are in alphabetical order, using the letter-by-letter (not word-by-word) method. This means that, when looking up terms and expressions made up of more than one word, you should ignore spaces and hyphens between words. For example, "F," "*F* distribution," and "*F* ratio" are separated by several pages, not grouped together as they would be using the word-by-word method. The only exception to the letter-by-letter rule is entries with a comma, such as "Association, Measure of."

2. In terms containing numbers, the numbers are spelled out and alphabetized accordingly. For example, to find "2 × 2 design," look under "Two-by-Two Design."

3. Greek letters are anglicized, spelled out, and alphabetized accordingly. Consult the table "The Greek Alphabet" on the inside front cover for equivalents. For example, to find α, you would look under "alpha."

4. For other symbols, consult the table "Frequently Used Symbols" on the inside front cover, get the equivalent in words, and look up the words in the ordinary way. For example, to find $| \ |$, you would look in the table to learn that it meant "absolute value" and then consult that entry in the alphabetical listing.

5. When an entry contains other terms defined in this dictionary, they are indicated by an asterisk (*), especially those terms most likely to be helpful for reading that particular entry.

6. If a term has more than one meaning, definitions are separated by letters (a), (b), and so on, with the more common definitions usually coming first.

Abscissa The horizontal axis (or x axis) on a graph.

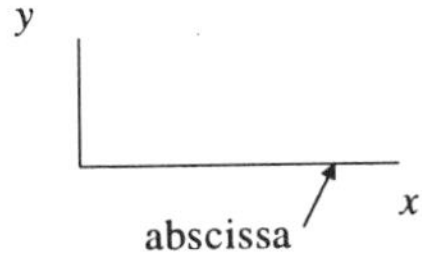

Absolute Frequency The actual number of times a particular value occurs in a *distribution as opposed to its *relative frequency or the *proportion of times it occurs.

Absolute Value (of a Number) The value of a number regardless of its sign (positive or negative).

For example, the absolute value of +8 and –8 is the same, 8. Symbolized: $|8|$. (The absolute value is the positive value, because a number without a sign is positive.)

Absolute Zero Point A value on a scale indicating that none of the variable being measured is present.

Abstraction A cognitive process in which common elements in diverse events or objects are identified and pulled out of their context (abstracted) to study them. Doing this makes it possible to classify and analyze *data that could not otherwise be studied together. Abstraction increases a researcher's ability to generalize but at the cost of some of the empirical details of each case.

For example, say you wanted to do a comparative study of the relationship between democracy and economic equality in modern nations. You might construct a "Democracy Index" (made up of some measures of freedom of the press, open elections, independent judiciary, and so on) and an "Equality Index" (made up of measures of the distribution of income, wealth, employment opportunities, and so on). You could then rank the nations using the two indexes and compute a *correlation coefficient between nations' ranks on one index and their ranks on the other. On the basis of this work, you might be able to come to conclusions about whether there was a general relationship between economic equality and democracy.

Only by using such abstractions as your democracy and equality indexes can you work at a *level of generality high enough to make comparisons. To the extent that you focused on the specific details of the economic and political situations in each country, it would be more difficult to make comparisons. And, conversely, the more you tried to make comparisons, the more difficult it would be to understand the concrete realities of the economic and political life of each nation.

Acceptance Error Another term for *beta error, or Type II Error.

Accidental Error Error in measurement that cannot be predicted or controlled because the researcher is ignorant of its cause(s). Compare *bias, *random error.

Accidental Sample A sample gathered haphazardly, for example, by interviewing the first 100 people you ran into on the street who were willing to talk to you. An accidental sample is *not* a *random sample. The main disadvantage of an accidental sample is that the researcher has no way of knowing what the *population might be. See *convenience sample, *probability sample.

Acquiescent Response Style The supposed tendency of some subjects, quite apart from what they actually believe, to be agreeable out of politeness and say "yes" to all statements in an interview or on a questionnaire. Compare *social desirability bias.

Today, this worry about the accuracy of responses is smaller than it once was. There is not a great deal of evidence that such yea-saying is very common, no more common, at any rate, than a nay-saying "quarrelsome response style." Also, as a matter of routine good practice, most question writers now compose their *scales and *indexes in such a way that persons would have to answer questions in opposite ways to convey their beliefs—for example:

"abortion should be legal," agree/disagree? "abortion should be illegal," agree/disagree?

Action Research A type of *applied research designed to find the most effective way to bring about a desired social change. Compare *basic research, *evaluation research.

Active Variable An experimental or manipulated *independent variable as opposed to one over which the researcher exerts no control. Compare *attribute variable, *background variable.

AD Abbreviation for the *average deviation.

Additive Said of a relation in which the effects of the *independent variables on a *dependent variable can simply be added together to find their total effect. Contrast *interaction effect.

Ad Hoc Literally, Latin for "for this." Said of an explanation or a solution improvised for a specific purpose.

Ad Infinitum Latin for "continuing without end."

Adjusted R^2 An *R^2 (R-squared) adjusted to give a truer (smaller) estimate of how much the *independent variables in a *regression analysis explain the *dependent variable. The adjustment is made by taking into account the number of independent variables. The adjusted R^2 is a measure of *strength of association. Also called "epsilon-squared." Compare *coefficient of determination, *omega-squared.

Admissible Hypothesis A hypothesis that is open to consideration because it is not mathematically or logically self-contradictory or otherwise impossible.

Age Effects Effects attributable to subjects' ages, as when adults in their sixties have different values than those in their thirties. Compare *maturation effects.

Age effects are often difficult to distinguish from *period effects (people in the 1960s had different values than those in the 1990s) and *cohort effects, because people in their thirties in the 1960s were in their sixties in the 1990s!

Aggregate A group of persons, or other *units of analysis, that have certain traits or characteristics in common without necessarily having any direct social connection with one another. Also called "aggregation." Compare *holism, *disaggregate.

For example, "all female physicians" is an aggregate; so is "all European cities with populations over 20,000." Gross National Income is an aggregation of data about individual incomes.

Aggregate Data Information about *aggregates or groups such as races, social classes, or nations. Sometimes contrasted with *micro-data.

Agreement Coefficient A measure of the relation of a single item on a *scale or an *index to the rest of a scale or index; also the similarity of one rating to another.

Ahistorical Said of an interpretation, theory, or point of view that ignores the influence of the past on the present and/or that assumes time is an unimportant variable.

AI *Artificial intelligence.

Aleatory Relating to chance, luck, randomness, or uncertainty. A word sometimes used in *probability theory. For example, "aleatory variable" means *random variable.

Algorithm (a) A set of clearly defined rules for solving a problem in a limited number of steps. (b) A formula. (c) Used broadly in methodological writing to mean any step-by-step procedure to solve a problem. Named after the ninth-century Arab mathematician al-Khwarizmi.

Alienation, Coefficient of (a) A measure of the *lack* of relationship between two *variables (sometimes symbolized: k). When the coefficient of alienation is high, it is hard to make predictions about one variable by knowing the value of another. The stronger the correlation between two variables, the weaker the coefficient of alienation will be. (b) A measure of how well a *model fits actual data. The lower the coefficient, the better the fit.

In either case, the coefficient of alienation is equal to the square root of the coefficient of *nondetermination, that is, to the square root of $(1 - r^2)$. Compare coefficient of *determination.

Alpha (a) Usually called *Cronbach's alpha to distinguish it from the alpha in *alpha level. It is a measure of internal *reliability of the items in an *index. This (Cronbach's) alpha ranges from 0 to 1.0 and indicates how much the items in an index are measuring the same thing. (b) Symbol for the *intercept in a *regression equation. (c) Symbol for the *odds ratio.

Alpha Error An error made by rejecting a true *null hypothesis (such as claiming that a relationship exists when it does not). Also called *Type I Error. See *beta error, *hypothesis testing.

Alpha Level (a) The chance a researcher is willing to take of committing an *alpha error or *Type I Error, that is, of rejecting a *null hypothesis that is true. (b) The probability that a Type I Error (wrongly rejecting the null hypothesis) has been committed.

The smaller the alpha level, the more significant the finding because the smaller the chance that the finding is due to chance alone. Thus an alpha level of .01 is a more difficult criterion to satisfy than a level of .05. Also called *level of (statistical) significance. See **p* value, *probability value, *probability level.

Alphanumeric Variable A variable that can be expressed as a letter, number, other symbol, or some combination of letters, numbers, and symbols.

Alternative Hypothesis In *hypothesis testing, any hypothesis alternative to the one being tested, usually the opposite of the *null hypothesis. Also called the *research hypothesis. Rejecting the null hypothesis shows that the alternative (or research) hypothesis *may* be true. Symbolized: H_1 or H_a.

For example, researchers conducting a study of the relation between teenage drug use and teenage suicide would probably use a null hypothesis something like this one: "There is no difference between the suicide rates of teenagers who use drugs and those who do not." The alternative hypotheses might be these: "Drug use by teenagers increases their likelihood of committing suicide," and "drug use by teenagers decreases their likelihood of committing suicide." Finding evidence that allowed the rejection of the null hypothesis (that there was no difference) would increase the researchers' confidence in the *probability* that one of the alternative hypotheses was true.

Alternative Methodologies A catchall term referring to any *nonexperimental and/or nonquantitative research methods.

Anachronism An error made by affirming something that is chronologically impossible, such as by attributing *cause to something that followed the effect.

For example, to claim that Merton's writings influenced Durkheim's would be an anachronistic mistake; it is impossible because Durkheim died long before Merton published anything.

Analog (also spelled: analogue) Said of data or computers that use a system of representation that is physically *analogous* to the thing being represented. Compare *digital.

For example, a thermometer can use height of a column of mercury to indicate heat; the higher the column, the higher the temperature. Or, analog watches use the physical movement of hour and minute hands to represent the passing of time; the more the hands have moved, the more time has passed.

Analysis (a) The separation of a whole into its constituent parts so as to study them. (b) The study of the elements of a whole and their relationships. (c) Loosely, but perhaps most commonly, any rigorous study of anything. Compare *synthesis.

Analysis of Covariance (ANCOVA) An extension of *ANOVA that provides a way of statistically eliminating the (*linear) effects of variables one does not want to examine in a study. These *extraneous variables are called *covariates, or control variables. (Covariates should be measured on an *interval or *ratio scale.) ANCOVA allows you to remove covariates from the list of possible explanations of variance in the *dependent variable. ANCOVA does this by using *statistical* techniques (such as *regression to *partial out the effects of covariates) rather than direct experimental methods to control extraneous variables. Compare *multiple regression analysis. Note: Be careful not to confuse ANCOVA with *analysis of covariance *structures.*

ANCOVA is used in experimental studies when researchers want to remove the effects of some *antecedent variable. It is also used in *nonexperimental research, such as surveys of nonrandom samples, or in *quasi-experiments when subjects cannot be assigned randomly to *control and *experimental groups. Although fairly common, the use of ANCOVA for *nonexperimental research is highly controversial.

Analysis of Covariance Structures A sophisticated statistical method for testing *causal models. It combines the techniques of *factor analysis and *multiple regression analysis thus allowing researchers to study the effects of *latent variables on each other. Analyses are frequently done with the *LISREL computer program—so frequently that the software brand name is sometimes used to identify the analytical techniques it can perform.

A latent variable is one that cannot be observed directly. It is a *construct, that is, a theoretical entity inferred from a pattern of relations (a *structure) among observable variables. Analysis of covariance structures can be used to test complex causal models in which the independent variable and the dependent variable are latent. See *confirmatory factor analysis. Compare *canonical correlation analysis.

For example, take the apparently simple statement: The more intelligent a person is, the more likely he or she is to be successful. Both intelligence and success are constructs, latent variables that are constructed out of observations. To begin to study the relationship between intelligence and success, one might sketch in the following kind of *path diagram. (A full LISREL path diagram would be much more complex and would include a detailed notation system.) Boxes stand for observed variables; those on the left are measurable aspects of intelligence; those on the right, measurable components of success. Circles represent the latent variables.

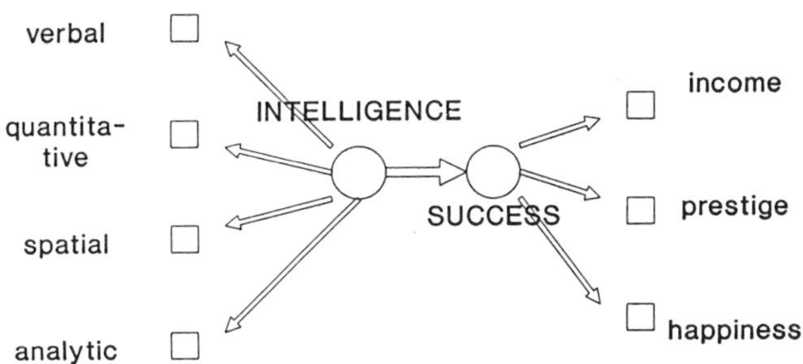

Analysis of Covariance Structures

Analysis of Variance (ANOVA) A test of the *statistical significance of the differences among the *mean scores of two or more groups on one or more *variables or *factors. It is an extension of the **t* test, which can only handle two groups, to a larger number of groups. More specifically, it is used for assessing the statistical significance of the relationship between *categorical *independent variables and a *continuous *dependent variable. The procedure in ANOVA involves computing a ratio (**F* ratio) of the *variance within the groups (*error variance) to the variance between the groups (*explained variance).

Note that the name "analysis of *variance*" is misleading because, strictly speaking, ANOVA involves analyzing *sums of squares, not variances. Note also that the following example is greatly simplified, especially because it does not illustrate a major advantage of ANOVA, which is that you can test several *factors in the same experiment. See *factorial experiments.

Suppose, for example, that a professor wanted to try different teaching methods. He randomly assigned members of his class of 30 students into three groups of 10 students each. All three groups were given the same required readings, but class time was spent differently in each. Group 1 ("Discuss") spent class time in directed discussions of the assigned readings. Group 2 ("No Class") was excused from any obligations to attend classes for the first half of the semester, but they were given additional text materials they could use to help them understand the assigned readings. Group 3 ("Lecture") was instructed using the professor's ordinary lecture methods. The students' scores on the mid-term examination are listed in Table 1. Students in the three groups obviously got different average scores. Of course, the professor wanted to know whether the differences were statistically significant, that is, whether they were bigger than would be likely due to chance alone. To find out, he entered the information from Table 1 into his computer and conducted an analysis of variance. As Table 2 shows, the results were highly statistically significant (at the $p < .001$ level). This means the odds are less than 1,000 to 1 that differences in the groups' average scores were just a fluke; the teaching methods almost certainly made a difference.

Table 1 Students' Mid-Term Scores, by Method of Instruction

Group 1 *Discuss*	*Group 2* *No Class*	*Group 3* *Lecture*	
94	78	87	
92	76	85	
91	72	84	
89	71	84	
88	68	81	
88	68	80	
86	67	80	
86	66	79	
83	64	72	
83	60	68	
880	690	800	(Totals)
88	69	80	(Means)

Table 2 ANOVA Summary Table: Three Teaching Methods

Source	*SS*	*df*	*MS*	*F*
Between groups	1820	2	910.00	35.10*
Within groups	700	27	25.93	
Total	2520	29		

*$p < .001$.

How to Read an ANOVA Summary Table "Source" means source of the variance. "Between groups" is explained variance, that is, explained by the treatments the different groups received. "Within groups" is unexplained or error variance, because differences among individuals within a group cannot be explained by differences in the treatments the groups received. "SS" is *sum of squares (total of squared *deviation scores). "Degrees of freedom" is abbreviated to "df." "MS" stands for mean squares, which are calculated by dividing the SS by the df. "*F*" is the *F* ratio, which is statistically significant at the .001 level ($p < .001$).

ANCOVA *Analysis of covariance.

Anecdotal Evidence Evidence, often in story form, derived from casual, unsystematic, and/or uncontrolled observation. Usually used to dismiss someone's evidence, as in "mere anecdotal evidence." Compare *case study.

ANOVA *Analysis of variance.

Antecedent (a) A condition that precedes another and is thought to influence or to cause it. (b) The first term in a ratio. For example, in the ratio 14:1, 14 is the antecedent; 1 is the *consequent.

Antecedent Variable A variable that comes earlier in an explanation or in a chain of causal links—as in a *path analysis.

For example, if the dependent variable were occupation at age 50, education level would usually be an antecedent variable, and place of birth would be a variable antecedent to education.

Antilog See *logarithm.

Antimode The least common score or value in a distribution. Compare *mode.

A Posteriori Literally, Latin for "from what comes after"; said of conclusions reached by reasoning from observed facts (*after* observation) or of research that proceeds in an *inductive way. Loosely, *empirical. Compare *a priori.

A Posteriori Comparison A comparison that a researcher decides to make *after* the data have been collected and studied. This is usually done because the results have suggested a new way to approach the data. Compare *a priori comparison, *post hoc comparison.

Applications Software Computer programs designed for specific purposes (applications) such as word processing or accounting.

Applied Research Research undertaken with the intention of applying the results to some specific problem, such as studying the effects of different methods of law enforcement on crime rates. One of the biggest differences between applied and *basic research is that in applied work the research questions are most often determined, not by researchers, but by policymakers or others who want help. Types of applied research include *evaluation research and *action research.

Approximation Error Another term for *rounding error.

A Priori Literally, Latin for "from what comes before." (a) Used to describe preexisting (prior) conditions among groups of subjects, especially potential *confounding variables. (b) Said of conclusions reached on the basis of reasoning from self-evident propositions—without or before examining facts—or of research that proceeds in a *deductive way. Loosely, theoretical. Compare *a posteriori.

The expression is often used to describe a conclusion for which someone believes there is no empirical evidence, as in "one conclusion is as likely to be true as the other, a priori, which is why we need to gather more data to resolve the question."

A Priori Comparison A comparison that a researcher decides to make before (*prior* to) performing the experiment or gathering the data. Compare *a posteriori comparison. See *planned comparison.

A Priori Probability Another term for *theoretical probability.

Aptitude-Treatment Interaction A *trait-treatment interaction research design in which the trait is aptitude.

Archive (often used in the plural) (a) A place where public records or other kinds of information are stored. (b) The information thus stored.

*Data base archives (such as the *General Social Survey) are becoming increasingly important in social and behavioral research.

Area Sample A kind of *cluster sample in which the clusters are selected on the basis of geographic areas. Area samples use geography to define the *sampling frame from which the sample is then drawn.

For example, say you want to survey residents of California about their *attitudes concerning property taxes. You do not have a list of all California residents from which to draw a sample. You could divide the state into "areas" (such as *census tracts) and take a *random sample of those areas. Then, within each of the areas you selected, you could survey all (or a sample) of the residents about their attitudes on property taxes.

ARIMA Autoregressive Integrated Moving Average. A complex set of statistical techniques for *time-series analysis that combines (integrates) *autoregressive analysis procedures with those of *moving averages.

Using ARIMA models, the researcher is able to construct *trend lines that take into account both the *systematic error (autocorrelation) and the unsystematic or *random error (or *noise).

Well known examples of findings based on this sort of work are the seasonally adjusted figures for unemployment and consumer spending that are often featured in the news.

Arithmetic Mean See *mean.

Array An ordered display of a set of observations, measurements, or statistics—such as a *frequency distribution.

For example, the observed grade point averages 3.2, 2.2, 3.1, 3.6, 2.8 in *ascending order give the array {2.2, 2.8, 3.1, 3.2, 3.6}.

Artifact An artificial result. More specifically, a mistaken or *biased result produced by the measuring instrument rather than the phenomenon being studied; or, something the researcher created by the way he or she gathered or analyzed the *data, not a condition present in the *subjects. Examples include *halo effect, *Hawthorne effect, *John Henry effect, *regression artifact. See *self-fulfilling prophecy.

Artificial Intelligence (AI) That branch of computer science that studies ways of getting computers to simulate human thought.

Ascending Order Said of data arranged so that each item in a series is higher than (ascends) the previous items. Arranging data in that way can be an important step on the way to constructing a *frequency distribution or calculating a *rank-order correlation. Compare *descending order.

ASCII (rhymes with "passkey") American Standard Code for Information Interchange. This computer character set is used as a sort of Esperanto for *software. It enables a user of one software *program (e.g., a word processor) to translate what he or she has written into a language that can be understood by another software program. ASCII is widely used to transfer statistical data files from one computer or program to another.

Association, Measure of Any *statistic that shows (in a single number) the degree of relationship between two *variables. Having a measure of association may enable you to estimate (or predict) the value of one variable when you know the value of another variable.

Examples of measures of association include *correlation coefficients, *lambda, and *gamma. While there is no essential difference between the latter two measures of association and correlation coefficients, common usage often separates them. Thus gamma and lambda are usually called measures of association; *Spearman's rho and *Pearson's product-moment statistic are usually called correlation coefficients.

Note that there can be considerable controversy about which measures of association are best to use for various purposes and kinds of data.

Association, Statistical (a) A relationship between two or more *variables that can be described statistically. (b) Any of several statistical techniques (such as *correlations and *regression analysis) that can be used to describe the degree to which differences in one variable are accompanied by (associated with) corresponding differences in another variable.

Association, Test of Another term for *test statistic. Not to be confused with a *measure* of association, which indicates the size of the relation between two variables. By contrast, a *test* of association gives the probability that an association of a given size could have occurred by chance, that is, whether it is *statistically significant.

Assumption A statement that is presumed to be true, often only temporarily or for a specific purpose. Compare *axiom, *hypothesis, *theory.

For example, researchers might make the assumption that there is no difference in the innate verbal ability of men and women so that they could use differences in grades in college-level literature courses to test a theory that college professors discriminate on the basis of sex.

Most statistical techniques, such as *regression analysis and *ANOVA, require that certain assumptions (e.g., *homoscedasticity) be made about the data. Serious violations of the assumptions can make the results misleading or meaningless.

Asymmetric Measure A *measure of association that has a different value depending on which *variable is *dependent and which is *independent. Compare *symmetric measure.

*Lambda and *Somers's d are examples of asymmetric measures of association.

Asymmetry Said of a *distribution that is *skewed or unbalanced.

Asymptote (a) A theoretical limit that a curve approaches but never reaches. (b) Any theoretical outer limit; see *limit. (c) A leveling off of performance quality or efficiency; see *learning curve.

Asymptotic Said of a curve that gets ever closer to a line but never touches it. For example, the *tails of a *normal curve are asymptotic to the x axis.

Attenuation A reduction in a *measure of association caused by measurement errors. Compare *artifact.

Attitude A positive or negative evaluation of and disposition toward persons, groups, policies, or other objects of attention. Attitudes are learned and relatively persistent. See *Bogardus Social Distance Scale.

Attitude Scale A series of questions designed to measure the strength of attitudes and beliefs. A common format for such measures is a *Likert scale. Compare *Guttman scale, *index.

Attribute A *qualitative variable or trait, often used in contrast with a *quantitative variable or trait. This is the same basic distinction as that between *categorical (attribute) and *continuous (quantitative) variables. Compare *attribute variable.

For example, a person's sex is an attribute (or qualitative, categorical variable), while the number of square feet in his or her living room is a quantitative, continuous variable.

Attribute Variable A variable that is a characteristic or trait of a subject, which therefore researchers cannot manipulate but can only measure.

For example, in a study of the effects of vitamins on health, researchers could vary (manipulate) the amount and kind of vitamins subjects received, but they could not manipulate, only measure, their gender and ethnicity.

Attrition Losing subjects over the course of the research project. Also called "mortality." Attrition may be a source of *bias if the subjects who are lost make the *sample less *representative of the *population.

For example, attrition is a common problem in *panel studies in which the same subjects are studied at two or more times. Attrition may occur, for instance, when subjects move and cannot be located. If many subjects are lost to the study and they are in some way unusual in comparison with the remaining subjects, it may be hard to draw valid conclusions about what happened to the group over time.

The U.S. census has a built-in problem with attrition. It tries to count all people in the country, but the process takes several months, during which time thousands of people die. Because the death rate of the elderly is higher than the average rate, they will be overrepresented in the final count—unless adjustments are made.

Autochthonous Variability Change that comes from influences within a causal system as opposed to from outside it. Compare *endogenous and *exogenous variables.

Autocorrelation Correlation between members of a series of observations, such as weekly oil prices or interest rates. More technically, autocorrelation occurs when *residual error terms from observations of the same variable at different times are correlated. Such correlations can raise several kinds of interpretive problems. In *regression analysis of *time-series data, for example, autocorrelation may arise from the tendency of effects to persist over time, even when *independent variables change. In regression analysis, autocorrelation can be reduced by using *generalized rather than *ordinary least squares to compute the *regression equation. Also called "serial correlation." See *multicollinearity, *ARIMA.

For example, declining interest rates usually lead people to buy more on credit; but lower interest rates do not always produce the expected effect, at least in the short run, and certainly not immediately. People's credit purchases (dependent variable) may continue unchanged even when economic conditions (independent variables) that "ought" to increase them have changed. If there are autocorrelations between credit purchases at week 1 and week 2, and week 2 and week 3, and so on, this will obscure any long-term relation between interest rates and credit purchases.

Autoregressive Said of a series of observations in which the value of each depends (at least in part) on the value of one or more of the immediately preceding observations. Called autoregressive because one explains later observations by earlier ones, that is, one **regresses* later values *on* earlier values. See *autocorrelation, *Markov chain.

Average See *mean.

Average Deviation (AD) A measure of the *variation in a group of scores. It is calculated by taking the *mean or average of the *absolute values of the *deviation scores (i.e., the differences between the scores and their mean). The larger the average deviation, the greater the *spread of scores in a group of scores. The AD is less commonly used as a measure of variation than are the *variance and the *standard deviation. Also called "mean deviation."

Axiom A maxim or statement that is considered so accurate or self-evident that it is widely accepted as a foundation on which arguments can be built or a truth from which other truths can be deduced. Compare *assumption, *postulate.

In contrast to mathematics, there are few genuine axioms in the social and behavioral sciences. Two statements that might qualify as axioms (at least for some researchers) are as follows: (1) Out-group hostility breeds in-group solidarity; (2) individuals seek to maximize pleasure and minimize pain.

Axis A vertical or a horizontal line used to construct a *graph. See *abscissa (*x* axis), *ordinate (*y* axis), *Cartesian coordinates.

Background Variables Aspects of subjects' "backgrounds" that may influence other variables but will not be influenced by them. Background variables are usually demographic characteristics—such as age, sex, ethnicity, and parents' income—that the researcher cannot manipulate. Also called "subject," "organismic," "classification," and "individual-difference" variables. While there can be subtle differences among these usages, the basic idea is the same: Background variables can be causes, but they are not *independent variables, in some strict senses of that term, because they cannot be manipulated by a researcher; however, researchers can and frequently do *control for background variables. Compare *antecedent variable.

For example, your sex and your age (background variables) might influence your income (think of age and sex discrimination), but a change in your income certainly would not change either your sex or your age.

Backward Elimination A computer procedure for *regression analysis that is used to identify the *independent variables that are good predictors of the *dependent variable in order to find the best *fitting equation or model. Compare *forward selection and *stepwise regression.

The routine is to begin the analysis with all the variables in the equation and remove (eliminate) them one at a time according to whether they meet specific criteria (levels of significance of their *F ratios). The variable with the smallest *partial correlation is examined first. If it does not meet the criteria, it is eliminated; then the variable with the second smallest partial is examined, and so on until no more variables are eliminated.

Bar Chart Another term for a *bar graph. Also called "bar diagram."

Bar Graph A way of depicting *frequency distributions for *categorical (nominal or discrete) variables, such as religious affiliation, ethnic group, or state of residence.

The following example presents the Republican party affiliation of members of various religious categories; about 31% of Protestants surveyed reported affiliation with the Republicans, roughly 17% of Catholics did, and so on. Note that the bars do not touch in a bar graph as they do in a *histogram.

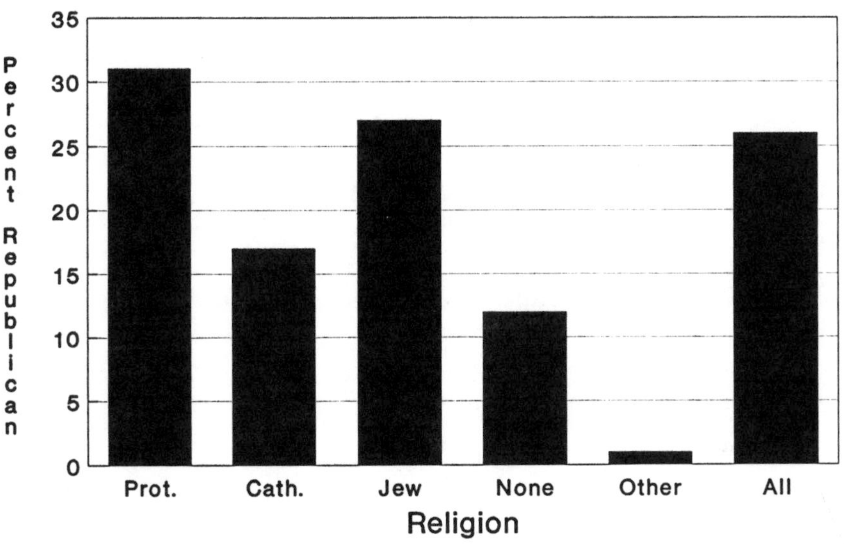

Bar Graph

Baseline (a) The average rate or level of some *variable before an experimental *treatment is applied or before some measure of the effect of a new variable is taken. (b) The horizontal, or *x axis, that is, the *abscissa.

For example, for definition a, if a political party wished to test the effects on party finances of a new advertising campaign, it could get baseline data by measuring the rate of contributions a week before the campaign began ("the baseline") and compare that with the rate of contributions for the week after the campaign began.

B

Basement Effect Another term for *floor effect.

BASIC Acronym for Beginner's All-Purpose Symbolic Instruction Code. A *programming language widely used for writing microcomputer programs.

Basic Research Research undertaken with the primary goal of advancing knowledge and theoretical understanding of the relations among variables. Often contrasted with *applied research.

Baud A measure of how quickly digital data can be transmitted; often the speed at which a *modem can send *bits over a telephone line.

For example, 1200 baud equals 150 characters (*bytes) per second, 2400 equals 300, and so on.

Battery of Tests A group or series of tests, usually psychological tests.

Bayesian Inference Statistical inference based on *Bayes's theorem and on the researcher's *subjective beliefs about the topic being studied. Named after Thomas Bayes, an eighteenth-century English mathematician. His method of inference is controversial, although his theorem is not. The method of inference involves working "backward," from effect to *cause, by estimating the *conditional probability of a cause given that certain events (effects) have occurred. See *prior and *posterior probability.

Bayes's Theorem A method for evaluating the *conditional probability of an *event. See *Bayesian inference.

Before-After Design Any research design in which the subjects are given a *pretest and a *posttest.

Behavioral Sciences Disciplines that study the actions (behaviors) of human beings and other animals. Most commonly included in lists of the behavioral sciences are psychology, sociology, and social anthropology; also, economics and political science.

Behaviorism (a) A theoretical position in psychology and related disciplines contending that the only scientific subject matter is behavior or actions—not beliefs, attitudes, desires, or other mental states. It is most commonly associated with the work of John B. Watson in the early twentieth century and B. F. Skinner more recently. (b) Advocacy of research based on empirical observation (of behaviors); this usage is perhaps most closely associated with political science and is often called "behavioralism."

Behrens-Fisher Test An extension of the *t test of the *statistical significance of the difference between two means; it relaxes the requirement of equal population *variances. It is somewhat controversial and not widely used.

Bell-Shaped Curve A symmetrical curve, usually plotting a continuous *frequency distribution, such as a *normal distribution, which looks like a cross section of a bell. See *normal distribution for an illustration. The *Student's *t* distribution is also bell-shaped, although it is rarely referred to that way.

Bernoulli Distribution Another name for the *binomial distribution.

Bernoulli Process Two classes of events and their associated probabilities. See *Bernoulli trial.

Bernoulli's Theorem In a *probability experiment, the larger the number of trials, the closer the *empirical probability will come to the *theoretical probability.

For example, the more flips of a coin, the closer the number of actual number of heads will be to the theoretical probability of 50%.

Bernoulli Trial In *probability theory, a trial or experiment with two possible outcomes, such as heads/tails, win/lose, 7/not 7. One of the two is usually called "success," and its probability is termed "p"; the other is called "failure," and its probability is labeled "q." Because $p + q = 1.00$; $1 - p = q$; $1 - q = p$. Named after the Swiss mathematician, Jacques Bernoulli (1654-1705).

Best Fit See *goodness of fit.

Best Linear Unbiased Estimator A *regression line computed using the *least squares criterion when none of the *assumptions are violated. Abbreviated: BLUE.

Beta Greek letter used to symbolize several statistical concepts, including *Type II Errors, standardized *regression coefficients, and *population parameters of regression coefficients.

Beta Coefficient A *regression coefficient for a *sample expressed in *standard deviation units (i.e., *z-scores). Specifically, the beta coefficient indicates the difference in a *dependent variable associated with an increase (or decrease) of one standard deviation in an *independent variable—when *controlling for the effects of other independent variables. Also called *standardized regression coefficient and *beta weight.

Note: A *regression coefficient expressed in nonstandardized units is usually symbolized by b. Usage is confusing because beta is also used to symbolize the population parameter of b.

B

Beta Error An error made by accepting or retaining a false *null hypothesis—more precisely, by *failing to reject* a false null hypothesis. This might involve, for example, claiming that a relationship does not exist when it in fact does. Also called *Type II Error. Compare *alpha error. See *hypothesis testing.

Beta Level The probability of making a *beta error, that is, failing to reject a false *null hypothesis. Compare *alpha level.

Beta Weights Another term for *standardized regression coefficients, or *beta coefficients. Beta weights enable researchers to compare the size of the influence of *independent variables measured using different *metrics or scales of measurement.

For example, imagine a *path analysis studying the influence of age and income on an attitude. Subjects could be adults ranging in age from 18 to 80. Their incomes might vary from $4,000 for a high school senior working after school to $200,000 for a tax lawyer. By reporting years and dollars as *standard scores, rather than in the original metric, beta weights allow easier comparisons of the relative influence of age and income.

Between-Group Differences Usually contrasted to differences within the groups being studied in an *analysis of variance. Between-group differences are what the researcher is interested in; they are considered large only if they are large in comparison with within-group differences.

For example, say an experiment is conducted. The dependent variable is measured after a treatment, with the results as reported in the following table. The between-group difference (between the means of the groups) appears significant because it seems quite a lot larger than the differences among subjects within each group. (One would use ANOVA or a *t* test to test for statistical significance.)

Scores

	Control Group	*Experimental Group*
	72	91
	71	89
	68	88
	67	86
	66	85
	64	83
Total	408	522
Mean	68	87

Between-Subjects Design A research procedure that compares different subjects. Usually contrasted to a *within-subjects design, which compares the same subjects at different times or under different *treatments.

Between-Subjects Variable (or Factor) An *independent variable or *factor for which each subject is measured at only one *level or under one *condition. See *within-subjects variable.

Between Sum of Squares A measure of *between-group differences. It is calculated by squaring and summing *deviation scores. It is used in comparison to within-group differences to compute the **F* ratio in an *analysis of variance. Symbolized: $SS_{between}$. See *mean squares.

Bias (a) Anything that produces *systematic error in a research finding. More formally, bias is the difference between the *expected value of a *sample statistic and the *population parameter the statistic estimates. See *biased estimator. (b) Also, the effects of any factor that the researcher did not expect to have an influence on the *dependent variable. Compare *random error.

For example, suppose you wanted to survey the opinions of New York City residents (the population). If you stood on a busy street corner at noon and asked the first 200 people who walked by to respond to your survey, your results would be almost surely biased. Perhaps your corner is at an intersection where out-of-town conventioneers usually stay, or your corner might be one where only very poor people are found or where men seldom pass by at that hour. You would be very lucky (and you would never really know) if some such factor weren't at work to bias your results by making your 200 respondents unrepresentative of the general population of the city.

Biased Estimator When the *expected value of a *sample statistic tends to over- or underestimate a *population parameter, it is called a biased estimator.

For example, the *standard deviation of a sample is a biased estimator; it underestimates the population standard deviation. To correct for that bias, when computing the standard deviation, the *sum of squares is divided by $n - 1$ rather than n.

Bimodal Distribution A distribution having two *modes or peaks. Strictly speaking, to call a distribution bimodal, the peaks should be the same height. It is quite common, however, to call any two-humped distribution bimodal, even when the highest points are not exactly equal.

In the following illustration, the number of students getting various scores on a 12-item test is plotted on the graph: 19 students got a score of 4 correct; another 19 got 8 right.

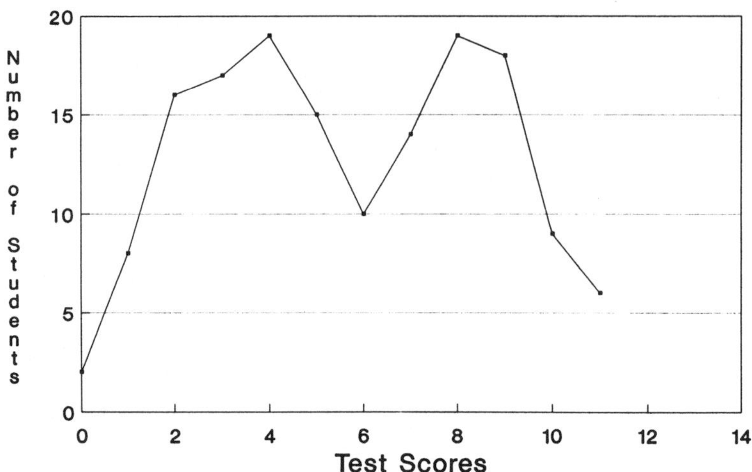

Bimodal Distribution

Binary Said of a number system or coding system that uses only 2 digits, generally 0 and 1.

Binomial Distribution A *probability distribution for a *dichotomous or two-value *variable (binomial = "two-names"), such as success/failure, profit/loss, or in/out. Also called "Bernoulli distribution."

For example, suppose you take an ordinary deck of playing cards, shuffle it, and draw a card, note what you draw, replace the card, and repeat the process five times. Say you record only one of two events: getting a club or not (clubs/not clubs). The probability distribution is given in the following table. Reading it, you can see that the probability of getting clubs on all five draws is very small (.001). The probability of getting exactly one club is .3955. To calculate the probability of getting two or more clubs, add together the probabilities of getting exactly 2, 3, 4, and 5 = .3672.

Probability Distribution for Drawing Clubs

Number of Clubs	*Probability*
0	.2373
1	.3955
2	.2637
3	.0879
4	.0146
5	.0010

Binomial Probability (a) A kind of probability calculation used when there are only two possible outcomes (binomial = "two names") such as heads/tails, win/lose, true/false for each of a series of trials. (b) The chances associated with a series of trials when there are only two possible outcomes. See *binomial distribution.

For example, suppose you are taking a true/false test tomorrow. There will be a total of 25 questions. To pass, you need get at least 18 correct. You could use binomial probability calculations to figure out how likely you are to pass by guessing alone.

Binomial Variable A variable with only two values or two "names" (a *dichotomous variable), such as up/down, left/right, rich/poor.

Biometrika Pioneering British statistics journal founded in 1901 by Karl Pearson (of the Pearson correlation) in which many of the statistical techniques most widely used today were first described. Many statistical tables (e.g., F, t, and chi-square distributions) in the back of texts were originally put together by the editors of that journal.

Biquartimin A method of (*oblique) rotation of the *axes in a *factor analysis.

Biserial Correlation A *correlation coefficient computed between a *dichotomous and a *continuous variable. The dichotomous variable is actually an interval-level variable but one that has been *collapsed to only two levels (such as success and failure). The biserial correlation provides an estimate of what the correlation would have been if the collapsed dichotomous variable had been left as a continuous variable. The estimate is usually high. Compare *tetrachoric correlation.

Biserial *r* See *biserial correlation.

Bit A binary digit (1 or 0). It is the smallest unit of information recognized by a computer. Several bits (usually 8) are combined to make a *byte.

B

Bivariate Pertaining to two variables only.

Bivariate Association A relation (covariation) between two variables only. Among the many measures of bivariate association are *eta, *gamma, *lambda, *Pearson's *r*, *Kendall's tau, and *Spearman's rho.

Bivariate Regression Coefficient A regression coefficient showing the relation between two variables only. A number indicating the degree of relationship between two *variables by estimating the difference in the *dependent variable associated with a one-unit increase in the *independent (*predictor) variable. See *simple regression, *regression equation. Compare *multiple regression analysis.

Biweight Mean A measure of *central tendency designed to correct for extreme values by letting the researcher treat *outliers differently (i.e., give them less weight) than other values. See *trimmed mean.

Black Box Any mechanism whose internal workings are hidden. Said of input-output *research designs where what happens in between is impossible to study or is ignored.

For example, studies of the effects of education on students often treat schooling as a black box. Students' characteristics upon entering and upon leaving are compared but without directly considering which parts of the school experience might have produced any changes or how they could have done so.

Blank Experiment An experimental *control produced by introducing an irrelevant treatment from time to time to keep subjects from becoming automatic in their responses.

Blind Analysis Diagnosis or analysis made from test or experimental data without direct contact with or knowledge of the subjects or when the person doing the analysis does not know which treatment, if any, the various subjects received. Compare *double-blind procedure.

Block In *experimental design, a group of similar subjects receiving treatments. See *randomized-block design.

Block Design An experimental design in which subjects are grouped into categories or "blocks." These blocks may then be treated as the experiment's *unit of analysis. Compare *randomized-block design.

Block Sampling (a) A sampling design in which respondents are grouped into representative categories or "blocks," which are then sampled. (b) Another term for *area sampling. Compare *cluster sampling, *stratified sampling.

BLUE *Best Linear Unbiased Estimator. A *regression line computed using the *least squares criterion when none of the *assumptions is violated.

BMDP Bio-Medical Data Package. A statistical package containing several software programs. Compare *SAS, *SPSS.

Bogardus Social Distance Scale An attitude scale for measuring how closely people would be willing to associate with members of social and ethnic groups other than their own. Respondents are asked whether they would be willing, for example, to live in the same town as, in the same neighborhood as, invite home for dinner, and have a relative marry a member of the social group in question. Named after its creator, Emory S. Bogardus.

Boilerplate Chunks of text (or other data) that are used repeatedly, word for word, in different documents. The term originally came from old newspaper printing technology.

Bonferroni Inequality A way of estimating the probability of making at least one *Type I Error when conducting a series of **t* tests on the means of three or more groups.

Bonferroni Test Statistic A method for testing the *statistical significance of (*planned,* not post hoc) multiple comparisons of *treatment effects, as in *ANOVA designs and *regression analysis. Also called "Dunn Multiple Comparison Test."

Boolean Algebra A form of algebra that deals with logical relations rather than numbers; or, a form of symbolic logic similar to algebra. Boolean algebra is important in computer design, set theory, and *probability theory. Named after the English mathematician, George Boole (1815-1864).

Boot *verb*: Also "boot up." To start a computer; to get it ready to work by loading the operating system into its memory. Derived from the term "bootstrap," as in "pull yourself up by your own bootstraps," meaning, to get yourself going.

Bootstrap Methods A recently developed and developing group of procedures that provide alternative ways to estimate *standard errors by repeated resampling from a sample. See *jackknife method, *nonparametric statistics.

The phrase "pull your self up by your own bootstraps," which tells you to rely on your own resources, is apt for these methods. The researcher's own resources are the sample. Rather than make assumptions about an *underlying population distribution to estimate the standard error, one estimates it on the basis of repeated random samples (with replacement) from one's sample. Taking 100 such subsamples is common and 1,000 is not unusual. While huge computing resources are required, the underlying mathematics is fairly uncomplicated in comparison with most advanced techniques.

Box-and-Whisker Diagram A type of graph in which boxes and lines show a *distribution's shape, *central tendency, and *variability. The "boxplot," as it is often called, gives a highly informative picture of the values of a single variable and is especially helpful for indicating whether a distribution is *skewed and has *outliers. See *exploratory data analysis.

In the following example, two box-and-whisker diagrams are used for comparing distributions. The grade point averages (GPAs) of individual students in two groups are diagrammed. Here is some of the information necessary to interpret the diagrams. (Terms and symbols vary, but the following conventions are fairly common and illustrate the main concepts.)

1. The upper and lower boundaries of each box (called *hinges) are drawn at the 75th and 25th *percentiles; this means that the box represents the *interquartile range (IQR), that is, the middle 50% of the values in the distribution.
2. The line marked with the asterisk, - - * - -, shows the distribution's median.
3. The "whiskers" are the lines extending from the boxes. They reach to the largest and smallest GPAs that are less than 1 interquartile range (IQR) from the ends of the boxes.
4. Any points beyond the high and low points of the whiskers are *outliers (if they are less than 1.5 IQRs from the end of the box) and are marked with an "O." If they are more than 1.5 IQRs from the end, they are extreme outliers and are indicated by an "E."
5. Comparing the two boxplots, we can see that the variability in Group II is much greater than it is in Group I. Also, Group I's median GPA is much lower than Group II's. This is true despite the fact that the highest single GPA was earned by a student in Group I (the extreme outlier, E) and even though the lowest GPAs were earned by students in Group II (the outliers marked by the Os).

Box-Score Method An elementary first step in synthesizing research in *meta-analysis, named after its similarity to score keeping in baseball. Basically, one just keeps count of the various research reports and whether each supports or fails to support the hypothesis being studied.

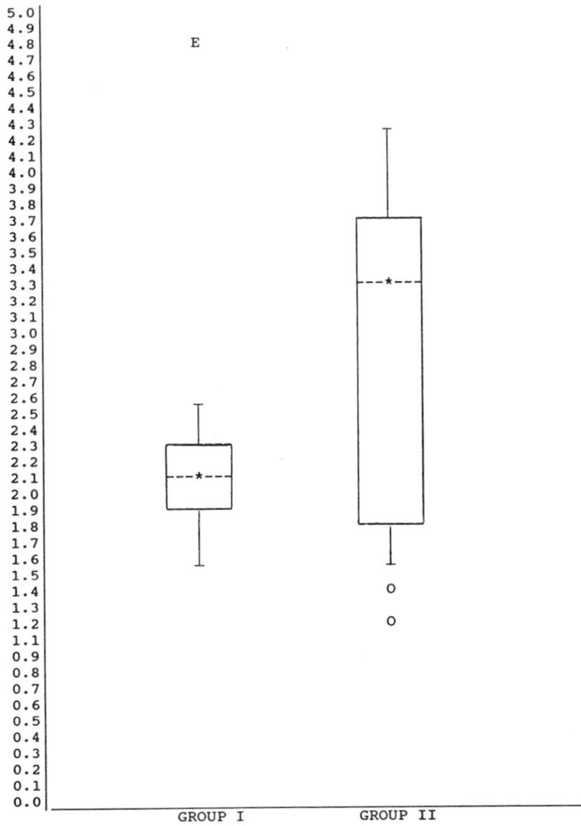

Box-and-Whisker Diagram

B

Bracketing (a) Another term for *collapsing data. (b) Providing upper and lower limits for a quantity.

Buffer (a) In brains and computers, a place for (or a process of) storing information briefly until one has time to deal with it. (b) Unscored test items included to reduce interaction between other items. Compare *blank experiment.

Byte A unit of information used by digital computers, usually equal to 8 *bits. For example, in *ASCII, the uppercase letter B is symbolized by the byte 01000010; C is 01000011.

C

C (a) A *programming language developed at Bell Laboratories. Because of its efficiency and because Bell Labs was barred from copyrighting the program, it is very widely used, especially by professional programmers. Compare *BASIC. (b) Symbol for *Pearson's coefficient of contingency.

CAD Computer-assisted design.

CAL Computer-assisted learning.

Canonical Analysis Sometimes used as a generic category of forms of analysis into which fit more specialized types, including *multiple regression analysis, *discriminant analysis, *MANOVA, and *canonical correlation analysis. Usually used to refer to the latter only, that is, to correlations between sets of independent and sets of dependent variables.

Canonical analyses were theoretically possible in research from the 1930s; they became practical only with the widespread availability of computers.

Canonical Correlation Analysis A form of *regression analysis for use with two or more independent variables and two or more dependent variables. The independent and dependent variables are each grouped into *linear composites or sets of variables; then correlations between those composites are calculated. Today, canonical correlations are increasingly superseded by *LISREL methods.

For example, suppose researchers were interested in the relation of students' health to their school achievement. They might want to use several measures of health (e.g., number of absences due to illness, nutritional information, body weight, dental records, school nurse's evaluation) and several measures of achievement (grades, scores on a reading test, scores on a mathematics achievement test, teacher evaluation, and so on). The two clusters of measures could be studied with canonical correlations.

Cap In *set theory, the symbol ∩, meaning "and." It is used to indicate the *intersection of two sets. Compare *cup.

C

Capital Productive wealth; resources one can use to generate income or additional resources. Compare *cultural, *human, and *social capital.

Examples include the balance in an interest-bearing savings account, tools one could use to make products to sell, and fertile farmland.

CARS Computer-Assisted Reference Service. Located at major research libraries in the United States, CARS enables users to search for bibliographic citations by topic in a large *data base. There is usually a modest fee charged for the service.

Cartesian Coordinates The numbers associated with points on a graph. The graphs one typically sees in the social and behavioral sciences display only the upper-right-hand corner of the Cartesian chart (the positive numbers only). Named after the French mathematician, René Descartes (1596-1650).

In the following example, five coordinates are plotted. Reading clockwise from the upper right, they are (1) $X = 3$, $Y = 2$; (2) $X = 4$, $Y = -1$; (3) $X = 4$, $Y = -2$; (4) $X = -3$, $Y = -3$; (5) $X = -3$, $Y = 4$.

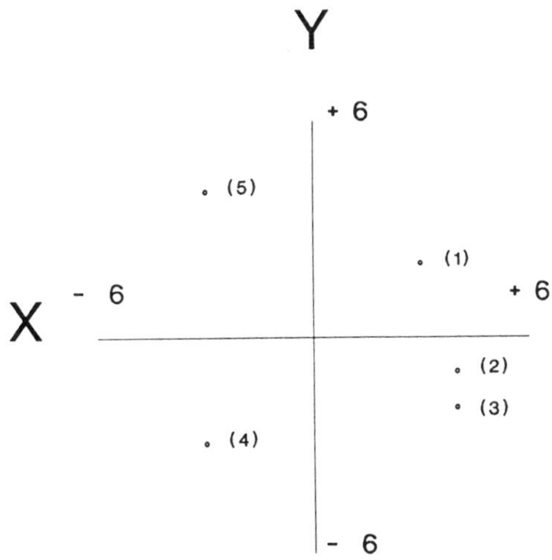

Cartesian Coordinates

C

Cartesian Product All the possible pairs of two *sets.

For example, if the two sets were two dice, the Cartesian product would be the 36 possible combinations of those two sets (dice): 1 + 1, 1 + 2, 1 + 3, and so on.

Cases The *subjects, whether persons or things, from which *data are gathered. A case is the smallest unit from which the researcher collects data. Compare *unit of analysis.

Case-Study Method Gathering and analyzing data about an individual example as a way of studying a broader phenomenon. This is done on the assumption that the example (the "case") is in some way typical of the broader phenomenon. The case may be an individual, a city, an event, a society, or any other possible object of analysis. The advantage of the case-study method is that it allows more intensive analyses of specific empirical details. The disadvantage is that it is hard to use the results to generalize to other cases. See *abstraction, *comparative method, *generalizability.

For example, a political scientist wishing to study why some candidates for public office are successful and others are not might study a particular election campaign in great depth in the hope of finding some general lessons about the electoral process.

Catastrophe Theory A theory of how living systems grow and differentiate. Long periods of slow change are punctuated by dramatic ("catastrophic") change. Originally developed in biology in the 1970s by René Thom, it has been applied to sociological, linguistic, and economic change as well.

Categorical Variable A variable that distinguishes among subjects by putting them into a limited number of categories, indicating type or kind, as sex does by categorizing people into male or female. Also called "discrete" or "nominal" variable. Compare *attribute, *continuous variable.

Causal Conclusion A conclusion drawn from a study designed in such a way that it is legitimate to infer *cause. Most people who use the term "causal conclusion" mean that an experiment, in which subjects are *randomly assigned to *control and *experimental groups, is the *only* *design from which researchers can properly infer cause. Compare *correlational research design, *natural experiment, *ecological fallacy.

Causal Diagram A graphic representation of *cause and *effect relations among *variables. Arrows indicate the direction of causal influence. See *path diagram for an example.

Cause An event, such as a change in one variable, that produces another event, such as a change in a second variable. See *necessary condition, *sufficient condition.

Before reading further, be forewarned. There is no concept in this dictionary more troublesome than "cause." Highly respected researchers disagree about what constitutes a cause and especially about how restrictive a set of conditions must be met before it is legitimate to talk of cause. Many social scientists, and even some philosophers, would agree with the following. Others, naturally, would not.

To attribute cause, for X to cause Y, three conditions are necessary (but not sufficient): (1) X must precede Y; (2) X and Y must covary; (3) no rival explanations account as well for the covariance of X and Y.

Causal relations may be simple or multiple. In simple causation, whenever the first event (the cause) happens, the second (the effect) always does too. Multiple causation is much more common in the social and behavioral sciences. Multiple causes may be such that any one of several causes can produce the same effect (for example, monetary inflation may be caused by rising wages, rising prices, declining productivity, or some combination of the three). Multiple causes also may be such that no one of them will *necessarily* produce the effect, but several of them in combination make it more likely (for example, prejudiced attitudes may be produced by repressive child rearing, general ignorance, low self-esteem, and/or lack of contact with people different than oneself).

Ceiling Effect A term used to describe what happens when many *subjects in a study have scores on a *variable that are at or near the possible upper limit ("ceiling"). The ceiling effect makes analysis difficult because it reduces the amount of variation in the variable. Compare *floor effect.

For example, suppose a group of statistics professors wanted to see whether a new method of teaching increased knowledge of elementary statistics. They could give students in their classes a test, try the new method, and then give the students another version of the same test to see whether their scores went up. But, if one of the professors had students who knew a lot of statistics already, who scored at or near 100% on the first test, she could not tell whether the new method was effective in her class; the scores of her students were so high (at the ceiling), they could hardly go up, even if the students learned a great deal of statistics with the new method.

Cell (a) The space formed by the intersection of a row and a column in a statistical table. (b) Any single group in an *analysis of variance design.

For example, in the table below, each of the numbers (except for the 100s) is in one of the table's cells. The percentage of Seniors who plan to Seek Work is in one cell, as is the percentage of Juniors who Don't Know, of Sophomores who plan to go on to Graduate School, and so on. The result in this case is a 4×3 *matrix.

Students' Plans Upon Graduation, by Class

	Freshman	*Sophomore*	*Junior*	*Senior*
Seek Work	73	58	57	58
Graduate School	5	11	18	30
Don't Know	22	31	25	12
Total	100	100	100	100

Censored Data or Samples Data or samples that are incomplete in some way, as when certain values are unknown or ignored.

Take, for example, a study conducted in 1993 of the college graduation rate of individuals born in 1970. Some people born in 1970 may not have completed college by 1993, but they could easily do so later on, after the end of the study. The data in this study would be censored, that is, the number of people from the 1970 *cohort who got their degrees after 1993 would be unknown.

Censored Regression Model See *tobit analysis.

Census In *statistics, a survey of an entire *population—in contrast to a survey of a *sample.

Census Tract A small area of a city or other densely populated region in the United States formed to make gathering census data easier. Census tracts usually contain between 3,000 and 6,000 people.

Centile An abbreviation of *percentile.

Central Limit Theorem A statistical proposition to the effect that, the larger a sample size, the more closely the *sampling distribution of the mean will approach a *normal distribution. This is true even if the population from which the sample is drawn is not normally distributed. A sample size of 30 or more will usually result in a sampling distribution of the mean that is very close to a normal distribution.

The central limit theorem explains why *sampling error is smaller with a large sample than it is with a small sample.

Central Tendency, Measure of Any of several statistical summaries of data designed to find a single number that best represents several numbers. Examples include the *mean, the *mode, and the *median.

A batting average is probably the best known measure of central tendency in the United States. A grade point average might be a more important example to the typical college student.

Central Tendency (of a Distribution) A point in a distribution of scores that corresponds to a typical, representative, or middle score in that distribution—such as the *mode, *mean, and *median.

Centroid (a) A *weighted combination of the observed *dependent variables in a *MANOVA. (b) In *factor analysis, the "centroid method" is a way to extract factors.

Ceteris Paribus Latin phrase meaning "all other things being equal"; also often used to mean if all other things remain unchanged. The phrase is generally used to qualify a conclusion, as in "this is true ceteris paribus," meaning this is true if all other things are/remain equal/unchanged.

Many aspects of *research design (such as *random assignment to *experimental groups or statistically *controlling for a variable) can be seen as attempts to approach the goal of ceteris paribus.

CFA *Confirmatory factor analysis.

Chain A series of values in which a value at one point depends in some way on the previous values in the series.

Chain Path Model Said of measurements of a variable taken from the same sample at three or more different times when the cause of the value of the measurement for each time is the immediately previous measurement. Also called *Markov chain.

For example, say we took measurements of some variable at four times, T1 → T2 → T3 → T4. Using a chain path model, we would assume the cause of the value at time 4 (T4) is T3, but T2 and T1 have no effect. Similarly, the cause of T3 is T2, but T1, while causing T2, has no direct effect on T3.

Chance Error Another term for *random error.

Chance Variable Another term for *random variable and *stochastic variable; also called *variate.

Chance Variation Another term for *random variation.

Chi-Square Distribution A family of theoretical *probability distributions, each of which has a different degree of freedom. The *chi-square test is based on it.

C

Chi-Square Test A *test statistic, that is, one used to assess the *statistical significance of a finding. It is also used as a *goodness-of-fit test.

The most familiar use of the chi-square test, and the one illustrated in the following example, occurs when a researcher wants to see if there are statistically significant differences between the observed (or actual) frequencies and the expected (or hypothesized, given the *null hypothesis) frequencies of two variables presented in a *cross-tabulation or *contingency table. The larger the observed frequency is in comparison with the expected frequency, the larger the chi-square statistic and the more likely the difference is statistically significant.

For example, say that a researcher gave a pass/fail test of knowledge of alcoholism to a sample of 100 subjects, 42 men and 58 women; 61 subjects passed, and 39 failed. Say the researcher was interested in whether there were differences in alcoholism knowledge by gender. She could use the chi-square test to test the *null hypothesis of no statistically significant differences between the sexes. To do so, she might arrange the information about her subjects in the following tables. Table 1 gives the total (or *marginal) frequencies for the two variables. Table 2 shows what the (approximate) frequencies of passes and fails on the two tests would have been if the null hypothesis were true, that is, what you would expect if there were no difference in how well the men and women did on the exam. Table 3 shows the actual or observed number of men and women who passed or failed the exam. Comparing Table 2 and Table 3, it is clear that the actual and expected frequencies are not identical. For example, 26 men were expected to pass, but only 19 did; 23 women were expected to fail, but only 16 did; and so on. But are these differences statistically significant, that is, unlikely to be due to chance alone? Computing the chi-square statistic can tell you. The answer (calculations not shown) is that the null hypothesis of no difference between men and women should be rejected. The differences are greater than what could be expected by chance alone; they are significant at the .01 level.

Table 1 Marginal Frequencies

	Pass	*Fail*	*Totals*
Men			42
Women			58
Totals	61	39	100

Table 2 Expected Frequencies

	Pass	*Fail*	*Totals*
Men	26	16	42
Women	35	23	58
Totals	61	39	100

Table 3 Observed Frequencies

	Pass	*Fail*	*Totals*
Men	19	23	42
Women	42	16	58
Totals	61	39	100

Circular Reasoning Said when one conclusion depends on a second, which in turn depends on the first. Compare *tautology.

For example, "Unemployed people are lazy. How do we know this? Because they are unemployed, which proves they're lazy; if they weren't lazy, they'd have jobs."

Class Frequency The number of observations of a particular *variable that fall in a given *class interval.

For example, if researchers were studying income distribution in a particular city and 2,149 individuals earned between $30,000 and $39,999, the class frequency for the class interval $30,000-39,999 would be 2,149.

Classical Statistical Inference What most people mean by "statistical inference." The word "classical" is often added to make a contrast with *Bayesian inference.

Classification Variables Another term for *background variables.

Classificatory Variable A *categorical variable, that is, one that values a variable by classifying or categorizing—such as upper/middle/lower class or jumbo/large/medium/tiny shrimp. Compare *nominal and *discrete variables.

Class Interval A convenient grouping of the data on a *continuous variable that makes it easier to analyze; the interval between the boundaries (or limits) of a class, such as between 21 and 40 million in the following example. By turning continuous variables into *categorical variables, class intervals make it possible to do *frequency distributions and *cross tabulations—at the cost, however, of throwing away some detailed information.

For example, the following table classifies nations by population size. This makes it easier to see the big picture, easier than it would be if we used a list of all 170 nations and their exact populations. On the other hand, a major disadvantage of using classes is that it obscures large differences, such as the one between Mauritius with a population of about 1 million and Venezuela with around 19 million, both of which are grouped together in the same category.

C

Distribution of Nations by Population Size (1990)

Population (in millions)	*Number of Countries*
Less than 1	44
1-20	86
21-40	17
41-60	9
61-80	4
81-100	1
100+	9

Class Limits The upper and lower values of a *class interval.

Closed Question Format In surveys and interviews, researchers most often offer subjects a limited number of predetermined responses to questions (closed format) rather than allow them to choose their own words for answering the questions (*open question format).

For example, "What sort of job is the president doing overall? (a) excellent (b) good (c) fair (d) poor (e) don't know." Using the closed question format means that a respondent who wants to say "very good for foreign policy but not so hot on domestic issues" is forced to select among options (a) to (e).

Closed System A theoretical system that does not admit evidence or arguments from different perspectives. In other terms, a causal system that allows no *exogenous causal variables.

Freudianism, Marxism, and behaviorism have been accused of being closed systems. Indeed, most theoretical systems have been so accused—by opponents.

Cluster Analysis Any of several procedures in *multivariate analysis designed to determine whether individuals (or other units of analysis) are similar enough to fall into groups or clusters.

Cluster Sample A method for drawing a *sample from a *population in two or more stages. It is typically used when researchers cannot get a complete list of the members of a population they wish to study but can get a complete list of groups or "clusters" of the population. It is also used when a random sample would produce a list of subjects so widely scattered (e.g., 6 in California, 3 in Maine, 4 in Illinois, 5 in Texas) that surveying them would be prohibitively expensive. Generally, the researcher wishes to get clusters containing subjects as diverse as possible, whereas in *stratified sampling the goal is often to find strata with subjects as similar to one another as possible.

The disadvantage of cluster sampling is that each stage of the process increases *sampling error. The margin of error is therefore larger in cluster sampling than in simple or stratified random sampling; but, because cluster sampling is usually much easier (cheaper), this error can be compensated for by increasing the sample size. See *central limit theorem.

For example, suppose someone wanted to survey undergraduates to get their opinions on various social and political questions. There is no complete list of all college students. But there are complete lists of all 3,000+ colleges in the country. The researchers could begin by getting such a list of colleges (which are "clusters" of students). They could then select a sample of, say, 100 colleges. Once the clusters (colleges) were identified, the researchers could go to each school and get a list of its students; subjects to be surveyed would be selected (perhaps by simple *random sampling) from each of these lists.

COBOL Acronym for Common Business Oriented Language. A *programming language. Compare *BASIC, *C, *FORTRAN.

Code (a) Rules specifying how data are to be represented. See *codebook. (b) Rules for converting data from one form to another. See *coding. (c) A *computer program as in "she wrote the code for that operating system."

Codebook A list of the *variables in a study and how they have been coded so that they can be read and manipulated by a computer. See *coding.

For example, a typical entry in a codebook would be as follows: Variable 1, Sex: 1 = female; 0 = male.

Coding (a) "Translating" data from one language or format into another—usually to make it possible for a computer to operate on the data thus coded. See *effects, *dummy, and *contrast coding. (b) Writing a set of instructions telling a computer how to handle data. See *programming.

For example, (a) if one of your variables were "race," you might code these as 1 for "black," 2 for "white," and 3 for "other." (b) "Arrange the data in ascending numerical order, sum the values, find the mean, median, and mode," might be a way of coding instructions for what a computer was to do with a data file.

Coefficient (a) A number used as a measure of a property or characteristic. (b) In an equation, a number by which a variable is multiplied. *For a specific coefficient, see under the type or kind*; to find coefficient of determination, for instance, look under "determination, coefficient of."

For example, (a) a coefficient of inequality between incomes could be calculated by dividing the larger income into the smaller. Thus, if the average (mean) income of U.S. men working full-time were $25,000 per year, and that of women working full-time were $15,000, the coefficient of inequality between men and women would be 15,000/25,000 = .6. (b) In the equation, $Y' = a + 3.2X$, 3.2 is the coefficient. See *regression coefficient.

Cognitive Science The interdisciplinary study of cognition, that is, the processes of acquiring, creating, and disseminating knowledge. It is composed in varying proportions of cognitive psychology, computer science (*information theory), philosophy (*epistemology), and linguistics.

Cohort A group of individuals having a statistical factor (usually age) in common. Compare *social category.

For example, all persons born in 1961 form a cohort.

Cohort Analysis Studying the same *cohort over time. See *panel study, *time-series analysis.

For example, individuals who graduated from high school in 1985 form a cohort whose subsequent educational experiences could be followed in a cohort analysis. For example, how many went on to college immediately? How many went on eventually? Of those who attended college, how many went to a two-year college? How many went to a four-year college? How many graduated? And so on.

Cohort Effects The effects of membership in a cohort, usually an age group. Also called "generation effects." Often contrasted with *period effects.

For example, the experience of having grown up in the 1950s might influence people's attitudes and outlooks in ways quite different from the influence of having grown up in the 1960s.

Collapsing Combining groups or categories of a variable in order to reduce their number. Also called "bracketing."

For example, suppose we surveyed 100 people about the number of movies they saw last year and got the following results. Table 1 uses five categories, less than 5, 6 to 10, and so on. Table 2 collapses the five categories into two, 15 or fewer, and 16 or more.

Table 1

< 5	22
6-10	18
11-15	12
16-20	28
>20	20

Table 2

0-15	52
16+	48

Collinear Having a common line. See *multicollinearity.

Commonality Analysis A method of *partitioning *variance in *multiple regression problems. Its purpose is to identify the parts of the variance in the *dependent variable attributed uniquely to each of the *independent variables and the parts that are due to various combinations of independent variables. Commonality analysis is controversial, especially when used in *explanatory (rather than *predictive) research.

Common Factor Variance The variance that two or more *factors share. See *communality, *factor analysis.

Common Metric A scale of measurement shared by more than one study or into which the results of several studies have been transformed. *Transformation to a common metric is often done in a *meta-analysis so that the results of different studies can be compared.

Communality The proportion of the total variance that is *common factor variance (i.e., shared by two or more variables). It is calculated by summing the squared *factor loadings (see below) of a variable. Symbolized, h^2.

	Factor 1	*Factor 2*				
Variable	.7	.1				
Loadings squared	.49	.01	=	.50	=	h^2

C

Communications Software A *computer program that allows a computer to use a *modem to link to another computer. "Kermit" is a widely used version of such software.

Communications Theory The study of the transfer of information. It tends to emphasize parallels between the ways humans and computers do this. Compare *information theory, *artificial intelligence, *cognitive science.

Comparative Method The study of more than one event, group, or society to isolate factors or *variables that explain patterns. The term is perhaps most often used to describe research whose comparisons are cross-national. Almost all systematic research is comparative, however, in the broad sense of the term. For example, experimental research involves comparing what happens to *control and *experimental groups. The term "comparative method" is often used when the research involves secondary analysis of historical data. (When data are contemporary, the term "cross-cultural" is sometimes used instead.) Compare *natural experiment.

There are two basic strategies in comparative research: (1) Study events or groups that differ in many ways but that have one thing in common—for example, different societies that have experienced revolutions; (2) study societies or groups that are highly similar but differ in one important respect, such as modern, industrialized nations that have different kinds of education systems.

Complement (of A) In *set theory, "not A." Also called "negation of A."

For example, if a set is made up of the numbers from 1 to 10, and a subset "A" is 2, 5, 8, 9, and 10, the complement of A is the rest of the numbers in the set, that is, 1, 3, 4, 6, and 7.

Complex Comparison A comparison of two or more groups with another. Comparing Group A with Group B would be a simple comparison. Comparing Group A plus Group B with Group C would be a complex comparison. Compare *pairwise comparison.

Composite Score A score made up of two or more scores either by adding the scores together or by taking an average.

Computer Program A set of instructions written in a form a computer can read ("machine readable") that tell it how to perform specific tasks.

Computer Simulation Using a computer to build a *model of what would happen in a real world situation under certain conditions. Computer simulations are used in a wide variety of fields from economic forecasting to weather forecasting. Compare *Monte Carlo methods.

Concentration, Coefficient of Another term for *Gini coefficient.

Concept An abstract idea that categorizes data. It often implies generalization from particulars—although Plato wouldn't agree. Compare *construct, a term used more often in quantitative research to express the same idea (concept) as "concept."

For example, if you saw an unusual breed of dog for the first time, you would probably still recognize it as a dog—even though you had never seen it before—because it would fit into your general concept or idea of what a dog is. Compare *schema.

C

Concomitant Variable A variable a researcher wishes to *control for. Also called *covariate.

Concomitant Variation Said of two or more phenomena that vary together or covary. See *correlation, *covariance, *cause.

The term was introduced by J. S. Mill (1806-1873) to describe a method for determining a causal link between two phenomena: the procedure is to investigate whether, when a supposed cause is present, the effect is present, and, when the supposed cause is absent, the effect is absent.

Concordance, Coefficient of See *Kendall's coefficient of concordance.

Concurrent Validity A way of determining the *validity of a measure by seeing how well it correlates with some other measure the researcher believes is valid.

For example, if a psychologist wanted to see whether a new IQ test were a valid measure of intelligence, he or she could correlate subjects' scores on the new test with their scores on an old IQ test that he or she thought was a good measure of intelligence. If the scores were highly correlated, this would be evidence of the validity of the new test—or, at least, that the two tests were measuring the same thing.

Or, one might check the validity of a test of quantitative ability by seeing whether people in occupations that presumably require it (e.g., accountants) tend to get higher scores on the test.

Condition A *treatment or a *level of an *independent variable in an *experiment.

For example, a study comparing the effects of drugs A, B, and C has three conditions (Drug A, Drug B, Drug C). The independent variable (drug treatment) has three levels (A, B, and C).

Conditional Event In *probability theory, an event that can occur only in conjunction with another event. See *conditional probability. Contrast *independent event.

For example, say you rolled a pair of dice one at a time. Getting a total of 9 (the conditional event) for the pair of dice is conditional upon the first die having come up 3 or higher.

Conditional Odds *Odds that take into account other variables. Compare *conditional probability.

For example, the odds (unconditional) of graduating from high school in a particular state might be 80% to 20%, or 4 to 1. Taking into account the variable sex, the conditional odds for females might be 85 to 15, or 5.67 to 1.

C

Conditional Probability (a) The chance that an event will occur, given that some other event has already occurred. Symbolized: $p(B|A)$, which is read, "the probability of event B, given event A." (b) The chance that one condition exists given that another does. See *Bayesian inference.

For example, (a) the probability of drawing an ace at random from a deck of 52 playing cards is 4 out of 52, or 1 out of 13. Let's say you drew a card, got an ace, and did not put it back in the deck. Call that draw event A. What is the conditional probability (given event A) of drawing another ace (event B)? Given that you did not replace the first ace, the (conditional) probability of drawing a second ace is 3 out of 51, or 1 out of 17. Compare *gambler's fallacy.

An example of (b) might be the likelihood that a patient has the HIV virus, given that his blood test is positive.

Conditioning Effect Another term for *interaction effect.

Confederate Someone who pretends to be a subject in an experiment but who is actually helping the experimenter in some way.

Confidence Bounds Another term for *confidence limits.

Confidence Coefficient Another term for *confidence level. It is 1.0 minus the *alpha level. Thus an alpha level of .05 results in a confidence coefficient of .95.

Confidence Interval A range of values of a *sample statistic that is likely (at a given level of probability, called a *confidence level) to contain a *population parameter. The interval that will include the population parameter a certain percentage (*confidence level) of the time. The wider the confidence interval, the higher the confidence level. See *confidence level for an example.

Confidence Level A desired percentage of the scores (usually 95% or 99%) that would fall within a certain range of *confidence limits. It is calculated by subtracting the alpha level from 1 and multiplying the result times 100; for example, $100 \times (1 - .05) = 95\%$.

For example, say a poll predicted that, if the election were held today, the Republican candidate for Senator would win 60% of the vote. This prediction could be qualified by saying that the pollster was 95% certain (confidence *level*) that the prediction was accurate plus or minus 3% (confidence *interval*); this means the Republican candidate has a 95% chance of winning between 57% and 63% (confidence *limits*) of the vote.

C

Confidence Limits The upper and lower values of a *confidence interval, that is, the values defining the range of a confidence interval.

Confirmatory Factor Analysis *Factor analysis conducted to test hypotheses (or confirm theories) about the factors one will find. See *exploratory factor analysis, *LISREL.

Conflict Theory A perspective on society and social relations contending that the main determinant of social phenomena is the tendency of individuals and groups to have opposing interests over which they come into conflict. Among the many classical authors who could be called conflict theorists, Karl Marx and Max Weber are probably the best known. Compare *functionalism.

Confound (a) *verb*: To study combined treatments in such a way that their separate effects cannot be determined. (b) *noun*: A variable that obscures, or makes it impossible to interpret, the relations among other variables. See *confounded.

For example, to study the effects of fertilizer on your lawn when the fertilizer must be applied with water is to confound the effects of watering and of fertilizing. Water is the confound.

Confounded Said of two or more *variables whose separate effects cannot be isolated.

For example, if one political science professor used Textbook A in her classes and another professor used Textbook B, and students in the two classes were given achievement tests to see how much political science they had learned, the *independent variables (the textbooks and the professors' teaching effectiveness) would be confounded. There would be no way to tell whether any differences in achievement (the *dependent variable) between the two classes were caused by either or both of the independent variables.

Confounding Variable A variable that obscures the effects of another. See *confound and *confounded for examples.

Consensual Validation The use of agreement (consensus) of two or more experts to determine whether a statement is true.

Consequent The second term in a ratio. In the ratio 3:2, 2 is the consequent. The first term (3) is the *antecedent.

Conservative (Measure or Estimate) Said of a statistic that tends to underestimate; that is, if it errs, it is more likely to do so by being overly cautious.

For example, *omega squared is a conservative measure of *strength of association, because it is more likely to underestimate than to overestimate that strength—especially in comparison with *eta squared, which can sometimes overestimate the strength of an association.

Constant (a) A measure or value that is the same for all units of analysis. (b) A quantity that does not change value in a particular context. (c) In a *regression equation, the *intercept (also called *regression constant and *Y* intercept) is often referred to as "the constant"; the *beta coefficients are also constants but are less often so called. Compare *variable, *universal constant.

For example, (a) in research that studied variables explaining unemployment among women only, sex would be a constant; all subjects (units of analysis) are female. An example of (b) would be a price that does not change regardless of fluctuations in supply or demand. And (c), in the regression equation $Y' = a + bX$, the value of a would be the constant for that equation.

Construct (a) Something that exists theoretically but is not directly observable. (b) A *concept developed (constructed) for describing relations among phenomena or for other research purposes. (c) A theoretical (not *operational) definition in which concepts are defined in terms of other concepts.

For example, intelligence cannot be directly observed or measured; it is a construct. Researchers infer the existence of intelligence from behavior and use *indexes (such as size of vocabulary or the ability to remember strings of numbers) to "construct" a measure of the construct "subject's intelligence."

Construct Validity The extent to which *variables accurately measure the constructs of interest. In other words: How well are the variables *operationalized? Do the *operations really get at the things you are trying to measure? How well can you generalize from your operations to your construct? In practice, construct validity is used to describe a *scale, *index, or other measure of a variable that *correlates with measures of other variables in ways that are predicted by, or make sense according to, a theory of how the variables are related. See *concurrent, *content, *convergent, and *criterion-related validity. Absolute distinctions among these kinds of validity are difficult to make, in large part because procedures for assessing them tend to be similar if not identical. *Convergent and *discriminant validity, for instance, are used as tests of construct validity.

For example, if you were studying racist attitudes, and you believed that racism (the construct) was more common among people with low self-esteem, you could put together some questions that you thought were a good *index of racism. If subjects' scores on that index were strongly (*negatively) correlated with their scores on a measure of self-esteem, this would be evidence that your index had construct validity. The index is more likely to be a good measure of racism if it correlates with something your theory says it should correlate with than if it does not. All this assumes, of course, that your theory is right in the first place about the relation between self-esteem and racism *and* that you have a valid measure of self-esteem.

Content Analysis Any of several research techniques used to describe and systematically analyze the content of written, spoken, or pictorial communication—such as books, newspapers, television programs, or interview transcripts.

For example, in a series of interviews, you could ask people open-ended questions about different ethnic groups. Later, the audiotapes of these interviews could be transcribed (perhaps entered into a computer program) so that the number of positive and negative adjectives used by interviewees when talking about various ethnic groups could be counted.

Probably the most famous use of content analysis was done in the late 1960s. Several psychologists and statisticians used word frequency analysis to identify previously unknown authors of some of the "Federalist Papers."

Content-Referenced Test Another term for *criterion referenced test.

Content Validity A measure has content validity when its items accurately represent the thing (the "universe") being measured. Content validity is not a statistical property; it is rather a matter of expert judgment. Compare *construct, *concurrent, and *convergent validity.

It is always easier to give clear examples of invalidity than validity. For instance, a test of U.S. history that only had questions about Civil War battles would not be content valid; its questions would not be representative of the subject.

Contextual Effects The impact on individuals of operating in certain contexts. Compare *cohort effects.

For example, attending a high school in which most of the other students plan to go to college (one context) might influence a student differently than another context, such as a high school in which very few of his or her classmates planned to go to college.

Contingency A relation between variables such that one determines or depends upon (is contingent upon) another. See *conditional probability.

Contingency Coefficient A measure of the association between two categorical variables. It is a version of the *chi-square test, that is, the contingency coefficient is a function of chi-square.

Contingency Effect Another term for *interaction effect.

Contingency Table A table of frequencies classified according to two sets of values of *categorical variables. Also called a *cross-tabulation. It is called a contingency table because what you find in the rows (the usual place for the *dependent variable) is *contingent* upon what you find in the columns (the usual place for the *independent variable).

Table 1 Religious Affiliation and Attitude Toward Legal Abortion

	Religion			
Favor Legal Abortion	*Catholic*	*Protestant*	*Other*	*Total*
Yes	31.0% (63)	70.2% (278)	72.3% (73)	59.1% (414)
No	69.0% (140)	29.8% (118)	27.7% (28)	40.9% (286)
Total	100.0% (203)	100.0% (396)	100.0% (101)	(700)

Table 2 Attitude Toward Legal Abortion by Gender and Religious Affiliation (numbers only)

	Gender							
	Women				*Men*			
	Catholic	*Protestant*	*Other*	*Total*	*Catholic*	*Protestant*	*Other*	*Total*
Yes	40	140	51	231	23	138	22	183
No	64	58	23	145	76	60	5	141
Total	104	198	74	376	99	198	27	324

For example, Table 1 (hypothetical data) shows the results of a survey of 700 individuals concerning how religious affiliation is related to attitudes about legal abortion. Table 2 also shows the gender of the respondents and is thus an example of a multivariate (more than two variables) contingency table.

Continuity Correction Another term for *Yates's correction for continuity.

Continuous Variable A variable that can be expressed by a large (often infinite) number of measures, that is, a variable that can be measured on an *interval or a *ratio scale. Compare *categorical variable. See *discrete variable for further discussion.

For example, height and grade point average are continuous variables. Persons' heights could be 69.38 inches, 69.39 inches, and so on; GPAs could be 3.17, 3.18, and so on.

Contrast Coding Another term for *orthogonal coding. Compare *dummy and *effect coding.

Control Card A series of instructions for a computer program telling it what operations to perform on a particular set of data. So called because these instructions (and the data) were at one time entered on computer punch cards. The cards have largely disappeared, but the term lingers on among some researchers.

Control for Any one of several ways of statistically subtracting the effects of a variable (a *control variable) to see what a relationship would be without it.

For example, to compare the average incomes of various ethnic groups, we might wish to control for education level. In that way, we could measure the effects of ethnic group membership apart from differences in the educational levels among the groups. This would be important, for example, if we were showing how much of the difference in income persisted even when people from different groups had the same education level. See *analysis of covariance and, for an example, *crossbreaks, Table 2.

Control Group In experimental research, a group that, for the sake of comparison, does not receive the treatment the experimenter is interested in. Compare *experimental group.

For example, psychologists studying the effects of television violence on attitudes might give subjects a questionnaire to measure their attitudes, divide the group into two, and show a videotape of a violent program to one half (the experimental group) and show a nonviolent program to the other half (the control group). A second attitude questionnaire then would be given to the two groups to see whether the programs affected their scores.

Controlled Variable A term occasionally used for an *independent variable, so called because independent variables are controlled by the experimenter.

Control Variable An extraneous variable that you do not wish to examine in your study; hence you *control for it. Also called *covariate.

C

Convenience Sample A sample of subjects selected for a study not because they are *representative but because it is convenient to use them—as when college professors study their own students. Compare *accidental sample, *bias.

Convergent Validity The overlap between different tests that presumably measure the same construct. See *concurrent validity, *construct validity.

Converging Evidence Said of the results of multiple studies that lead to the same conclusion. Compare *meta-analysis, *triangulation.

Coordinates Numbers that can be used to plot points on a graph. See *Cartesian coordinates for an example.

Correlated Groups Design A *research design in which some of the *variance in the *dependent variable is caused by a correlation between groups of subjects—or among sets of their scores.

The most common form of this research design is a before-and-after study. For example, fifth graders could be given a vocabulary (pre-) test. Half of them could then receive an experimental vocabulary enrichment program; the other half, the regular language curriculum. At the end of a semester, they could be given another vocabulary test (a posttest). The dependent variable is the scores on the posttest. Many of the differences in the students' scores (the variance) on the posttest could be explained by their pretest scores. For example, students with very large vocabularies before the experiment would still have large vocabularies after it was over. Thus, regardless of the treatment they receive, the scores of students on the pre- and posttests almost certainly will be at least somewhat correlated, probably highly correlated.

Correlation The extent to which two or more things are related ("co-related") to one another. This is usually expressed as a *correlation coefficient.

Correlational Research Design A design in which the variables are not manipulated. Rather, the researcher uses measures of *association to study their relations. The term is usually used in contrast with *experimental research.

Correlation Cluster A group of variables that correlate with one another. Compare *factor analysis.

Correlation Coefficient A number showing the degree to which two *variables are related. Correlation coefficients range from −1.0 to +1.0. If there is a perfect *negative correlation (−1.0) between A and B, whenever A is high, B is low, and vice versa. If there is a perfect *positive correlation (+1.0) between A and B, whenever one is high or low, so is the other. A correlation coefficient of 0 means that there is no relationship between the variables. (A zero correlation may also occur when two variables are related but their relationship is not *linear.) See *association, measure of, *correlation matrix, *regression analysis.

There are numerous ways to compute correlation coefficients depending on the kinds of variables being studied. Among the most common are *Pearson's product-moment, *Spearman's rho, and *Kendall's tau.

The term "correlation" is used by some to refer to any measure of association and by others to refer only to the association of variables measured at an *interval or *ratio level.

Correlation Matrix A table of *correlation coefficients that shows all pairs of correlations of a set of variables.

In the following example, correlations between subjects' age, income, and scores on two attitude scales are shown. Note in Table 1 the series of diagonal correlations of 1.0. These figures reflect the fact that a variable always correlates perfectly with itself. These correlations are often omitted, as they are in Table 2, because they are self-evident. The upper-right (or lower-left) portion of the table is usually omitted as well, because it just repeats (as a sort of mirror image) what is printed in the lower left. In short, most correlation matrices are simplified to look like Table 2, not Table 1.

Studying either table, you could conclude that the two scales were highly correlated (.91) with one another and that the scores on the scales were more strongly correlated with age (.74 and .68) than they were with income (.33 and .42).

Table 1

	Age	*Income*	*Scale 1*	*Scale 2*
Age	**1.00**	.49	.74	.68
Income	.49	**1.00**	.33	.42
Scale 1	.74	.33	**1.00**	.91
Scale 2	.68	.42	.91	**1.00**

Table 2

	Age	*Income*	*Scale 1*	*Scale 2*
Age	—			
Income	.49	—		
Scale 1	.74	.33	—	
Scale 2	.68	.42	.91	—

Correlation Ratio A kind of correlation—symbolized by and commonly known as *eta squared—that can be used when the relation between two variables is *curvilinear (or nonlinear). It is a measure of *strength of association, which is independent of the form of the relation—unlike r^2, which only shows linear relationship between variables.

Counterbalancing In a *within-subjects *factorial experiment, presenting *conditions (*treatments) in all possible orders to avoid *order effects. See *Latin square.

For example, an experimenter might wish to study the effects of three kinds of lighting (A, B, and C) on performance of a visual skill. Subjects could first be placed in Condition A and be given a test of the skill; then they could be put in Condition B and get a second test; and so on. By Condition C and the third test, subjects' scores might tend to go up simply because they would have had the practice of the first two tests. Or their scores might go down because they would tend to become fatigued.

The effects of practice and fatigue could be counterbalanced by rotating the lighting conditions so that subjects would experience them in all possible orders. Because there are six possible orders (ABC, ACB, BAC, BCA, CAB, CBA), subjects could be divided into six groups, one for each possible order.

Covariance A measure of the joint or (co-) *variance of two or more variables. See *covariation, *analysis of covariance.

For example, suppose we want to see if there is a relation between knowledge of politics (variable X) and political tolerance (variable Y). Our tests of these two variables are each measured on a scale of 1-20.

We give the two tests to a *sample of 10 people. The scores and the calculation of the covariance are shown in the table below. Column 1 assigns a number to each individual taking the two tests. Columns 2 and 4 are their results on Test X and Test Y. Columns 3 and 5 subtract the mean of each variable from each individual's score (to get the *deviation scores). Column 6 shows the *product of multiplying Column 3 times Column 5 (the *cross product). You total Column 6 and divide by the number of cases minus 1 (10 – 1 = 9) to get the covariance of X and Y (Cov_{XY}), which equals 11.4.

Example of How to Compute a Covariance

Column 1	*Column 2*	*Column 3*	*Column 4*	*Column 5*	*Column 6*
case	X	$X - \overline{X}$	Y	$Y - \overline{Y}$	$(X - \overline{X})(Y - \overline{Y})$
01	18	5	16	4	20
02	9	–4	10	–2	8
03	12	–1	11	–1	1
04	17	4	14	2	8
05	13	0	13	1	0
06	8	–5	13	1	–5
07	17	4	16	4	16
08	14	1	11	–1	–1
09	16	3	12	0	0
10	6	–7	4	–8	56
Total	130	0	120	0	103
Mean	13		12		**11.4** (covariance)

Covariance Analysis See *analysis of covariance.

Covariance Structure Models See *analysis of covariance structures, *LISREL models, *confirmatory factor analysis.

Covariate A variable that a researcher seeks to *control for (statistically subtract the effects of) by using such techniques as *multiple regression analysis (MRA) or *analysis of covariance (ANCOVA).

Covariation (a) A state that exists when two things—such as the price and the sales of a commodity—vary together. Measures of *association are designed to capture the degree of covariation. (b) The numerator of a *covariance. See *covariance, *correlation.

Cov_{XY} *Covariance of X and Y.

CPS *Current Population Survey.

Criterion Group A group used to validate a test because its characteristics are known.

For example, if we wanted to validate a screening test for prospective locksmiths, we could give the test to master locksmiths to see if they performed well on it. If they did not perform well, the test probably would not be a valid measure of skills needed to be a good locksmith.

Criterion-Referenced Test A test that examines a specific skill that a student is expected to have learned (the criterion). It measures a student's achievement without comparing it with the scores of other students. Also called a "content-referenced test." Compare *norm-referenced test.

Criterion-Related Validity The ability of a test to make accurate predictions. The name comes from the fact that the test's validity is measured by how well it predicts an outside criterion. Also called "predictive validity."

For example, the extent to which students' SAT scores predict their college grades is an indication of the SAT's criterion-related validity.

Criterion Scaling A method of reducing the number of categories of *categorical and *ordinal variables in a *multiple regression analysis. The goal is to make the analysis more manageable by reducing the number of coded *vectors. The technique gets its name from the fact that it involves using the *mean of each group on the criterion (dependent) variable. It is often used in *repeated-measures designs.

Criterion Variable Another term for *dependent variable, or the presumed effect in a study. The term is usually used for nonexperimental studies. In such usage, the *independent variable is called the *predictor variable.

Critical Ratio The formula that gives the values that define the *critical region.

Critical Region The area in a *sampling distribution representing values that are "critical" to a particular study. They are critical because, when a *sample statistic falls in that region, the researcher can reject the *null hypothesis. (For this reason, the critical region is also called the "region of rejection.") If, for example, the mean of a sample falls within the critical region, then it is unlikely that the difference between the sample mean and the *population mean is due to chance alone.

Critical Theory A term applied to several approaches to research and scholarship, most of which blend *relativism with left-wing political commitments.

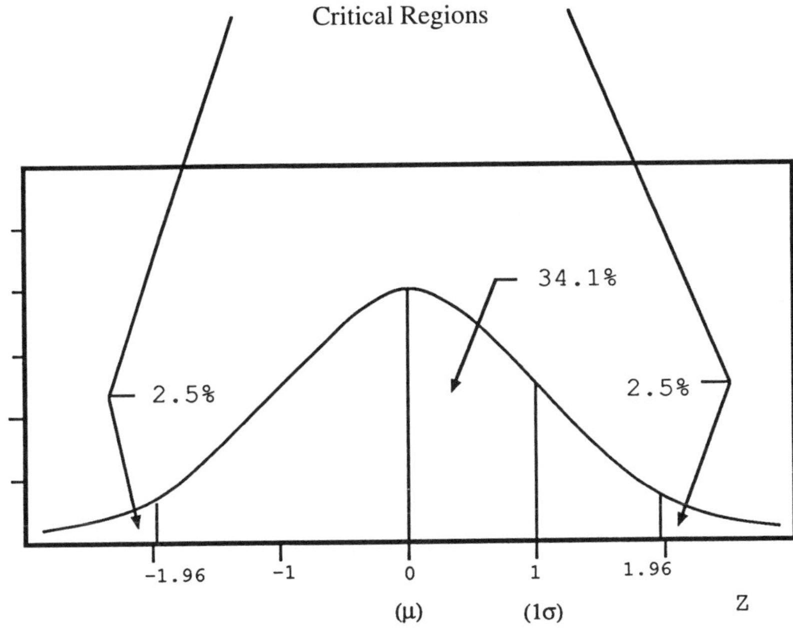

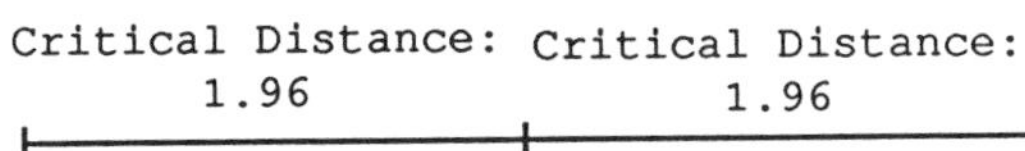

Critical Regions
SOURCE: L. Mohr, *Significance Testing* (Newbury Park, CA: Sage, 1990), p. 39.

Critical Values (a) The values that determine the *critical regions in a *sampling distribution. The critical values separate the obtained values that will and will not result in rejecting the *null hypothesis. See the illustration under *critical regions.

(b) Tables of values for *test statistics, which when exceeded enable the researcher to reject the null hypothesis. Such tables are used to interpret the results of a *t test, a *chi-square statistic, or an *F ratio. The values on such tables are in the *metric of these tests; they are not expressed in *raw data.

Cronbach's Alpha A measure of internal *reliability or consistency of the items in an *index. Cronbach's alpha ranges from 0 to 1.0 and indicates how much the items in an index are measuring the same thing.

For example, if survey researchers asked a series of questions to measure a particular variable, they could use Cronbach's alpha to determine the extent to which people answered the questions in the index in the same way. If, for instance, all respondents who said "yes" to question 1 always said "yes" to questions 2 and 3, the alpha for those three would be 1.0.

Crossbreaks Also called cross-tabulations ("tabs") and cross partitions. A way of arranging data about categorical variables in a matrix so that relations can be more clearly seen. This is not to be confused with a *factorial table, in which two or more variables are related to a third. While not all researchers make these distinctions in the terms, the concepts are quite distinct. Compare *contingency table.

For example, Table 1 is a 2 × 2 crossbreak table. It shows the relation between race and high school dropout rates. Table 2, on the other hand, is a 2 × 2 factorial table where the influence of two variables (race and education) on a third, average annual income, is shown. (Figures for both tables are approximate for 1990.)

Table 1 Percentage of High School Dropouts Among Persons 16-24 Years Old

	Race	
Dropout	*Whites*	*Blacks*
Yes	12.0	13.2
No	88.0	86.8

Table 2 Adult Males' Annual Income by Race and Education Level (full-time workers 25+ years old)

	High School Graduates	*College Graduates*
Whites	$26,500	$41,100
Blacks	$20,300	$31,400

Cross-Cultural Method See *comparative method.

Crossed Factor Design The usual way two or more factors are combined in a *factorial design. When every level of one factor appears with every level of the other factor(s), they are said to be (completely) crossed. The opposite of crossed is "nested." See *nested design for an illustration contrasting the two designs.

Cross-Level Inferences Making inferences about one *level of analysis based on data about another, such as making inferences about individuals based on data about groups. See *ecological fallacy.

Crossover Interaction Another term for *disordinal interaction.

Cross Partition A combination of two or more *partitions.

Say, for example, we were studying unemployment rates. We could look at them in general (for all people) or we could partition the data by group. We could examine unemployment among men and women (one partition) or among different ethnic groups (a second partition). Cross partitions would combine the first two partitions (Sex by Ethnicity) so that we could study groups such as white women, Hispanic men, and so on.

Cross Products Short for cross-products deviation scores. A step in the calculations to determine the *covariance; the cross products are obtained by multiplying the *deviation scores of one variable times those of another. See *covariance (Column 6) for an example.

Cross-Products Ratio Another term for *odds ratio.

Cross-Sectional Data Data gathered at a particular point in time. Compare *time-series data, *panel study.

Cross-Sectional Study A study conducted at a single point in time by, so to speak, taking a "slice" (a cross section) of a population at a particular time. Compare *panel study, *longitudinal study.

Cross-sectional studies provide only indirect evidence about the effects of time and must be used with great caution when drawing conclusions about change. For example, a cross-sectional survey might show that respondents aged 60-65 are more likely to be racially prejudiced than respondents aged 20-25; but this does not necessarily mean that, as the younger group ages, it will become more prejudiced—nor does it necessarily mean that the older group was once less prejudiced.

Cross-Tabulation A way of presenting data about two variables in a table so that their relations are more obvious. Also called a *contingency table or a *crossbreak table. It can be used for *categorical variables only and shows the joint *frequency distributions of the two variables. Compare *factorial table. The following table is an example of a cross-tabulation of religious preference and political party affiliation:

Political Party Affiliation by Religious Affiliation (in percentages)

	Religious Affiliation					
Political Party	*Protestant*	*Catholic*	*Jewish*	*None*	*Other*	*All*
Democrat	36	45	35	28	56	38
Independent	33	38	39	61	44	36
Republican	31	17	26	11	0	26
Total	100	100	100	100	100	100

C

Crucial Experiment An experiment or other study that decisively tests a theory or hypothesis. There is some controversy about whether any one experiment can be crucial in this sense, particularly in the social and behavioral sciences.

Cultural Capital Resources (such as verbal fluency and educational credentials) that one can use to obtain income or other resources. Compare *capital, *social capital, *human capital.

Cultural Relativism The belief that human thought and action can be judged only from the perspective of the culture out of which they have grown.

For example, a person who is generally opposed to male chauvinism, but who is also a cultural relativist, might conclude that one should not condemn male chauvinism if it could be seen as an integral part of the culture of a particular ethnic group. Of course, this relativistic judgment could itself be relative to another cultural group, middle-class Western intellectuals perhaps.

Cumulative Frequency For any value or *class interval in a *frequency distribution, the total up to and including that value or interval.

For example, here are the grades of 43 students on a final exam. The cumulative frequency for the class interval 70-79 is 13, which is the total up to and including that interval (4 + 9 = 13).

Final Examination Grades of 43 Students

Interval	*Frequency*	*Cumulative Frequency*
90-99	12	43 (4 + 9 + 18 + 12)
80-89	18	31 (4 + 9 + 18)
70-79	9	13 (4 + 9)
60-69	4	4

Cumulative Scale A *scale, strictly speaking. See *Guttman scale, *index.

Cup In *set theory, the symbol ∪, meaning "or." It is used to indicate the *union of two sets. Compare *cap.

Current Population Survey An annual survey conducted by the U.S. Census Bureau. About 60,000 households are sampled and studied, mainly about income and employment status.

Curvilinear Regression Another term for *polynomial regression.

Curvilinear Relation (or Correlation) A relationship between two *variables that, when plotted on a graph, form a curve rather than a straight line (a *linear relationship). See *eta squared, *polynomial regression analysis.

For example, the relationship between children's vocabulary scores when entering school and their parents' incomes is curvilinear in some less developed countries where wealthy parents often hire servants (who tend to have smaller vocabularies) to take care of their children. Such a relationship is plotted in the following example.

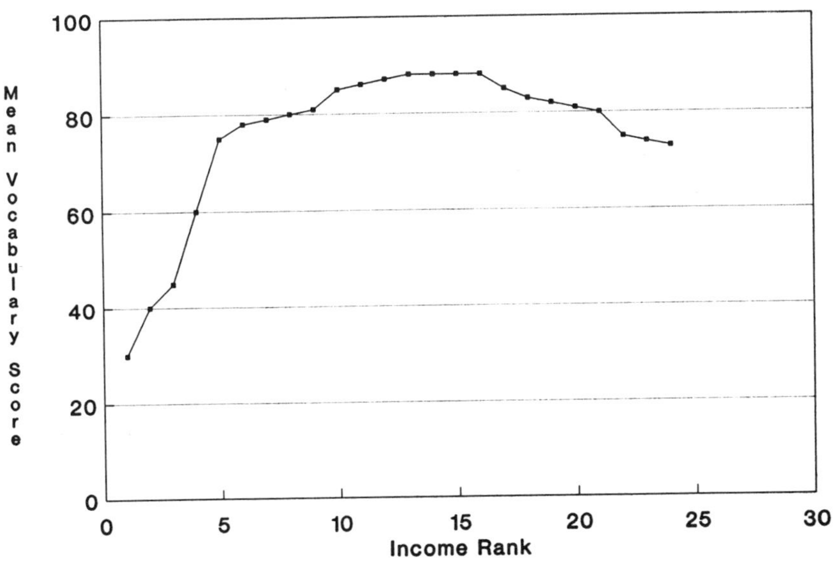

Curvilinear Relation

CV Coefficient of variation.

Cybernetics A discipline specializing in the study of communication systems, particularly as they relate to control mechanisms, as when computers run robotic assembly lines. Compare *artificial intelligence, *information theory.

D

D Abbreviation for a standardized *effect size index. It reports the difference between the *means of two groups in terms of their common *standard deviation. When $d = 1.00$, for example, the mean of one group is one standard deviation above that of the other group. A lowercase *d* is used for the *parametric statistic; an uppercase *D* is used for the *nonparametric statistic. See *Somers's *d*, *Kim's *d*.

Dandekar's Correction A method of adjusting the calculation of a *chi-square statistic for a *2 × 2 table. Compare *Yates's correction.

Data Information collected by a researcher. ("Data" is the plural term; the singular is "datum," but usage varies.) Data are often thought of as statistical or quantitative, but they may take many other forms as well—such as transcripts of interviews or videotapes of social interactions. Nonquantitative data such as transcripts or videotapes are often *coded or translated into numbers to make them easier to analyze.

Data Base A collection of data organized for rapid search and retrieval, usually by a computer; often a consolidation of many records previously stored separately.

Data Curve A line formed by connecting the *data points on a graph. For an example, see *frequency polygon or *learning curve.

Data Entry The process of preparing data for use by a computer or of putting data into a computer, usually by using a keyboard.

Data File A collection of *data records organized for retrieval and analysis.

Data Matrix A grid for storing and subsequently locating data, usually in a computer format.

For example, suppose a survey organization interviewed 1,500 people. Each *respondent was asked 90 questions. The results of the survey could be put in the following type of data matrix. The rows represent the persons interviewed (the *units of analysis) and the columns their answers to the questions (the *variables). In the example, the x shows the location (the *cell) of respondent number 0001's answer to question number 1 (Q1); y shows where 0004's answer to Q3 would be placed; and z indicates where 1500's answer to Q2 would be.

Data Matrix of Hypothetical Survey

Respondent	*Question*	*Q1*	*Q2*	*Q3*	*Q4*	.	.	.	*Q90*
0001		x							
0002									
0003									
0004				y					
0005									
.									
.									
.									
1500			z						

Data Point An individual piece of data, a datum. Often, the point at which two values intersect on a graph, as in the following example where the data point for a subject who is 66 inches tall and weighs 150 pounds is circled.

Data Reconstruction In *meta-analysis, any of various methods for using research findings to calculate data not reported. This is done so that the person doing a meta-analysis can compare or combine the results of different studies that do not report their results in the same way.

Probably the most common form of data reconstruction occurs when a study reports the total number of subjects and the percentage of them that fall into various categories, for example, "of the 1,500 people interviewed, 52% were females, 18.6% of whom had four or more years of college education." A researcher could reconstruct the absolute numbers from these percentages: 780 females were interviewed; 145 of them had four or more years of college.

Data Record A grouping of data composed of one or more lines. There is one record for each subject or *case in a study. A record is part of a *data file. The columns indicate the location of the data about each

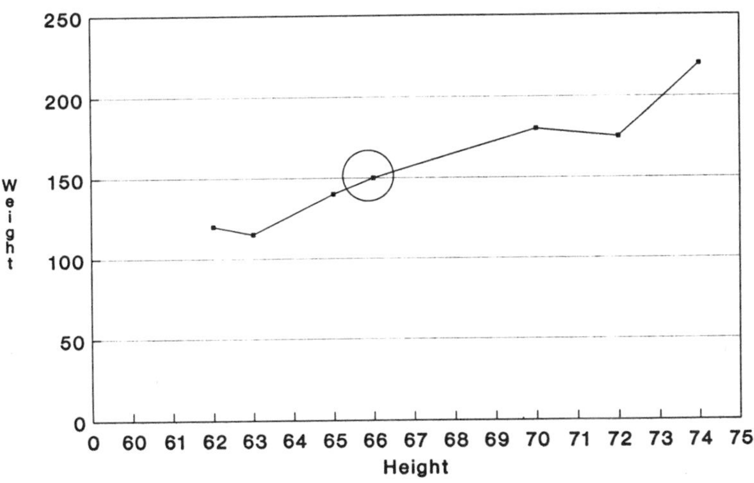

Data Point

variable for each case, as in the following example giving the age, height, and weight for three subjects. (Compare *data matrix.)

	Variable 1 (age)	*Variable 2 (height)*	*Variable 3 (weight)*
Case/Record 1	27	72	173
Case/Record 2	35	70	180
Case/Record 3	25	63	125

Data Set A collection of related data items, such as the answers given by respondents to all the questions on a survey.

Datum A single piece of *data.

Debriefing Explaining the purposes of an experiment to subjects after their participation in it is over. This is particularly required, legally as well as ethically, when the experiment has involved deceiving subjects or has in any way put them at risk of some harm. See *dehoaxing, *desensitizing.

Decidable Said of problems that are solvable, particularly with an *effective procedure or an *algorithm.

Decile One of the points that divides a *frequency distribution into 10 equal parts: 10% of the cases fall below the first decile, 20% below the second, and so on.

For example, if there were 120 million wage earners in the United States, a researcher might divide them into ranked tenths (or deciles) of 12 million each, the lowest-earning tenth, the second lowest earning, and so on. This would facilitate comparisons, such as of the average earnings of people in different deciles.

Decision Error A mistake made when deciding whether or not to reject the *null hypothesis. Compare *Type I Error and *Type II Error.

Decision Problem The problem of figuring out whether a problem is *decidable.

Decision Rule A statement specifying when a statistic we are about to compute will lead us to reject or not reject the *null hypothesis.

For example, a decision rule could read as follows: If the difference between the diabetes mellitus rates for samples of ethnic groups A, B, and C are equal to or greater than $x\%$, we will reject the null hypothesis of no difference between the groups.

Decision Table A table depicting the alternatives to be considered in a given problem, along with the outcomes of each alternative and action(s) to be taken.

For example, suppose you went to a doctor who told you that you had a terrible degenerative disease. The *probability is very great (.90) that it will kill you within in a year. You can reduce your chances of death from the disease (but only somewhat, to .80) by a radical change of diet. There is an operation, but it is risky: 50% of those who have the operation are cured, but 50% die on the operating table. The following decision table shows your options and the likely outcomes. Without any other information, it looks like your best choice is to have the operation.

Decision Table

Options	*Outcomes, Probability of Survival*
Do nothing	.10
Change diet	.20
Operation	.50

Decision Theory An interdisciplinary area of research that focuses on how to select good ways of making decisions on the basis of evidence.

It originated in problems of economic decision making but has become increasingly associated with statistics and hypothesis testing. See *game theory, *minimax principle.

Decision Tree A graphic representation of the alternatives in a decision-making problem.

For example, suppose you were considering buying some high risk stock. The cost of the stock is $5,000. If the company in which you are investing is successful, your stock will be worth $40,000. If it fails, you lose the $5,000. On the basis of past performance of such companies, you estimate that the probability of success for this one is .10 or 10%. The solution to the problem of whether or not to invest can be summarized in the following decision tree.

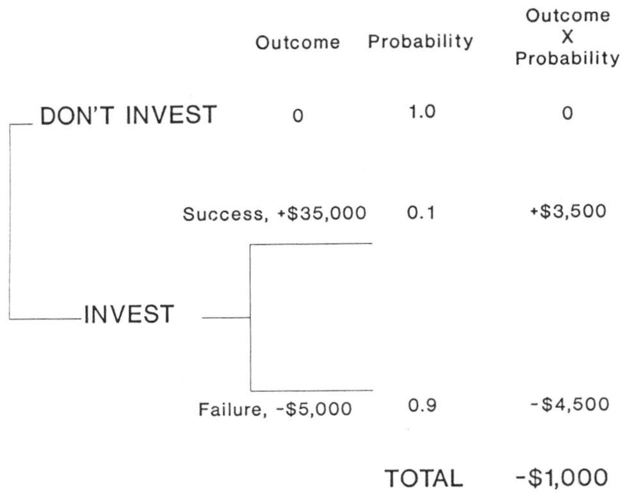

Decision Tree

Decode To translate or determine the meaning of *data that have been *coded.

Decomposition (a) Splitting a *time series into its component parts: *trends, regular *fluctuations, and random fluctuations. (b) A similar division of a *correlation coefficient into direct effects, indirect effects, and dependence on common causes. Compare *partition.

Deduction (a) A conclusion that follows logically from known (or assumed) principles, that is, that uses *deductive methods. (b) The process of reasoning that moves from general principles to conclusions about particular instances. See *deductive. Compare *induction.

Deductive Said of conclusions derived by reasoning rather than by data gathering; or, research methods using such reasoning. A *hypothesis is often arrived at by deduction from a *theory or other assumed truth; the hypothesis could then be tested using *inductive (data gathering) research methods. For example:

(a) prejudice is the product of ignorance;

(b) education reduces ignorance;

(c) therefore the prejudice level will go down as the education level goes up.

The assumptions or theories are a and b; c is the deduction. It can be turned into a research hypothesis. For instance, one could do survey research to see whether education levels and prejudice levels vary *inversely. Are people with low levels of education more likely to give prejudiced answers to survey questions, and vice versa?

Default In computer jargon, said of a disk or a drive or a value. It is the one the computer *software assumes you mean when you don't tell it otherwise, that is, when you "default" on your obligation to specify what you mean.

For example, if you give the computer the instruction "save this file" but do not specify where to save it, the computer will save it on the default disk. The term is sometimes used more broadly, as in ".05 is the default *alpha level used in this research;" this means: "unless I say otherwise, it is .05."

Degrees of Freedom Usually abbreviated "df." The number of values free to vary when computing a statistic. This number is necessary to interpret a *chi-square statistic, an *F ratio, and a *t score.

Many people find the concept of df difficult but the practical application relatively easy; that is, statistics texts contain clear rules for how to calculate and use the df to interpret a statistic.

The degrees of freedom in a *cross-tabulation provide the clearest example. The df are computed by multiplying the number of rows minus 1 times the number of columns minus 1; df = $(R - 1)(C - 1)$. Thus the more categories the variables are broken into, the higher the degrees of freedom.

For example, suppose a professor with 130 students gave a test and tabulated the scores. Table 1 is a *two-by-two (2×2) table; it has 2 rows and 2 columns. Using the formula, df = $(R - 1)(C - 1) = (2 - 1)(2 - 1) = 1 \times 1 = 1$. Table 1 has 1 df, which means, among other things, that, if you know one of the *cell values *and* the totals (or *marginals), you can figure out the other three. For instance, if 40 men passed, it is easy to figure out how many men failed (70 – 40 = 30), how many women passed (90 – 40 = 50), and how many women failed (40 – 30 = 10).

Table 2 is a 2 × 5 table. Using the formula df = $(R - 1)(C - 1) = (2 - 1)(5 - 1) = 1 \times 4 = 4$. This means that, if you know four of the cell values and the marginals, you can compute the other six—because they are no longer free to vary once four are determined.

D

Table 1 Test Grade by Sex

	Pass	*Fail*	*Total*
Men			70
Women			60
Total	90	40	130

Table 2 Test Grade by Sex

	A	*B*	*C*	*D*	*F*	*Total*
Men						70
Women						60
Total	20	50	20	30	10	130

Dehoaxing A form of *debriefing of subjects in an experiment after their participation is concluded. When the experimental design requires deceiving ("hoaxing") subjects about themselves, dehoaxing involves convincing them that they have been deceived. The idea is to eliminate any undesirable effects the deception might have had. Compare *desensitizing. Dehoaxing should also be considered after a *participant observation study in which the investigator has not revealed that he or she was doing research.

For example, if a learning experiment involved studying the effects of believing that one is not good at learning a particular subject, the researchers might give all subjects an aptitude test in a field. The *experimental group might be told that they did quite poorly and demonstrated low aptitude, regardless of how they actually performed. The *control group might not be informed one way or another about their scores. Then, both groups could be given the same kind of learning task to see whether the experimental group (those who had been falsely told they were low-aptitude subjects) performed any differently than the control group. It is generally considered the researcher's ethical responsibility in such circumstances to dehoax the subjects, to convince them that they were deceived and that, in this example, they are not in fact low in aptitude. It may sometimes be difficult to convince subjects; the researcher's credibility can be reduced by the fact that he has just admitted lying ("I was lying before, but now I'm going to tell you the truth").

D

Deliberate Sampling Another term for *quota sampling. See *purposive sampling.

Delphi Technique A method of survey research developed by the RAND Corporation requiring repeated surveying of the same respondents on the same issue or problem so that they can come to an informed consensus.

For example, managers in a large organization might be sent questionnaires asking them to rank a list of the organization's priorities and to explain their reasoning. Further surveys (a minimum of four) provide each respondent with information about how the others have answered.

Delta A Greek letter most often used to symbolize one form or another of difference. For example, delta-L^2 is the difference between two L^2s.

Demand Characteristics Any of the numerous potential cues available to subjects in experimental research regarding the nature and purpose of the study that might influence the subjects' reaction to the experimental treatment.

For example, an experimenter might, without knowing it, nod encouragingly when subjects acted in ways that seemed to be supporting the research hypothesis—that is, the experimenter seems to be "demanding" certain behavior from subjects. One way to reduce this problem is to use *double-blind procedures.

Denominator Another term for the *divisor; in division, the part of the fraction that is below the line.

Density Function The equation for a *theoretical relative frequency distribution. Also called "probability function."

Dependent Event In *probability theory, said when the occurrence of one event changes the probability that another will take place. See *conditional probability. Compare *independent event.

Dependent Samples Another term for *correlated samples or groups. Said of research groups that are not drawn independently from a population.

Dependent samples occur most commonly in before-and-after studies when two measures are taken on the same subjects. Dependent samples require different *test statistics than independent samples.

Dependent Variable (a) The presumed effect in a study; so called because it "depends" on another variable. (b) The variable whose values are predicted by the *independent variable, whether or not caused by it.

For example, in a study to see if there is a relationship between students' drinking of alcoholic beverages and their grade point averages, the drinking behavior would be the presumed cause (independent variable); the grade point average would be the effect (dependent variable).

Note: Some authors only use the term "dependent variable" for *experimental research; for *nonexperimental research, they might use *criterion variable or "outcome variable." Most commonly, however, dependent variable is used in both experimental and nonexperimental research.

Derived Statistics Statistics calculated on the basis of other simple (or primary) descriptive statistics. Compare *raw data.

For example, say you had *data describing the total number of murders last year in all U.S. cities and the total populations of those cities. You could use those primary statistics to compute the murder rates—statistics derived by dividing the number of murders in each city by its population. Other examples of derived statistics include *percentile ranks and *standard scores. Compare *data reconstruction.

Descending Order An order that begins with the highest value and moves to the lowest. The opposite of *ascending order.

Descriptive Research Research that describes phenomena as they exist. Descriptive research is usually contrasted with *experimental research in which environments are controlled and *subjects are given different *treatments.

Descriptive Statistics Procedures for summarizing, organizing, graphing, and, in general, describing quantitative information. Often contrasted with *inferential statistics, which is used to make inferences about a *population based on information about a *sample drawn from that population.

Desensitizing A form of *debriefing subjects after their participation in an experiment. The purpose of desensitizing is to enable subjects to cope with any negative information they may have acquired about themselves as a result of an experiment. Compare *dehoaxing, *Milgram experiments.

Design Short for *research design, that is, the plan a researcher will follow when conducting a study.

Determination, Coefficient of A statistic that indicates how much of the *variance in one variable is determined or explained by one or more other variables; more strictly, how much the variance in one is associated with variance in the others. It is calculated by squaring the *correlation coefficient. Thus it is abbreviated r^2 in *bivariate analyses and R^2 in *multivariate analyses. Also called "index of determination." See *strength of association.

D

For example, one might find a statement like the following in a research report: "Education level attained explains 22% of adult occupational status ($r^2 = .22$)."

Determinism The theory that all events and behaviors are determined or caused by prior events, conditions, and the operation of natural laws. Under the assumptions of extreme determinism, there are no random events and people do not have free will. "Soft" versions of determinism, which allow for free will, exist; they are more common among social and behavioral scientists than the strict variety.

Deterministic Model A causal model that contains no random or probabilistic elements; one in which all causes and values are known and all the variance in the dependent variable(s) can be explained. Compare *stochastic model.

Deviation Score A statistic indicating how much the *mean score of a group of scores misrepresents (deviates from) an individual score. It is obtained by subtracting the mean from the individual score. Also known as an *error score. See *covariance for an example.

df *Degrees of freedom.

Diachronic Said of research that studies events as they occur or change over time. Often contrasted with *synchronic. Compare *panel study, *event history analysis.

Dialectic A method of reasoning that proceeds by developing contradictions to propositions and then discovering ways to resolve those contradictions so as to discover new ideas and advance thought. Although employed by many philosophers since ancient Greece, the dialectic is perhaps best known as it was used by Karl Marx, who held that history progresses dialectically, through the conflict of opposites.

Dichotomous Variable A *categorical variable that can place subjects into only two groups, such as male/female, alive/dead, or pass/fail.

Difference of Proportions A method for comparing proportions for *dichotomous variables. One proportion is subtracted from the other. The result ranges from −1.0 to +1.0, with zero indicating that the two variables have identical conditional probabilities on a dependent variable.

For example, a medical treatment that resulted in Cure or No cure studied for men and women could use the difference of proportions method to describe its results. If the proportion of women treated who were cured was .60 and the proportion of men was .45, then the difference of proportions would be .15.

Difference Sign Test A test of *time-series data to see if a *linear trend exists. It is calculated by counting the number of times the series increased—for example, the number of times the Dow-Jones average went up over the past year. See *sign test.

Diffuse Comparisons Techniques used in *meta-analysis to compare the amount of heterogeneity in the analyzed studies' *significance levels and *effect sizes. The more heterogeneity or "diffuseness," the harder it is to meaningfully integrate the studies. See *focused comparisons. Compare *divergent validity.

Diffusion of Treatments A threat to the *validity of a study arising from communication among the subjects, in particular when the communication results in the experimental *treatment being spread ("diffused") among *control group subjects. Also called "diffusion effect." Contrast with *double-blind procedure.

For example, if a new technique were being tested in a chemistry laboratory to see if it led to quicker and more accurate analyses, it could be tried out by a sample of the lab workers. They would be the *experimental group. The rest of the workers would be the *control group. To measure the effectiveness of the new technique, the productivity and efficiency of the two groups of workers would be compared. If, however, the experimental group liked the new technique and told their friends in the control group about it, and they also started using it, the validity of any comparison between the two groups would be doubtful at best—because of the diffusion effect.

Digital Data (a) Information represented by numbers (digits) such as time on a digital watch; often contrasted with *analog data such as time represented by movement of a watch's hands. (b) Loosely used to mean *binary, as in "digital computer," that is, a computer that uses information represented in the form of 1s and 0s. The 1s and 0s represent electronic computer switches that are "on" (1) or "off" (0).

Dimensionality The number of aspects or "dimensions" a construct has. Is "tolerance," for example, one attitude or a cluster of related attitudes? If it is one attitude, it is said to be a unidimensional construct; if more than one, a multidimensional construct.

***D* Index** See **D*.

Directional Hypothesis (or Test) An *alternative hypothesis that specifies the direction of difference (greater or smaller) from a *null hypothesis. Sometimes called a *one-tailed test.

For example, say the null hypothesis were as follows: There is no difference in manual dexterity between Group A and Group B. An example of a directional alternative hypothesis would be this: Group A's average dexterity quotient is greater than B's.

D

Direct Relationship (or Correlation) A relation between two *variables such that, whenever one goes up or down, so does the other. Also called *positive relationship. Compare *inverse relationship.

For example, hours spent studying and grade on an examination might be directly related; that is, the more hours you studied, the better you would do; the fewer, the worse.

Disaggregate To separate out for purposes of analysis the parts of an *aggregate statistic.

For example, if we were interested in trends in average SAT scores over the past 20 years, we might want to disaggregate the data so that we could look at separate trends for males, females, blacks, whites, students in and not in college preparatory programs, and so on.

Discrete Variable Commonly, another term for *categorical (or *nominal) variable. Compare *continuous variable.

More formally, a discrete variable is one made up of distinct and separate units or categories. When a variable is discrete, only a finite number of values separates any two points. While all categorical variables are discrete, in some usages, there might be dispute about whether to label particular variables discrete or continuous. This matters because it determines the statistical techniques that are appropriate to use.

For example, the number of people in a family is clearly a discrete variable. So are flips of a coin; if you flip a coin 10 times, you can't get 3.27 tails, only 3 or 4. But the distinction is not always so clear. Take personal income. It looks like a continuous variable, and it is usually treated as one in research. One weekly income might be $411.01, another, $411.02; there are millions of possible values stretching from zero to Ross Perot's income. More strictly, however, income is discrete.

Income does not come in units smaller than one cent; there is only one value between $411.01 and $411.03 (i.e., $411.02). By contrast, weight is a truly or a strictly continuous variable. No matter how close the weights of people are, there is always an intermediate value, although an ordinary scale might not capture it.

Discriminant Analysis (DA) A form of *regression analysis designed for classification. It allows two or more *continuous *independent variables (or *predictor variables) to be used to place individuals or cases into the categories of a *categorical *dependent variable. DA also provides a means of calculating a weighted combination of all independent variables so as to be able to cut the dependent variable into discrete categories. Also called discriminant "function" analysis. Called "multiple" discriminant analysis when subjects are to be placed in more than two categories.

DA was originally used for work such as deciding whether a collection of thigh bones dug up by paleontologists belonged to early hominoids, chimps, or baboons. Continuous variables, such as the bones' length, weight, circumference, and so on, were used to "discriminate" among them and place them in the right categories.

As a second example, illustrating another use of DA, suppose researchers wanted to use data about previous high school students to figure out which current students were and were not likely to graduate. The categorical dependent variable would be graduation yes/no. The continuous predictor variables might be number of days absent, grade point average, score on a verbal ability test, and so on. A successful discriminant analysis would enable the researchers to predict, with some accuracy, who would be likely to graduate and who wouldn't, and to compare the relative importance of each of the predictor variables.

Discriminant Function Some combination of the observed *independent variables in a *discriminant analysis that aids in distinguishing (discriminating among) categories of the *dependent variable.

Discriminant Validity A measure of the *validity of a *construct that is high when the construct *fails* to *correlate with other, theoretically distinct, constructs. Discriminant validity is the mirror image of *convergent validity.

For example, suppose a researcher is writing a questionnaire containing several questions designed to measure the construct "patriotism." The researcher worries that respondents may just be giving the answers they think are "proper" or that they think the researcher wants to hear (*social desirability bias). So he or she includes questions that measure the construct "socially desirable responding." If the two measures were *not* correlated, the measure of patriotism would have more discriminant validity, that is, it would be unrelated to a measure of something to which it should not be related if it is valid.

Disjoint Sets In *set theory, sets with no common elements, that is, that are "joined by" no common elements, such as the set of all males and the set of all females.

Disordinal Interaction Said of an *interaction effect when the lines on a graph plotting the effect cross. When the lines do not cross, the interaction is called *ordinal. The two graphs below show a disordinal and an ordinal interaction. In neither case are the lines parallel. If they were parallel, there would be no interaction. In an ordinal interaction, the lines *would* cross if extended further. The fact that they are not extended to that point could mean that the researcher was not interested in those levels of the variables—in the example, no more than eight treatments of fertilizer and, of course, by logical necessity, no fewer than zero treatments.

Say a gardener had 9 rows of tomatoes with 9 plants in each row. She planted 3 different brands of tomato plant, A, B, and C, 3 rows each. She gave each of the 9 "columns" of tomatoes a different number of doses of fertilizer and kept a record of the total weight of tomatoes produced by each brand of plant at each dose level. Up to a certain point, fertilizer increases the tomato crop, but, for different brands, it does so *at different rates,* which means there is an interaction effect. The top figure on page 73 shows a disordinal interaction; the bottom figure shows an ordinal interaction.

Doses

Type	*ROW*	*0*	*1*	*2*	*3*	*4*	*5*	*6*	*7*	*8*
	1	a	a	a	a	a	a	a	a	a
A	2	a	a	a	a	a	a	a	a	a
	3	a	a	a	a	a	a	a	a	a
	4	b	b	b	b	b	b	b	b	b
B	5	b	b	b	b	b	b	b	b	b
	6	b	b	b	b	b	b	b	b	b
	7	c	c	c	c	c	c	c	c	c
C	8	c	c	c	c	c	c	c	c	c
	9	c	c	c	c	c	c	c	c	c

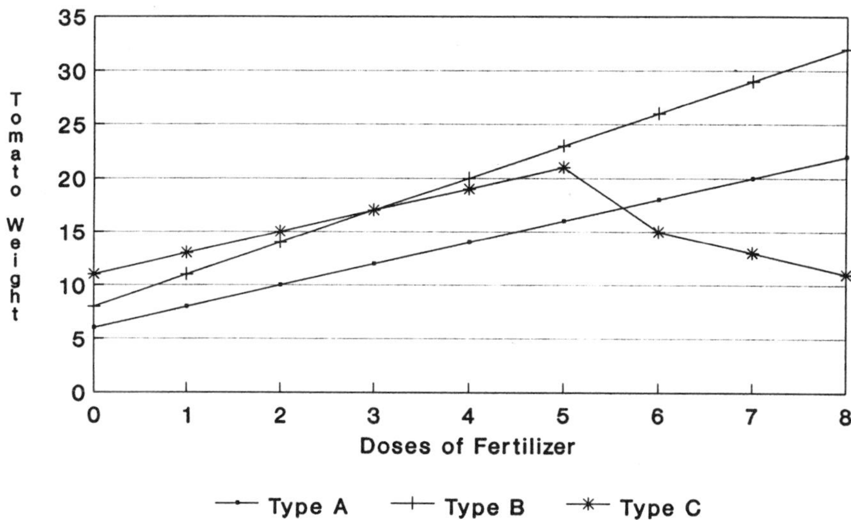

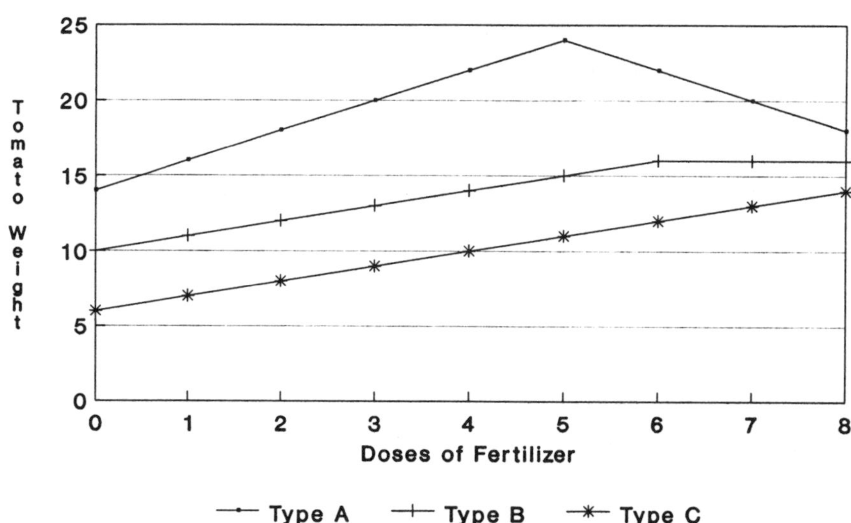

Disordinal/Ordinal Interaction

Dispersion, Measure of A statistic showing the amount of *variation or spread in the scores for, or values of, a *variable. When the dispersion is large, the scores or values are widely scattered; when it is small, they are tightly clustered. The two most commonly used measures of dispersion are the *variance and the *standard deviation.

Distribution A ranking, from lowest to highest, of the values of a variable and the resulting pattern of measures or scores, often as these are plotted on a graph. See *frequency distribution, *kurtosis, *normal curve, *sampling distribution, *skewed distribution.

D

Distribution-Free Statistics (or Tests) A term sometimes used for *nonparametric statistical tests; so called because they do not require assumptions about the form of the distribution of a *population from which a *sample is drawn. Examples include the *chi-square and *Wilcoxon tests. See also *bootstrap methods.

Disturbance Another term for *noise in *information theory; broadly used to mean *random error.

Dividend In mathematical division, the number that is divided—by the *divisor or *denominator. The part of a fraction that is above the line. Also called the *numerator.

Divisor A quantity used to divide another quantity (the *dividend). The part of a fraction that is below the line.

DK Common abbreviation for "Don't Know" in survey research.

Domain (a) A subgroup of a *population that is of special interest to the researchers *sampling it. (b) The content area studied in a *domain-referenced test. (c) In set theory, a set of numbers that can serve as a replacement for a variable; also called "replacement set." See *function.

Domain-Referenced Test A type of achievement test that measures a learner's absolute level of performance in a specific area or "domain," such as long division. Domain-referenced tests usually measure more specifically defined content areas than other achievement tests. Compare *criterion-referenced test, *norm-referenced test.

Domain Sampling Sampling items, such as questions on a questionnaire, in a particular subject area or *domain.

For example, a researcher might be interested in the domain of respondents' attitudes toward affirmative action. Rather than study all responses to all questions that are pertinent, the researcher could take a sample of the questions in the domain (which, in this usage, is a "*population" of items).

DOS Disk Operating System. Computer software that makes a kind of "map" of the disks so as to manage, store, and keep track of files on the disks. It allows one to run other software packages on a microcomputer.

Double-Blind Procedure A means of reducing bias in an *experiment by ensuring that both those who administer a *treatment and those who receive it do not know (are "blind" to) which subjects are in the *control and *experimental groups, that is, who is and is not receiving the treatment.

For example, in a study of the effectiveness of various headache remedies, 80 headache sufferers could be *randomly assigned to four groups. Group A would receive aspirin; Group B, ibuprofen; Group C, acetaminophen; and Group D, a *placebo. The pills might be color-coded but otherwise look the same so that the experimenter handing them out would not know which subjects were getting which, and, of course, the subjects would not know. When subjects experienced pain, they would be given pills depending upon their group and then asked about the relief they got from their pills. Their responses would be data used to evaluate the effectiveness of the various remedies. If the experiment used true double-blind procedures, the researchers analyzing the data would not know, until after they had reached their conclusions, which group received which remedy.

Double-Tailed Test Another name for a *two-tailed test, that is, one for which the *region of rejection of the null hypothesis is made up of (usually equal) areas at both ends of the *sampling distribution. See illustration at *two-tailed test. Compare *one-tailed test/hypothesis.

Download Transferring data from a large computer to a small one.

***D* Test** Also called the Kolmogorov-Smirnov *D* Test. A test of the *statistical significance of the difference between two *frequency distributions. It is a *nonparametric test.

Dummy Coding A way of *coding *categorical variables such that membership in a category is indicated by a 1 and nonmembership by a 0. So called because the zero is silent ("dumb") about nonmembership. One advantage of dummy coding is that it allows researchers to use statistical techniques that assume *interval-level data on variables measured only at the *nominal or *ordinal levels. See *dummy variable. Compare *effects coding, *orthogonal coding.

Dummy Table An empty or blank table (one that "says" nothing) constructed before data are collected and into which the data will be put once they are collected.

Dummy Variable A *dichotomous variable, usually *coded 1 to indicate the presence of an attribute and 0 to indicate its absence. Example: 1 = female; 0 = not female. This coding facilitates the use of *interval-level statistical techniques, which would be hard to interpret if the variable were coded otherwise, such as female = 2, male = 1. Also called "indicator variable." See *dummy coding, *multiple classification analysis.

When a variable has more than two categories, a series of dummy variables can be used. For example, say we wanted to use *regression analysis to study the effects of three kinds of growing conditions (A, B, C) on weight (Y) of pumpkins. The coding would be condition A: 1 = yes; 0 = other than A; B: 1 = yes; 0 = other than B; C: 1 = yes; 0 = other than C. The results of weight (Y) by condition for 15 cases put in dummy variable form would appear as in the following table. Upon examining the table, you might well ask: Whatever happened to C? C need not be included because it can be deduced from the coding of A and B. Indeed, it *must* not be included because the number of dummies must be 1 less than the number of categories to avoid *multicollinearity.

D

Case	*A*	*B*	*Y*
01	1	0	20
02	1	0	21
03	1	0	23
04	1	0	22
05	1	0	18
06	0	1	15
07	0	1	12
08	0	1	11
09	0	1	19
10	0	1	17
11	0	0	24
12	0	0	26
13	0	0	29
14	0	0	28
15	0	0	29

Duncan's Multiple-Range Test A test used after an *analysis of variance (ANOVA) has been conducted to determine which sample means differ significantly from one another.

Dunn Multiple Comparison Test Another term for the *Bonferroni test statistic, that is, a method for multiple comparisons of *treatment effects in *regression analysis and *ANOVA designs.

Duration Recording Measuring the amount of elapsed time a particular behavior lasts, such as using a stopwatch to record how long research subjects spend talking to one another.

Durbin-Watson Statistic A test for *autocorrelation, or serial correlation, in a *time-series, *OLS *regression analysis. As the autocorrelation increases, the Durbin-Watson goes down. The larger the autocorrelation, the less reliable the results of the regression analysis.

DV Common abbreviation for *dependent variable.

Dyad Two persons interacting; often thought of as the most elementary sociological unit.

Dynamic Model In economics and related disciplines, a model in which at least one variable is measured over time.

Dysfunction In *functionalism, used to describe any element of a system that hinders the overall operation of the system, as hostility between groups in a society might impede the functioning of the society.

E

E (a) Upper- or lowercase *E*, the usual symbol for *error, or *error score. See *residual. (b) Uppercase E, *expected value, as in $E(x) = .33$, which means the expected value of x is .33. (c) Lowercase e, the symbol for the "universal constant" (2.718281 . . .), which is an *irrational number that is the base of natural *logarithms and is used in many calculations, including the formula for computing the *normal distribution.

Ecological Correlation A correlation between two variables based on grouped data such as averages for a geographic area or for social groups. One can commit an *ecological fallacy by using such correlations to draw conclusions about individuals.

For example, the correlation between the Gross National Income for various nations and average education level for those nations would be an ecological correlation. Such a correlation would not, however, be valid evidence for an individual to use in deciding whether she or he should go back to school in hopes of earning a higher income.

Ecological Fallacy An error of reasoning committed by coming to conclusions about individuals based only on data about groups.

For example, if crime rates were higher in areas with a high concentration of elderly people, you would be committing an ecological fallacy if you concluded that elderly individuals are more likely to commit crimes.

Reasoning in the opposite direction, from data about a few individuals to generalizations about groups, is also a widespread form of fallacious thinking, but it does not have a well-known technical name.

Ecological Validity A kind of *external validity referring to the generalizability of findings from one group to another group. Usually used when a study does *not* meet the criteria. Compare *population validity.

For example, studies of 19-year-old college students might not be generalizable to 19-year-olds who were not attending college. If a study made such generalizations from one group to the other, it could be lacking in ecological validity.

Effect In *analysis of variance (ANOVA), "effect" refers to differences among group *means, differences presumably caused by differences in the characteristics of, or treatments received by, the groups. *Main effects are differences among group means for levels of a *variable (*factor) apart from the effects of other variables. *Interaction effects occur when the effect for one factor (variable) differs depending on the levels of another factor. See the example at *disordinal interaction.

Effect Coding Also called "effects coding." A way of coding *categorical variables in a *regression analysis. It uses 1, 0, and −1, unlike *dummy coding, which uses only 1 and 0. Effect coding gets its name from the fact that, when it is used, the *regression coefficients (betas) show the effects of the treatments. Compare *orthogonal coding.

Effect Coefficient In *path analysis, the total effect (i.e., direct plus indirect) of an *independent variable on the *dependent variable.

Effectiveness Ability to achieve goals well; or, the degree to which intentions are achieved. Often contrasted in *evaluation research with *efficiency, which is a measure of cost relative to output.

Effective Procedure A series of steps that enable one to solve a problem, an *algorithm.

Effect Size Any of several measures of the strength of a relation. By contrast, tests of the *null hypothesis only allow you to conclude that a relation is significantly larger than zero, but they do not tell you by how much. Effect size measures do. Thus the effect size is an estimate of the degree to which a phenomenon is present in a *population and/or the extent to which the null hypothesis is false. See *strength of association.

Efficiency (a) In *experimental design, said of a procedure that uses fewer resources for the same results or that gets more results using the same resources. (b) In statistics, a property of an *estimate of a *population *parameter; the better the estimate, the greater the efficiency. Efficiency is a measure of the *variance of an estimate's *sampling distribution; the smaller the variance, the better the estimator.

Efficient Estimator See *estimator and *efficiency, definition b.

Eigenvalue A statistic used in *factor analysis to indicate how much of the variation in the original group of variables is accounted for by a particular factor. It has similar uses in *canonical correlation analysis and *principal components analysis. Comes from the German for the "characteristic" (*eigen*) root of a *matrix.

Elaboration A process of studying *correlations between *variables by observing how they are affected when *controlling for the effects of other variables. One goal of elaboration is to uncover *spurious correlations.

Element In *set theory, any one of a set's members. See *vector.

Elementary Event See *event, elementary.

E

Emic *Culturally relative approaches to the study of anthropology that stress participants' understanding of their own culture. Derived, by an indirect route, from the linguistics term "phonemic." Usually contrasted with *etic.

Empirical Said of *data based on observation or experience and of findings that can be verified by observation or experience. Often contrasted with "theoretical." Compare *deductive, *objective.

Empirical Generalization A statement about observable regularities made without any attempt at explanation. Such factual statements can sometimes be useful, but, without being explained by a *theory, they usually add little to science. Compare *middle-range theory.

An example of an empirical generalization is the following: "Men in their twenties have an unusually high rate of killing themselves and others in automobile accidents." There are many possible explanations. Say we theorized that young men are socialized to a subculture that defines traditional manhood as reckless disregard for personal safety. If this theory is true, it could be used to explain other aspects of young men's behavior (e.g., smoking, drinking, participation in violent sports). Furthermore, with the traditional male culture theory, we could make predictions about other groups. For example, as women became more integrated into male-dominated society, their auto death rate should go up (along with their drinking and smoking rates). Or we might predict that the auto death rate for men somewhat separate from traditional male culture (e.g., homosexual men) would be lower.

Empiricism Any approach to research relying heavily on observation and experiment; also, the belief that only such an approach yields true knowledge. Compare *positivism, *idealism.

Empty Cells A problem in research using *cross-tabulations that arises from having too many categories or too few subjects. Whenever a category has no subjects that fit into it, you have an empty cell. See *cell.

For example, suppose you survey a *sample of 100 people on their attitudes. You are interested not only in the overall response of the sample but also in the attitudes of different groups of people. Among the categories you think are important are gender, age, race, education, and occupation. It is clear that with only 100 people answering your survey you would not have many people in each category. Some will almost surely be empty, for example, white female blue-collar workers over 60 with more than 12 years' education. Of course, you might have several people in that category, but, if you do, you will be short of people in other categories.

Empty Set A *set that contains no *elements. Also called "null set."

Encode To put into a *code, as by assigning numbers to categories. Encoding always involves simplifying observations. See *coding.

Endogenous Variable A variable that is an inherent part of the system being studied and that is determined from within the system. In other words, a variable that is caused by other variables in a causal system. Generally contrasted with *exogenous variable. See *path diagram. In the following figure, C and D are endogenous; A and B are exogenous.

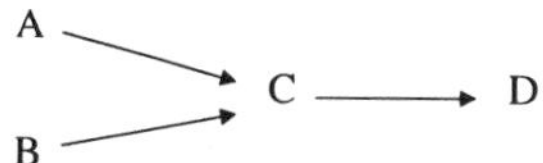

Entails Said of a statement that must logically follow from another statement. "A entails B" means that if, A is true, B must also be true. Such entailment is very rare in the social and behavioral sciences. Compare *necessary and *sufficient conditions.

Epistemology Literally, "the study of knowledge." That branch of philosophy concerned with the nature and criteria of knowledge. Methodological debates in the social and behavioral sciences are often the result of differences of opinion about epistemological issues. See *idealism, *empiricism, *materialism, *realism.

Epsilon Squared Another term for *adjusted R^2.

Equation A formal statement that two mathematical expressions, placed on either side of an equal sign (=), are equal, such as $12 \times 9 = 108$, or $Y' = bX + a$. See *model.

ERIC Educational Resources Information Center. Managed by the National Institute of Education, ERIC indexes and abstracts journal articles (in *Current Index to Journals in Education*, or *CIJE*) and other documents and research reports (in *Resources in Education,* or *RIE*).

Error The difference between an observed score and a predicted or estimated score. Symbolized as *e* or *E*.

Error Score The difference between an estimated value, such as a *mean, and the actual value of a subject on a variable. Also called *deviation score.

For example, say that the average (mean) verbal GRE score for students in your department is 560 and your score is 580. If the head of your department used the mean score to predict your score, his error score for you would be 20 (580 – 560 = 20).

E

Error Sum of Squares In *analysis of variance, the within-group sum of squares, that is, the part not explainable by the *treatment effects. Also called residual sum of squares. See *error variance.

Error Term The part of an *equation indicating what is unexplained by the *independent variables. The error term specifies how big the unexplained part is. Also called the *residual term because it is what is left over after one subtracts from the total *variance in the *dependent variable the part that can be explained by the independent variables. Also called "disturbance term."

Error Variance Any uncontrolled or unexplained variability, such as within-group differences in an *ANOVA. Also called *random error and "random variance." The error variance is the variance of the *error term.

ES *Effect size.

Estimate The value of an *estimator.

For example, we might use the *mean daily caloric intake of a sample of adults to estimate the mean daily caloric intake of a population of adults. The sample mean is our estimator; if we calculated it to be 2570, then 2570 would be the estimate given us by our estimator.

Estimation Using a *sample *statistic to determine the probable value of a *population *parameter. See *inferential statistics.

For example, let's say you wanted to know the average (*mean) verbal SAT score of students at your university. Rather than going through the files and getting the *data for several thousand undergraduates, you could take a *random sample of, say, 200 files. Suppose the mean verbal SAT score of those 200 students was 553. If you used that average score to estimate the score of the population of all students, this would be *point* estimation. If you said that the interval between 533 and 573 was likely to contain the mean score of the population, this would be *interval* estimation.

Estimator A *sample statistic that is used to determine a probable value of a *population parameter, as one might use a known *mean value of a sample to estimate the value of the population mean. See *estimate, *estimation. Good estimators should be "consistent," "*unbiased," and "*efficient."

Eta or Eta Squared A *correlation coefficient that can be used to express a *curvilinear relationship. It is read in the same way as other correlation coefficients. Also called *correlation ratio.

Eta squared is a measure of how much of the *variance in a *dependent variable (measured at the *interval level) can be explained by a *categorical (nominal, discrete) *independent variable. It can also be interpreted as a *PRE measure, that is, it tells us how much better we can guess the value of the dependent variable by knowing the independent variable.

Ethnographic Research Any of several methods of describing social or cultural life based on direct, systematic observation, such as becoming a participant in a social system. Ethnographic methods are most commonly used by anthropologists. See *descriptive research, *participant observation.

Ethnomethodology A type of *ethnographic research in sociology founded by Harold Garfinkel. It focuses on the commonsense understanding of social life held by ordinary people (the *ethnos*), usually as discovered by *participant observation. Often the observer's own methods of making sense of the situation become the object of investigation.

Ethology Research methods stressing observation and detailed descriptions of behavior in natural settings. The term originally referred to the study of animal behavior, but it has come to be used in research on human behavior when the methods are strongly observational and minimally interpretive. See *ethnographic research.

Etic Methods of study in anthropology stressing material and scientific, rather than cultural, explanations for social and cultural phenomena. Derived, by an indirect route, from the linguistics term phon*etic*. Compare *emic, with which etic is usually contrasted.

Evaluation Research Research, using any of several methods, designed to test the *effectiveness or impact of a social program or intervention. It is very often conducted by interdisciplinary teams of researchers. Evaluation research is a type of *applied research. Also called "program evaluation."

Evaluation research became important in the 1960s with the expansion of social welfare programs in that decade; it was curbed considerably during the Reagan and Bush administrations of the 1980s and 1990s.

Examples of evaluation research include studies designed to tell whether a school desegregation plan improved intergroup harmony, whether new sentencing guidelines deterred crime, or whether driver education reduced fatal accidents.

E

Event In *set theory, any group of *elementary events. A *subset. Also called "event class."

For example, if the *elementary* event were the 7 of clubs in a deck of cards, an event would be the 7s, the clubs, the black cards, and so on.

Event, Elementary In *set and *probability theory, a single *data point in, or element or member of, a *sample space.

For example, the 7 of clubs would be an elementary event in a deck of cards (the sample space). A particular college student would be an elementary event in the *population (or sample space) of all college students.

Event History Analysis Methods for studying the movement over time of subjects through successive states or conditions. The goal of the research is to study change from one state to the next and how long each of the states lasts. "Events" are changes from one categorical state to another. See *longitudinal study, *time-series data, *survival analysis. While *panel studies do research on subjects over time, they do so in successive *waves. Because they do not usually investigate what happened between the *waves, panel studies can be thought of as a series of *cross sections of the same group.

For example, one could use event history analysis to study marital status with the states or conditions being unmarried, married, divorced, remarried, widowed.

Exhaustive Said of a group of conditions, events, or values of a variable that, when taken together, account for (or "exhaust") all possibilities.

For example, age categories 0-19, 20-39, and 40+ are exhaustive; everybody fits into one of them. On the other hand, Christian, Islamic, and Jewish is not an exhaustive list of religious affiliations. It could be made so, however, by adding Other and None to the list. Compare *mutually exclusive.

Exogenous Variable A variable entering from and determined from outside the system being studied. A causal system says nothing about its exogenous variables. See *endogenous variable for an example.

Expected Frequency In *contingency table problems, the frequency you would predict ("expect")—if you knew only the *marginal totals and if you assumed the *null hypothesis of *independence of the variables.

For example, suppose that in a *sample of 100 adults you had 60 women and 40 men, and 70 of the 100 adults had graduated from high school and 30 had not. You could put the results in a contingency table as in the following:

	Men	*Women*	*Totals*
Graduates	a	b	70
Nongraduates	c	d	30
Totals	40	60	100

Given this information, we can compute the expected frequency for each of the cells, a, b, c, and d. To find the expected frequency for a cell, multiply its row marginal (total) by its column marginal (total) and divide the result by the total number of subjects. For example, the expected number of women high school graduates (cell b) would be 60 × 70 = 4200/100 = 42. You would expect 42 of your sample to be female high school graduates. If your expected frequencies were significantly different than the actual, observed frequencies (you could determine this with a *chi-square test), you could conclude that there was probably some relationship between the variables, that members of one sex were more likely to be high school graduates.

Expected Value (a) The *mean value of a variable in repeated samplings or trials. (b) The mean of the *sampling distribution of a statistic.

The idea grew out of gamblers' calculations of how much they could expect to win (or lose) in a fair game, in the long run, with a bet of a certain size. Say you play roulette making 1,000 bets of $1 on your favorite number. Each time you win, you get $35; each time you lose, the croupier takes your dollar. Your odds of winning on most wheels are 37 to 1, which means that in the long run you will lose about $55 for every 1,000 bets. If you tried the experiment once, you might do considerably better or worse. But, if you tried it many times, your average result for each 1,000 bets would be to lose about $55. The more times you made the 1,000 bets, the closer your average would get to the expected value of a $55 loss.

Note that the expected value is not necessarily the most common (modal) value. It can even be an impossible value: if, for example, the variable can have a value of either 1 or 2, the expected value is 1.5, a value that never occurs.

Experiment A study undertaken in which the researcher has control over some of the conditions in which the study takes place and control over (some aspects of) the *independent variables being studied. *Random assignment of subjects to *control and *experimental groups is usually thought of as a necessary criterion of a true experiment. Compare *natural experiment, *quasi-experiment, *secondary analysis, *descriptive research.

For example, if you interviewed moviegoers as they exited a theater to see if what they saw influenced their attitudes, this would not be experimental research; you had no control over who the subjects were or what film they watched or the conditions under which they watched it. On the other hand, if you chose a room, a film, and subjects to assign randomly to control and experimental groups and interviewed these subjects about the effects of the film on their attitudes, that would be an experiment.

Experimental Design The art of planning and executing *experiments. The greatest strength of an experimental research design, due largely to *random assignment, is its *internal validity: One can be more certain than with any other design about attributing *cause to the *independent variables. The greatest weakness of experimental designs may be *external validity: It may be hard to generalize results beyond the laboratory.

Experimental Error Differences in results among experiments repeated using identical procedures. When experiments are repeated, the results are rarely if ever *exactly* the same—even if the experiment is well designed and the experimenters make no mistakes. Compare *error term, *random variation.

Experimental Group A group receiving some *treatment in an experiment. Data collected about people in the experimental group are compared with data about people in a *control group (who received no treatment) and/or another experimental group (who received a different treatment).

Experimental Unit The smallest *independently treated* unit of study. Compare *unit of analysis.

For example, if 90 subjects were randomly assigned to 3 *treatment groups, the study would have 3 experimental units, not 90.

Experimenter Effect A type of *confounding effect that occurs when different experimenters working on the same experiment administer different *treatments or *conditions.

For example, say Al, Betty, and Chuck were running an experiment on subjects' reaction time as influenced by three types of visual cues (A, B, C). If Al always administered cue A, Betty cue B, and Chuck cue C, it would be impossible to tell if differences in subjects' reaction times were due solely to differences in the cues or in part to the way the experimenters administered them. Al, Betty, and Chuck should rotate. Compare *counterbalancing.

Explained Variance Variance in the *dependent variable that can be accounted for by variance in the *independent variable(s). Contrast *error variance.

Explanatory Research Research that seeks to understand variables by discovering and measuring causal relations among them. Generally used to describe *experimental versus *correlational research designs. Often contrasted, especially in discussions of *regression analysis, with *predictive research.

Exploratory Data Analysis Any of several methods, pioneered by John Tukey, of discovering unanticipated patterns and relationships, often by presenting quantitative data visually. The *stem-and-leaf display and the *box-and-whisker diagram are well-known examples. Compare *hypothesis testing.

Exploratory Factor Analysis *Factor analysis conducted to discover what *latent variables (factors) are behind a set of variables or measures. Generally contrasted with *confirmatory factor analysis, which tests theories and hypotheses about the factors one expects to find.

Exploratory Research Said of research that looks for patterns, ideas, or hypotheses rather than research that tries to test or confirm hypotheses.

Ex Post Facto Research Design Any *nonexperimental research design that takes place after the conditions to be studied have occurred, such as research in which there is a *posttest but no *pretest. Researchers often try to compensate for the lack of a pretest or *baseline data by *matching subjects or otherwise *controlling for variables that might have influenced outcomes.

External Validity The extent to which the findings of a study are relevant to subjects and settings beyond those in the study. Another term for *generalizability.

Extraneous Variable Any condition not part of a study (i.e., one that researchers are not interested in for the purposes of the particular study) but that could have an effect on the study's *dependent variable. (Note that, in this context, extraneous does not mean unimportant.) Researchers usually try to *control for extraneous variables by experimental isolation, by randomization, or by some statistical technique such as *analysis of covariance.

Extraneous Variance Variance caused by an *extraneous variable.

Extrapolation Inferring values by projecting *trends beyond known evidence. Compare *interpolation.

Suppose, for example, that you had some measures of the daily high temperatures for a week in June:

Monday	*Tuesday*	*Wednesday*	*Thursday*	*Friday*	*Saturday*	*Sunday*
72	74		78	80	82	

E

If you guessed that the temperature on Sunday would be 84, that would be an extrapolation. If you guessed that Wednesday's temperature had been 76, this would be an *interpolation, which is generally a safer inference than an extrapolation.

Extreme Outlier See *outlier, *boxplot.

Extreme Values The largest and smallest values in a distribution of values. See *range.

F

F (a) Uppercase *F*, the statistic that is computed when conducting an *analysis of variance. See **F* distribution, **F* ratio. (b) Lowercase italicized *f*, the usual symbol for *frequency in a table depicting a *frequency distribution. (c) Lowercase f, the symbol for *function, as in $Y = \mathrm{f}(X)$.

Face Validity Logical or conceptual validity; so called because it is a form of validity determined by whether, on the face of it, a measure seems to make sense. In determining face validity, one often asks expert judges whether the measure seems to them to be valid.

Factor (a) In *analysis of variance, an *independent variable, that is, a variable presumed to cause or influence another variable. (b) In *factor analysis, a cluster of related variables that are a distinguishable component of a larger group of variables. See also *latent variable. (c) A number by which another number is multiplied, as in the statement: Real estate values increased by a factor of three, meaning that they tripled. (d) In mathematics, a number that divides exactly into another number. For example, 1, 2, and 4 are factors of 8, because, when you divide each of them into 8, the result (quotient) is a whole number. See *factoring.

Factor Analysis Any of several methods of analysis that enable researchers to reduce a large number of *variables to a smaller number of variables, or "factors," or *latent variables. Factor analysis is done by finding patterns among the variations in the values of several variables; a cluster of highly intercorrelated variables are a factor. Factor analysis is only practical using a computer. *Principal components analysis is sometimes regarded as a form of factor analysis, although the mathematical models on which the two are based are different.

Factor analysis is often used in survey research to see if a long series of questions can be grouped into shorter sets of questions each of which describes an aspect or factor of the phenomena being studied.

Factor Equations In *factor analysis, equations analogous to *regression equations describing the regression of observed (*manifest) variables on unobserved (*latent) variables. Factor equations have no *intercept, or, rather, the intercept is fixed at zero.

Factorial Said of a whole number (positive integer) multiplied by each of the whole numbers smaller than itself. It is usually indicated by an exclamation point. Factorials are used extensively when calculating probabilities.

For example, 5 factorial, or 5!, means: $5 \times 4 \times 3 \times 2 \times 1 = 120$.

Factorial Experiments or Designs Research designs with two or more *categorical *independent variables (*factors), each studied at two or more *levels. The goal of factorial designs is to determine whether the factors combine to produce *interaction effects; if the treatments do not influence one another, their combined effects can be gotten simply by studying them one at a time and adding the separate effects. See *analysis of variance, *main effect.

For example, a study of the effects of puberty and a drug taken at three doses or levels on subjects' psychological states would be a factorial design. There would be an interaction effect between the drug and puberty if at some level(s) the drug was a depressant before puberty but a stimulant after.

Factorial Plot A graph of two or more *independent variables (factors) in which nonparallel lines for the different factors indicate the presence of *interaction. See *disordinal interaction and *interaction effect for examples.

Factorial Table A table showing the influence of two or more *independent variables on a *dependent variable. See *crossbreak for an example.

Factoring Breaking a number into its *factors, that is, breaking it into parts that, when multiplied together, equal the number.

For example, 24 can be factored into 2×12, 3×8, and 4×6. Each of these numbers (2, 3, 4, 6, 8, 12) is a factor of 24.

Factor Loadings The *correlations between each *variable and each factor in a *factor analysis. They are analogous to *regression (*slope) coefficients. See *factor equation, *structure coefficient.

Factor Rotation Any of several methods in *factor analysis by which the researcher attempts to relate the calculated factors to theoretical entities. This is done differently depending upon whether the factors are believed to be correlated (oblique) or uncorrelated (orthogonal).

Fail Safe N In *meta-analysis, the number of studies confirming the *null hypothesis that would be necessary to change the results of meta-analytic study that found a significant relationship.

Failure In *probability theory, one of the two ways a *Bernoulli trial can turn out.

For example, in flipping a coin, tails might be called *success and heads "failure." While the designations are mostly arbitrary, failure is reserved for occasions when the predicted event does not occur.

False Alarm See *signal detection theory.

Falsificationism The doctrine, originating with Karl Popper, that we can only refute ("falsify") theories; we can never confirm them. A good theory is one that we have tried repeatedly, but unsuccessfully, to disprove or falsify. Compare *null hypothesis.

F

***F* Distribution** A *theoretical distribution used to study *population *variances. It is the distribution of the *ratio of two *independent variables each of which has been divided by its *degrees of freedom. See **F* ratio, *chi-square distribution. The distribution is perhaps most widely used in *analysis of variance. Named after Sir R. A. Fisher.

Field Experiment An *experiment in a natural setting (the "field"), not in a laboratory. The researcher in a field experiment does not create the experimental situation, but she or he does manipulate it. School classrooms are a favorite location for field experiments. See *quasi-experiment.

Field Notes A record, usually written, of events observed by an *ethnographic researcher. The notes are taken as the study proceeds; because they will later be used for analysis, they should be as close to comprehensive (perhaps even stenographic) as possible.

Field Study Research conducted in a real-life setting, not in a laboratory. The researcher neither creates nor manipulates the subject of study but observes it. See *participant observation, *ethnographic research.

FIFO See *first in-first out.

File Any *program or *data set in a computer's memory.

File Drawer Problem In literature reviews and *meta-analyses, a problem of validity that arises because studies that come up with negative findings are often not published; rather, they are put in researchers' file drawers and are unavailable for review and analysis.

FILO See *first in-last out.

First In-First Out (FIFO) A rule determining the order in which data are processed by a computer. Also called "queue processing."

First In-Last Out (FILO) A rule determining the order in which data are processed by a computer. Also called "stack processing."

First-Order Interaction Effects Said of the *interaction of two *independent variables. Second-order interaction effects take place among three independent variables; higher orders are possible but are difficult to interpret.

F

First-Order Partial Said of a *partial correlation or a *partial regression coefficient that *controls for the (*linear) effect of one *independent variable. A second-order partial controls for two; a third-order, for three; and so on. A *zero-order correlation controls for no other variables.

Fisher's Exact Test A *test statistic for measures of *association that relate two *nominal variables. It is used mainly in 2×2 frequency tables when the *expected frequency is too small to trust the use of the *chi-square test. See *phi coefficient, *Yates's correction.

Fisher's Z (a) A measure of *effect size often used in *meta-analysis. Symbolized: Z_{FISHER}. (b) A statistic used to *transform *Pearson's correlation coefficients so that they can be used for *confidence limits and *significance tests. Also called *r-to-Z transformation.

Fishing Expedition Any random "looking around" in the data gathered in a study to see if you can find some significant relationship. This is generally considered bad practice, especially if one is reporting the results of *significance tests. See *post hoc comparisons. There are, however, good ways to go hunting (versus bad ways to fish) for interesting relationships; see *exploratory data analysis.

Fit Refers to how closely observed *data match the relations specified in a *model or how closely they correspond to an assumed distribution.

Fixed-Effects Model The typical *ANOVA design in which the populations studied are (or are treated as) fixed categorical variables—users of Drugs A, B, and C, at High, Medium, and Low levels, for example. Also called "Model I ANOVA." See *random effects model.

Floor Effect A term used to describe a situation in which many subjects in a study measure at or near the possible lower limit (the "floor"). This makes analysis difficult because it reduces the amount of variation in the variable. Compare *ceiling effect.

For example, a study of counseling strategies to reduce suicide could be more difficult to conduct with subjects who were black women in their sixties because this group has a very low suicide rate, one that could be hard to reduce further. It might be easier to conduct the study with white men in their sixties because they have a much higher suicide rate.

Flowchart (or Flow Diagram) A graphic illustration of progression through a system or the steps of a procedure.

The following example briefly suggests the steps by which some environmental stimuli might be "processed" to eventually go into long-term memory.

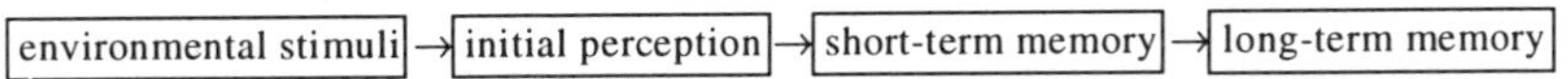

Fluctuations In *time-series data, any short-term back-and-forth movements that are unrelated to long-term *trends.

Sometimes fluctuations are so large they make trends difficult to see. Global warming is an example. Even if the planet is gradually getting warmer, it still gets very cold in the winter (regular fluctuation), and sometimes the temperature can be quite low in the summer (random, nonpredictable fluctuation).

Focused Comparisons Techniques of *meta-analysis for comparing *significance levels and *effect sizes by measuring the extent to which the studies' results are explained by an *independent variable.

Forecasting Prediction of the size of a future quantity, such as the inflation rate next year. Forecasting is often contrasted with *estimation, by which one tries to determine the size of some existing quantity.

Formative Evaluation *Evaluation research undertaken to find ways to improve, redesign, or fine-tune a program in its early stages. The focus is on the program's processes more than its outcomes, and the techniques are often *qualitative. Compare *summative evaluation.

FORTRAN Short for Formula Translation. A *programming language used for writing computer programs. Using commands such as "DO," "GO TO," and "READ," it "translates" English into a language a computer can use.

Forward Selection A computer method for choosing which variables should be included, and in which order, in a *regression model or equation. Compare *backward elimination and *stepwise regression.

For example, if you had 20 potential independent variables, the computer program would estimate 20 *simple regressions (one for each independent variable) and choose the "best" one, that is, the one that had the highest R^2 (explained the largest percentage of the variance in the dependent variable). Then this variable would be tried in combination with the remaining 19 to find a second that (in a *multiple regression equation) produced the "best" pair (the pair with the largest R-squared). Then it would use those two and search for a third, and so on, until adding more variables no longer led to a significant increase in the R-squared.

Fractal A curve or a surface created by repeated subdivisions of the curve or surface; a geometric shape that is infinitely ragged, curvy, or otherwise irregular. Fractals can be used to describe natural shapes such as crystals, clouds, or snowflakes and have many applied uses such as in weather forecasting and predicting patterns of population growth.

Fractile Any division of a *distribution into equal units or fractions, such as fifths (*quintiles), tenths (*deciles), or hundredths (*percentiles). See *quantile.

Frame See *sampling frame.

***F* Ratio (or Value or Statistic)** The ratio of explained to unexplained variance in an *analysis of variance, that is, the ratio of the *between-group variance to the *within-group variance. To interpret the F ratio, you need to consult a table of F values for a particular level of *statistical significance at the number of *degrees of freedom in your study. Named after Sir R. Fisher, the inventor of analysis of variance. See *F test.

Frequency The number of times a particular type of event occurs (such as the number of days it rained last year) or the number of individuals in a given class (such as the number of males under 21 years old who got speeding tickets this month).

Frequency Curve (a) A smooth curve depicting the data in a *frequency polygon. (b) The curve representing a *probability density function.

Frequency Distribution A tally of the number of times each score occurs in a group of scores. More formally, a way of presenting *data that shows the number of cases having each of the *attributes of a particular *variable.

For example, the frequency distribution of final exam grades in a class of 50 students might be as follows: 8 As, 20 Bs, 19 Cs, 1 D, and 2 Fs.

In this example, the variable is final grade; the attributes are A, B, C, D, and F; and the frequencies are 8, 20, 19, 1, and 2.

The following table presents a more elaborate frequency distribution of the data for this class. See the definitions of the various column heads (*class interval, *relative frequency, and so on) for more detail.

Final Examination Grades in a Class of 50 Students

Final Grade	*Class Interval*	*Frequency (f)*	*Relative Frequency*	*Cumulative Frequency*	*Cumulative Relative Frequency*
A	90-99	8	.16	50	1.00
B	80-89	20	.40	42	.84
C	70-79	19	.38	22	.44
D	60-69	1	.02	3	.06
F	50-59	2	.04	2	.04

Frequency Polygon A line graph connecting the midpoints of the bars of a *histogram.

The following example depicts the same data about the national debt as does the *histogram.

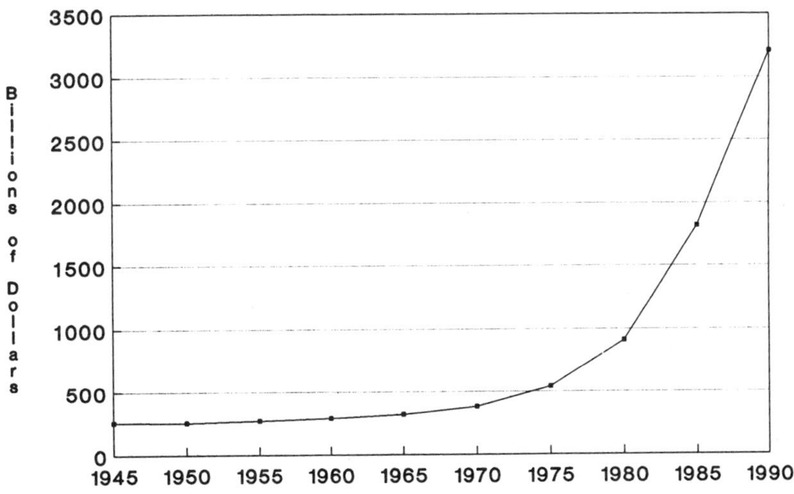

Frequency Polygon

Friedman Test A form of *analysis of variance that can be used when the *dependent variable is measured on an *ordinal scale.

***F* Scale** A widely used measure of the authoritarian personality (F for fascism) created in the aftermath of World War II by T. Adorno and colleagues. Not to be confused with the *F* ratio or *F* test.

***F* Statistic** See **F* test.

***F* Test** A test of the results of a statistical analysis, perhaps most closely associated with, but by no means limited to, *analysis of variance (ANOVA). The *F* test yields an **F* ratio or *F* statistic. This is a ratio of the *variance between groups (explained variance) to the variance *within groups (unexplained variance). To tell whether the *F* ratio is statistically significant, you have to consult an **F* distribution table. See *analysis of variance for an illustration.

F

Fully Recursive Model Said of a *recursive *path analysis model when all the variables are connected by arrows, that is, are causally linked. Also called "just-identified model."

Function (a) A *variable that can be expressed in terms of another variable; also, a variable that varies with another variable. The term is often used loosely, if not very correctly, to mean a *cause. For example, the phrase "learning is a function of time spent studying" means that spending time studying causes learning. The functional relationship can be expressed in an equation: $L = f(T)$, where L stands for learning and T for time spent studying and f means "is a function of."

(b) In *set theory, a functional relation exists when each *element, x, in one set, X, is paired with an element y in set Y; this is written $y = f(x)$, meaning "y is a function of x." The set X is called the "domain" and the set Y is called the "range." A function can be plotted on a graph if for every value of x there is exactly one value of y. In the equation $y = f(x)$, Y is the *dependent variable and is plotted on the *y axis, and X is the *independent variable plotted on the *x axis.

Functionalism Short for structural-functionalism. A perspective on social research based on the assumption that social phenomena that are widespread and long lasting (i.e., structures) probably fulfill a social function. Hence, to explain a social form (structure), a functionalist will look for its functions or usefulness for maintaining the society. Functionalism is an idea borrowed from anatomy, where the same assumption is made: Anatomical structures exist for a functional reason; the reason that, say, the kidney has the shape (structure) it does is that it could not function (well) otherwise.

For example, a functionalist might study income inequality (the structure) in a society by looking for the ways it was functional for the society as a whole. Perhaps inequality increases motivation and thus stimulates the overall productivity and economic well-being of the society.

Functional Relationship A relation that can be expressed in an *equation. See *function.

G

G^2 Symbol for the *likelihood ratio test of *goodness of fit.

Gambler's Fallacy The mistake of treating *independent events as though they were *dependent.

The familiar example has to do with tossing a fair coin. If after 5 consecutive heads you concluded that a sixth toss was more likely to come up tails, you would be committing the gambler's fallacy: You would be assuming that the sixth toss was dependent upon the previous five, when, in fact, each is independent of the others.

Or suppose you shuffle an ordinary deck of cards and draw a card from it at random. The card is red (a heart or a diamond). You replace the card, reshuffle the deck, and draw a second card; this too is a red card. You repeat the process and draw a third red card. You commit the gambler's fallacy if you believe that, because you drew three red cards in a row, your fourth draw is more likely to be a black card. Because you replaced the card and reshuffled each time, each draw was an independent event; that is, it had no influence on subsequent events (and was not influenced by prior events). On the other hand, had you not replaced the red card each time, that would have made drawing a black card more likely. See *sampling with replacement.

Game Theory A mathematical theory of competitive games in which each player wants to figure out the best way to play games given their rules. The games in question have to be strategic games, that is, not games of pure chance but games based on knowledge, including knowledge of what the other players are likely to know. The theory has been widely applied as a model of human action in such fields as economics and military strategy. See *maximin strategy, *minimax strategy, *zero-sum game.

Gamma Sometimes called "Goodman and Kruskal's gamma." A *measure of association for *ordinal variables. It is a *symmetric, *PRE statistic. Gammas range from –1.0 to +1.0. When calculating gamma, the ranks of the ordered categories are not treated as interval scales. Compare *Spearman's rho.

For example, if knowing how a sample of citizens ranked on one variable, such as opinion on gun control (strongly opposed, opposed, in favor, strongly in favor) always enabled you to predict how they would rank on attitude toward the death penalty (strongly opposed, opposed, and so on), the gamma indicating the association between those two variables would be –1.0. But, because, in fact, there are some people who oppose gun control and the death penalty, the gamma would probably be something like –0.8.

Gaussian Distribution Another term for *normal distribution.

Generalizability The extent to which you can come to conclusions about one thing (often a *population) based on information about another (often a *sample). Compare *external validity, *inferential statistics.

For example, when a national burger restaurant wants to see whether a new sandwich will sell, it promotes the sandwich in a few communities that are assumed to be representative of the nation. If that assumption is correct, the company can generalize from the sales figures in the handful of communities to how the new product will sell in the rest of the country.

Generalized Least Squares A means of calculation used (instead of *ordinary least squares) in *regression analysis when there is a nonrandom pattern to the *error terms (i.e., *heteroscedasticity in residual error terms) or when *autocorrelation or serial correlation bias the results.

General Linear Model (GLM) A common set of statistical *assumptions upon which are based *regression, *correlation, and *analysis of variance, in short, the full range of methods used to study one continuous dependent variable and one or more independent variables, whether continuous or categorical. The model is general in that the kind of independent variable is not specified.

The basic idea is that the relation between a dependent variable and the independent variables can be expressed as an *equation containing a *term for the weighted sum of the values of the independent variables—plus a term for everything that we do not know about, which is called an *error term. The method used to decide how much weight to give to the independent variable(s) is the *least-squares criterion.

General Social Survey (GSS) An annual survey of a representative sample of (about 1,500) American adults conducted by the National Opinion Research Center. Respondents are asked several questions about their backgrounds and for their opinions about many social and political issues. The results of these surveys are available to, and are widely used by, other researchers for *secondary analyses.

Generation Effects The effects on individuals of growing up in or being members of the same generation or age group. See *cohort effects.

Geometric Distribution A *probability distribution of the number of failures before the first success in a series of *Bernoulli trials. See *Pascal distribution.

In the following example, the table gives the probability of getting tails on the first, second, and so on flips of a coin and of getting a heart on the first, second, and so on draws (with *replacement) from an ordinary deck of cards. Consulting the table, you can conclude, for instance, that only about 3% of the time would you need five flips of a coin to get a tail. Only about 8% of the time would you need to draw five cards before getting a heart.

Probability of Getting the First Success on Each Trial

Trial	*Tails*	*Heart*
1	.50	.25
2	.25	.1875
3	.125	.1406
4	.0625	.1055
5	.03125	.0791

Geometric Mean See *mean.

GIGO Short for "garbage in, garbage out." A brutal way of putting an undeniable principle: No matter how good your computer and your statistical analysis package, if you put poor *data (data that are neither *reliable nor *valid) into your computer, it will give you poor results.

Gini Coefficient A measure of inequality or dispersion in a group of values, such as income inequality in a population. The larger the coefficient, the greater the dispersion. It is calculated by taking the mean difference between all pairs of values and dividing that by 2 times the population mean. Sometimes called the "coefficient of concentration."

GLM Abbreviation for the *general linear model.

Goedel's Proof The demonstration by Kurt Goedel (in 1931) that a formal system, such as logic or mathematics, cannot prove its own basic axioms. This has sometimes been taken more generally to indicate that we can have little certainty in our claims to knowledge. Compare *Heisenberg's uncertainty principle.

Goodman and Kruskal's Gamma and Lambda See *gamma, *lambda.

Goodness-of-Fit How well a *model, a theoretical distribution, or an *equation matches actual *data. See *goodness-of-fit test.

For example, in *regression analysis, the question is this: How closely does the *regression line (formed of the *predicted scores) come to summarizing the observed scores? The coefficient of *determination is a measure of the goodness-of-fit for a regression line.

Goodness-of-Fit Test The *chi-square test applied to a single categorical variable to see if the distribution among categories matches (fits) a theoretical expectation. The bigger the chi-square statistic, the poorer the fit; the smaller, the better.

For example, say a researcher wants to know if bankruptcies are randomly distributed throughout the year. The theoretical distribution in this case would be equal probability; the *expected frequency would be that 1/12 of the bankruptcies occur in each month (with slight adjustments for the longer and shorter months).

Graph A diagram showing a relationship between two variables. For examples see *bar graph, *curvilinear relation, *histogram, and *frequency polygon.

Greco-Latin Square An extension of the *Latin square method of allocating *treatments in a *within-subjects *factorial experiment. The extension is done by adding a different Greek letter to the Latin letter in each cell. As with the Latin square method, the goal is *counterbalancing *order effects.

Gross Before any deductions. For example, gross income is income before deducting expenses. Compare *net.

Grouped Data Data recorded as numbers of cases in *class intervals. Compare *raw data, *aggregate data.

Group Effect The influence on individuals of being members of one group rather than another, such as the effect on one's earnings of being female. See *contextual effects, *t test, *analysis of variance.

Grouping Another term for *collapsing.

GSS General Social Survey.

Guttman Scaling A method of scale construction created by Louis Guttman. It is was originally designed to be used after the data were collected to see if the items in an *index could be arranged as a *scale, that is, in the order of the strength of the items. See *Bogardus social distance scale.

For example, national surveys often ask questions about abortion roughly as follows:

Do you favor a woman's right to have an abortion if:

1. having the baby would threaten her life?
2. the fetus is deformed?
3. she is too poor to care for the child properly?
4. she does not want any more children?

If these items form a Guttman scale, the vast majority of people who answer the questions will do so in a scalar pattern: People who say yes to question number 4 will also say yes to questions 3, 2, and 1; those who say yes to number 3 will also say yes to 2 and 1 but not necessarily to 4, and so on. If these items do not form a scale, there will be no pattern to the answers; People who say yes to number 4 will be as likely as not to say no to numbers 3, 2, and 1.

H The usual symbol for the statistic that is computed when doing the *Kruskal-Wallis test of statistical significance.

H_0 The symbol for the *null hypothesis.

H_1 A symbol for an *alternative or *scientific hypothesis.

h^2 The usual symbol for *communality in *factor analysis.

H_a A symbol for the *alternative or *scientific hypothesis.

H

Halo Bias (or Effect) A tendency of judges to overrate a performance because the subject did well in an earlier rating or when rated in a different area.

For example, say a student has taken two courses from a professor and has done exceptionally well in each. In a third course, she or he writes a substandard paper. This paper might receive a higher grade than it deserves because of the student's earlier good work.

Hanning A technique for *smoothing data in a *trend line. Compare *running medians, *moving average.

Hard Sciences Natural sciences, especially physical sciences. Often contrasted with soft sciences such as psychology, sociology, political science, and economics. Some scholars think this distinction indicates a real difference; others dismiss it as mere "physics envy." Among the social and behavioral sciences, economics and psychology more often make successful claims to "hardness," largely because they have used quantitative research methods longer than the others.

Hardware In computer jargon, the physical components of a computer; the machine without any operating instructions or *software.

Harmonic Mean A *measure of central tendency used mainly in comparing average rates. See *mean.

Hawthorne Effect A tendency for subjects of research to change their behavior simply because they are being studied. So called because the classic study in which this behavior was discovered was in the Hawthorne Western Electric Company Plant in Illinois. In this study, workers improved their output regardless of changes in their working conditions. Compare *John Henry effect.

Heisenberg Uncertainty Principle Because we cannot study the atom without affecting it, we cannot know (we must be uncertain about) what it might be like without our interference, when we are not studying it. This principle has been extended by some writers to areas of research other than atomic physics. Compare *Goedel's proof.

Heterogeneous Generally, mixed or diverse. Used to describe *samples and *populations with high *variability.

Heteroscedasticity A situation in which there are considerably unequal *variances in the *dependent variable for the same values of the *independent variable in the different populations being sampled and compared in a *regression analysis or an *ANOVA. Comes from *hetero* meaning other or different and *scedasticity* meaning tendency to scatter. Heteroscedasticity violates the *assumption of *homoscedasticity; this violation, if serious enough, compels the use of *nonparametric statistics.

H

Heuristic (a) Generally, instructive or pedagogical. (b) More specifically, having to do with methods that aid learning by exploratory, or trial-and-error, methods; said of a *computer program that can learn from its mistakes (by eliminating trials that do not work) and/or that can teach people how to use the program by learning from their mistakes.

Heuristic Assumption An *assumption made more because it is useful for teaching or research purposes than because it is believed to be true.

Hierarchical Regression Analysis A type of *regression model that assumes that, when a higher order *interaction term is included, all the lower order terms (*main effects) are also included. Also called *incremental partitioning of variance.

Higher Order Partials (or Correlations) Fully, "higher order partial correlations." Correlations that *control for more than one *variable in a complex, *multivariate, relationship. A *zero-order correlation controls for no other variables; a *first-order correlation controls for one; a second-order correlation, for two; and so on. All beyond second order are higher order. Compare *partial relation.

For example, when computing a correlation between persons' education levels and their incomes, a researcher might wish to control for other variables that could influence the relationship of interest. If four variables were controlled (e.g., age, sex, parental income, and ethnicity), the correlation would be a higher order (fourth-order) partial correlation.

High-Level Language *Software for programming computers. The programmer writes programs in the high-level language, which then "translates" the program into language that the machine (*hardware) can understand. Examples include *BASIC, *C, *COBOL, and *FORTRAN.

Highspread The range of values between the *median and the highest value in a *distribution. Compare *lowspread.

Hinge The point in a *distribution that divides the scores at the ¼-¾ mark. The lower hinge is the score at the 25th *percentile, that is, the point in a distribution above which ¾ of the scores are located. The upper hinge (at the 75th percentile) is the point with ¼ of the scores above it and ¾ below it. See *exploratory data analysis, *box-and-whisker diagram.

Histogram A *bar graph for *variables measured at the *interval and *ratio levels. Because the data in a histogram are interval or ratio, the bars should touch; in a bar graph—which is for *nominal or for *ordinal data—they should not.

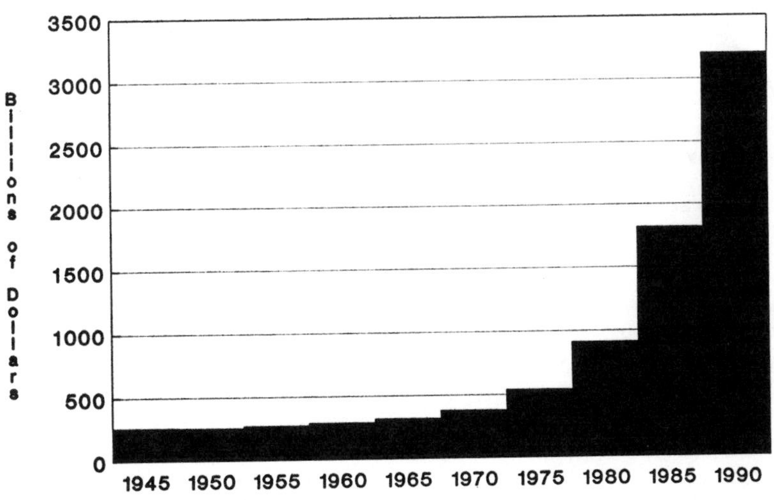

Histogram

Historical Sciences Disciplines in which *cause and effect are separated by relatively long periods—including, but not limited to, topics taught in traditional history courses.

For example, geology is a historical science; the formation of continents takes millions of years. On the other hand, while chemical reactions occur over time, the amounts of time are very small by human standards, so chemistry is not considered a historical science. In psychology, personality development, which takes years, could be thought of as a historical science; perception, which takes milliseconds, would not be.

Historicism The original form of *cultural relativism stressing that different eras can only be understood in their own terms. Like other forms of relativism, it can lead its adherents to doubt all claims to knowledge. Compare *anachronism.

History Effect An event that intervenes and makes it difficult if not impossible to interpret the relations among *independent and *dependent variables.

Suppose a city government began an experiment with sensitivity training (*independent variable) to improve intergroup relations among its employees with different racial and ethnic backgrounds. Attitudes are measured before the training begins and are to be measured again after 10 weeks. In the 9th week, a dramatic event occurs that would be very likely to influence subjects' attitudes (e.g., a race riot or a controversial affirmative action ruling). Any differences in attitudes measured after the 10th week of training *could* be due to the training, *or* the training effects might have been overwhelmed by the event (the history)—there is no way to tell. History effects are not always this dramatic and are perhaps more of a problem when they are less dramatic and easily can go unnoticed. History effects, in short, are always a potential *threat to validity for any nonlaboratory study that lasts more than a few hours.

Hold Constant To "subtract" the effects of a *variable from a complex relationship so as to study what that relationship would be if the variable were in fact a *constant.

For example, in a study of managerial behaviors and their effects on workers' productivity, a researcher might want to hold the education of the managers constant. This would especially be the case if she or he had reason to believe that different kinds or amounts of education might lead managers to behave differently.

Holism An *assumption that groups, collectivities, or wholes can be more than, or different than, the sum of their individual parts. This leads to an approach to research that stresses studying wholes or complete systems rather than analyzing individual parts. Compare *reductionism, *methodological individualism.

For example, a holist might say that an organization, such as General Motors, exists independently of the individuals who work for or own it. After all the individuals who today own or work for General Motors quit, retire, die, or sell their stock, the corporation could still exist—as long as those people were replaced by others. Because General Motors is not just the sum of its parts, it makes sense, holists would say, to talk of it "wanting," "planning," "deciding," and so on. Such desires, plans, and decisions are not reducible merely to those of individuals.

Homogeneous Generally, the same or similar. Used to refer to *populations and *samples that have low *variability.

Homoscedasticity A condition of substantially equal *variances in the *dependent variable for the same values of the *independent variable in the different populations being sampled and compared in a *regression analysis or an *ANOVA. Comes from *homo* meaning the same or equal and *scedasticity* meaning tendency to scatter (skedaddle?). *Parametric statistical tests usually assume homoscedasticity. If that assumption is violated, results will be of doubtful *validity. See *heteroscedasticity.

Honestly Significant Difference (HSD) Test See *Tukey's Honestly Significant Difference Test.

Hotelling's *t* Test An extension of the **t* test to *multivariate research problems.

HRAF *Human Relations Area Files.

HSD Test See *Tukey's Honestly Significant Difference Test.

Human Capital A kind of *capital (resources that can produce income) that exists within persons rather than external to them. Compare *cultural capital.

Knowledge, skill, and strength are examples of human capital. Economists often think of education as an investment in human capital.

Human Relations Area File (HRAF) A collection of anthropological information about more than 300 human cultures throughout the world divided into several hundred categories of information. The HRAF is widely used by researchers doing *secondary analyses of data on cross-cultural topics.

Hypergeometric Distribution A *probability distribution used for studying *sampling without replacement, that is, when each selection (or trial) changes the probability of the outcome of the next.

Hypothesis A statement of (or conjecture about) the relationships among the *variables that a researcher intends to study. Hypotheses are sometimes testable statements of relations. In such cases, they are usually thought of as predictions, which, if confirmed, will support a *theory. See *alternative hypothesis, *null hypothesis.

For example, suppose a social psychologist theorized that racial prejudice is due to ignorance. Hypotheses for testing the theory might be as follows: *If* (1) education reduces ignorance, *then* (2) the more highly educated people are, the less likely they are to be prejudiced. If an attitude survey showed that there was indeed an *inverse relation between education and prejudice levels, this would tend to confirm the theory that prejudice is a *function of ignorance.

Hypothesis Testing The classical approach to assessing the *statistical significance of findings. Basically, it involves comparing empirically observed *sample findings with theoretically expected findings—expected if the *null hypothesis is true. This comparison allows one to compute the *probability that the observed outcomes could have been due to chance alone. See *alpha error, *beta error.

For example, suppose you wanted to study the effects on performance of working in groups as compared with working alone. You might get 80 subjects to volunteer for your study (college sophomores are the typical subject pool). You could assign them randomly into two categories: those who would work in teams of four students and those who would work individually. You could provide subjects with a large number of math problems to solve and record the number of answers they got right in 20 minutes. Your *alternative or *research hypothesis might be that people who work in teams are more efficient than those who work individually. To examine the research hypothesis, you would try to find evidence that would allow you to reject your null hypothesis—which would probably be something like this: There is no difference between the average score of students who work individually and those who work in teams.

The outcomes of a decision in hypothesis testing are often depicted in a matrix as follows. (Compare the similar matrix illustrating *signal detection theory.)

Possible Outcomes of a Hypothesis Test

		Decision: Null Hypothesis Is True	Decision: Alternative Hypothesis Is True
REALITY	Null Hypothesis Is True	correct retention	Type I (alpha) Error
	Alternative Hypothesis Is True	Type II (beta) Error	correct rejection

Idealism A wide range of philosophical doctrines and perspectives methodologically important for their belief that the mind and its ideas (not external experience) are the ultimate source and criterion of knowledge. Compare *empiricism, *epistemology.

Ideal Type A term introduced by Max Weber to refer to a *model or a pure conceptual type. "Ideal" does not refer to the best or most desirable; rather, it means "pertaining to an idea." In modern English usage, "conceptual type" would capture Weber's meaning. See *concept, *construct.

For example, one could describe an ideal-typical bureaucracy; this would be as conceptually pure a bureaucracy as one could imagine, that is, a government that worked only according to bureaucratic principles. An ideal type is used as a category or a concept to guide research. Thus, if you defined how a pure (ideal-type) bureaucracy would work, you could use this as a standard to hold up to actual governments to see how bureaucratic they were. Without such a standard, it would be difficult to say whether one government was more bureaucratic than another.

Identification Problem An analytic difficulty that arises in *regression analysis when one has more unknowns than can be independently estimated from the available data; in other words, when there are too many unknowns in a causal *model for a solution to be possible.

Ideology A system of beliefs held by a group that tends to serve the self-interests of that group. In research reports, one generally reserves the term "ideology" for positions one *really* doesn't like at all.

Idiographic Used to describe research that deals with the individual, singular, unique, or concrete. Idiographic is often contrasted with *nomothetic.

Illusory Correlation See *spurious correlation.

Incremental Partitioning of Variance See *hierarchical regression analysis.

Independence In *probability theory, a state in which the occurrence of one event does not change the probability of another event, that is, when one event does not depend on another. Compare *gambler's fallacy, *sampling with replacement.

For example, one might conclude that the cards a gambler was dealt were independent of whether he was wearing his lucky ring.

Independent Event In probability theory, said of an occurrence that is not *conditional upon or conditioned by another. See *independence, *dependent event.

Independent Variable The presumed *cause in a study. Also a variable that can be used to predict the values of another variable. Compare *dependent variable.

Some authors use the term "independent variable" for experimental research only; for nonexperimental research, they use *predictor variable. Most writers, however, use the term "independent variable" for both experimental and nonexperimental research. Some even use it in pure *forecasting, where no causal connection is implied, as when variations in the starting date of the migrating season are used to predict the severity of winter temperatures.

Index (a) Any observable phenomenon that is used to indicate the presence of another phenomenon, as when church attendance is used to indicate religious commitment. Compare *proxy variable or measure. (b) A number, often a *ratio, meant to express simply a relationship between two variables or between two measures of the same variable. (c) A group of individual measures that, when combined, are meant to indicate some more general characteristic. Compare *scale.

For example (b), indexes measuring access to medical school for various groups could be calculated by dividing a group's percentage of students in medical schools by its share of the population of medical school age. If, say, women made up 50% of the 21- to 25-year-olds and were 40% of the medical students, their access index would be .8 (40/50 = .8). Or, if white males were 40% of the 21- to 25-year-old population and were 56% of the medical students, their index would be 1.4 (56/40 = 1.4).

For example (c), in survey research, political tolerance might be measured by an index composed of six questions about whether the respondent favored such things as free speech for religious outsiders, the right to demonstrate for political radicals, and so on. Scores on the index could range from 0 (for those answering none of the questions in the tolerant way) to 6 (for those answering all of the questions in the tolerant way). This kind of index is used to measure an *ordinal variable.

Indicators See *social indicators.

Indicator Variable (a) Another term for *manifest variable, that is, an observable variable one uses to study a *latent variable. (b) Another term for *dummy variable.

Indices Alternative way of pluralizing *index, and one that is more grammatically correct (or traditional) than "indexes."

Individual-Difference Variables Another term for *background variables.

Induction Using statistical methods to form generalizations by finding similarities among a large number of cases. The generalizations derived in this way are probabilistic. For example, if 90% of the members of the U.S. Congress were lawyers, the chances of any individual member of the Congress being a lawyer would be 9 out of 10.

Inductive Said of research procedures and methods of reasoning that begin with (or put most emphasis on) observation and then move from observation of particulars to the development of general *hypotheses. Often used to describe ethnographic research. Compare *deductive.

Inductive Statistics Another term for *inferential statistics.

Inference The act of using one statement (or judgment or proposition or generalization) to derive a new one. The truth of the new statement is held to follow logically (*deductively or *inductively) from the original statement.

Inferential Statistics Statistics that allow one to draw conclusions or inferences from data. Usually this means coming to conclusions about a *population on the basis of data describing a *sample. See *statistical inference.

Information Theory A statistical and mathematical theory of communication dealing with the nature, effectiveness, and accuracy of transmitting information between humans, between machines, and between humans and machines.

Institute for Social Research Founded by Rensis Likert and located at the University of Michigan, the Institute for Social Research (ISR) is perhaps best known as the parent organization of the Survey Research Center (SRC).

Instrument Any means used to measure or otherwise study subjects. In the language of social and behavioral research, an instrument can call to mind a mechanical device (as it does in ordinary language—a dentist's drill, a saxophone), but it is used more broadly to include written instruments, such as an attitude *scale or an *interview schedule.

Integer A whole number, whether negative or positive: 1, 2, 4, and 5 are integers; 1.2 and 4/5 are not.

Interaction Effect The joint effect of two or more *independent variables on a *dependent variable. Interaction effects occur when *independent variables not only have separate effects but also have combined effects on a *dependent variable. Put somewhat differently, interaction effects occur when the relation between two variables differs depending on the value of another variable. Also called "conditioning effect," "contingency effect," "joint effect," and "moderating effect." Compare *main effect, *additive relation.

When two variables interact, this is called a *first-order interaction; when three interact, it is a second-order interaction; and so on. Interaction effects may be *ordinal or *disordinal; see the entries under those terms for more details.

For example, suppose a cholesterol reduction clinic had two diets and one exercise plan. Exercise alone was effective and dieting alone was effective. As can be seen in the following graph, for patients who didn't exercise, the two diets worked about equally well. Those who went on Diet A and exercised got the benefits of both. But those who combined exercise with Diet B got a bonus, an interaction effect. All patients could benefit by dieting and exercising, but those who followed Diet B and exercised benefited more.

Intercept The point at which a *regression line crosses (or "intercepts") the vertical (*Y*) axis, that is, when the value on the *X* (horizontal) axis is zero. Another way to put it, the intercept is the point at which the expected value of the *dependent variable corresponds to a score of zero for the *independent variable. Also called "*y* intercept." See *regression constant.

For example, if we were to graph the correlation between life expectancy (the dependent variable) and average annual taxable income (the independent variable), the regression line that best summarized the data might look like the following. People with no taxable income (living on welfare and so on) have a life expectancy of about 60 according to these hypothetical data; 60 is the intercept, that is, the expected value of the dependent variable when the score on the dependent variable is zero.

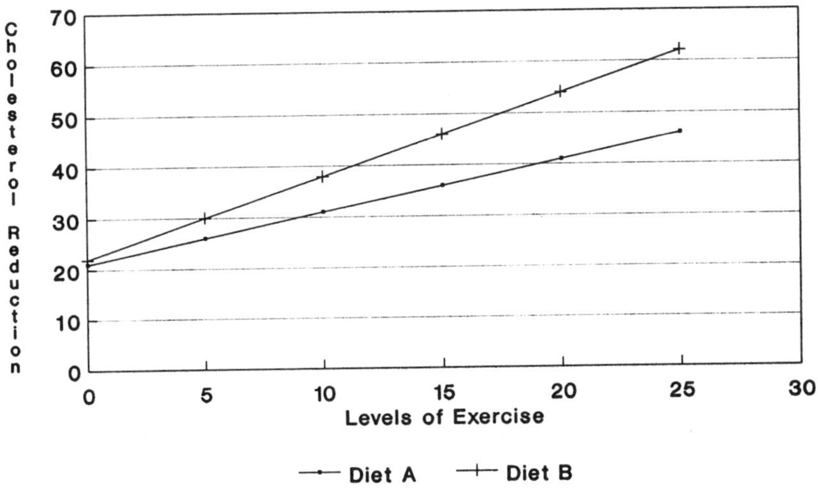

Interaction Effect

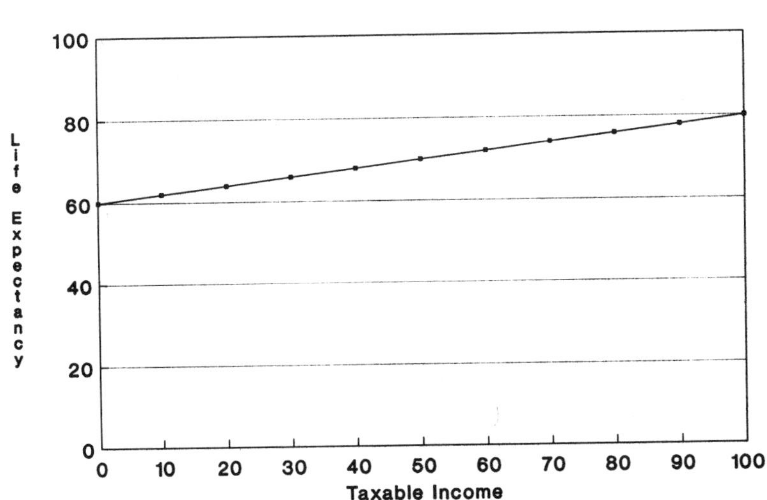

Intercept

Intercorrelation A correlation between *independent variables—as contrasted with a correlation between an independent variable and a dependent variable. See *multicollinearity.

Intermediary Variable Another term for *mediating variable; also *intervening variable.

Internal Consistency The extent to which items in a *scale are *correlated with one another, which is to say the extent to which they measure the same thing.

Internal Validity The extent to which the results of a study (usually an *experiment) can be attributed to the *treatments rather than to flaws in the research design; in other words, the degree to which one can draw valid conclusions about the causal effects of one variable on another. Compare *external validity.

Interpolation The act of estimating an unknown value by using its position among a series of known values. Compare *extrapolation.

For example, if the average weight of 5-year-olds were 50 pounds, and the average weight of 7-year-olds were 70 pounds, we might interpolate that 60 pounds is the average weight of 6-year-olds.

Interquartile Range (IQR) A measure of *dispersion calculated by taking the difference between the first and third *quartiles (i.e., the 25th and 75th percentiles). Also called "midspread." See *boxplot, *hinge.

Interrater Reliability Agreement among raters; the extent to which raters judge phenomena in the same way. Ratings often involve assigning numbers to qualitative assessments. Olympic judges provide a familiar example. While all the judges of an individual performance rarely award it exactly the same score, a very high level of agreement (interrater reliability) is the rule rather than the exception.

Interrupted Time-Series Design An approach that allows (indeed, requires) researchers to examine trends in the *dependent variable before, during, and after an intervention or *treatment. The purpose is to avoid such *threats to validity as *history effects and *pretest sensitizing.

Suppose, for example, that the management of a company thought that productivity could be increased if employees attended a special training seminar (the *treatment). To see whether the seminar was effective, the following design could be used.

Week 1	*Week 2*	*Week 3*	*Week 4*	*Week 5*	*Week 6*	*Week 7*
Pretest	Pretest	Pretest	Treatment	Posttest	Posttest	Posttest

Repeated pretesting (weeks 1-3) would establish a *baseline and might reduce *Hawthorne effect bias. Repeated posttesting could help establish whether any improvements in productivity lasted beyond the first posttest week (week 5).

Intersection In *set theory, the overlapping of two or more sets; said of the elements shared by subsets. Symbolized "*cap," as in $A \cap B$.

Intersubjective Agreement A state that exists when subjects (often researchers or other experts) agree. It is a main criterion of *objectivity.

Interval Estimate An estimate that includes a range of scores. Compare *point estimate.

For example, the following statement contains an interval estimate: "If the election were held today, we estimate that Candidate A would get between 51% and 57% of the vote." By contrast, the statement, "If the election . . . 54% of the vote," is a point estimate.

Interval Scale (or Level of Measurement) A scale of measurement that describes variables in such a way that the distance between any two adjacent units of measurement (or "intervals") is the same but in which there is no meaningful zero point. Scores on an interval scale can meaningfully be added and subtracted but not multiplied and divided. Compare *ratio scale.

For example, the Fahrenheit temperature scale is an interval scale because the difference, or interval, between (say) 72 and 73 degrees is the same as that between 20 below and 21 below. Because there is no true zero point (zero is just a line on the thermometer), it is an interval, not a ratio, scale. There is a zero, of course, but it is not a true zero; when it's zero degrees outside, there is still some warmth, more than when it's 20 below.

Intervening Variable A variable that explains a relation, or provides a causal link, between other variables. Also called "mediating variable" and "intermediary variable." Compare *moderating variable.

For example, the statistical association between income and longevity needs to be explained, because having money by itself does not make one live longer. Other variables intervene between money and long life; for instance, people with high incomes tend to have better medical care than those with low incomes. Medical care is an intervening variable; it mediates the relation between income and longevity. Graphically:

Income → Medical Care → Longevity

Interview Protocol A list of questions and instructions for asking those questions. Used when interviewing subjects.

Interview Schedule A list of questions and spaces for their answers used by interviewers when questioning respondents. Compare *questionnaire.

Intraclass Correlation A measure of homogeneity among the members of a group, class, or cluster.

Invariance The condition of being unchanged by specific mathematical *transformations, as an invariant *factor.

Inverse Relation (or Correlation) A relation between two variables such that, whenever one goes up, the other goes down, and vice versa. Also called "negative relation." Compare *direct relationship.

For example, the relation between the female employment and fertility rates is inverse (or negative): The higher the female employment rate, the lower the fertility rate.

Ipsative Measure (or Scale) A *rank-order scale in which a particular rank can be used only once. The opposite is usually called a "normative" scale.

For example, if you gave raters the following instructions, the results would be an ipsative scale: "Here are 11 movies; rank them from best to worst, giving the best a 10, the next best a 9, the next an 8, and so on down to the worst, which gets a 0." By contrast, if you said, "Here are 11 movies, rate them on a scale of 0 to 10," you would be asking for a normative scale. One rater could think the movies were all excellent and give them all 10s and 9s; another might believe they were terrible and give them all 1s and 2s.

When more than one rater uses an ipsative scale, the means, medians, and standard deviations of their rankings are always the same; but, when different raters use a normative scale, this is not necessarily (and rarely is) the case.

Irrational Number A number with infinite, nonrepeating decimals such as pi or the square root of 2 (1.414213562 . . .). Compare *rational number.

Isomorphic Having a form or structure similar to something else. Said of theories when one can be deduced from another because they are logically equivalent. Said of measurements when big units of measurement are used to measure big things and small units are used to measure small things.

For example, we don't measure the distance from Los Angeles to San Francisco in inches; we could, but we don't, because the measurement scale and the thing measured would not be isomorphic.

Iteration Generally, a repetition. A procedure in computation in which a set of operations is repeated.

IV Abbreviation for *independent variable.

Jackknife Method A method for estimating *standard errors. The basic approach is to take repeated subsamples of one's original sample, eliminating observations one at a time. The main advantage of the method is that it requires no assumptions about *underlying distributions; it is thus a *nonparametric method. See *bootstrap methods, which are an extension of the jackknife.

J Curve A curve describing a *frequency distribution that looks roughly like an uppercase letter J, that is, with minimum frequency at low levels of the *x axis and rapidly increasing frequencies at higher levels. Examples of such curves are often found illustrating the frequency of adherence to a norm or compliance with a standard of behavior. For instance, the graph on the next page shows the number of speeding tickets per hour given on a busy highway and the percentage of vehicles driving at or below the speed limit.

John Henry Effect A tendency of persons in a *control group (i.e., those who are not receiving an experimental *treatment) to take the experimental situation as a challenge and exert more effort than they otherwise would; they try to beat those in the *experimental group. This, of course, negates the whole purpose of having a control group.

For example, to see if a new power tool is worth the investment, a supervisor in a construction firm might provide some workers (the experimental group) with the new power tool; the rest of the workers (control group) continue using the old tool. The workers using the old tool might work very much harder to show that they were just as good and should get new the tool too. They might actually produce more, even though, under ordinary conditions (not influenced by the John Henry effect), workers using the new tool would be more productive.

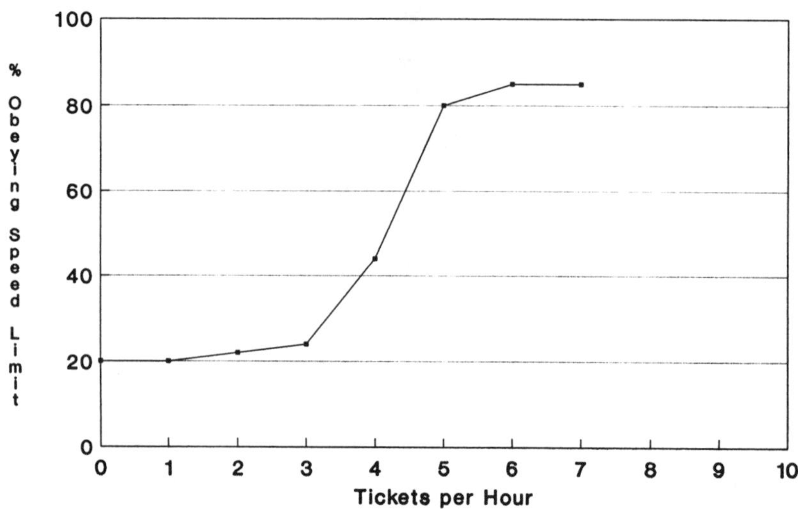

J Curve

Joint Contingency Table A table illustrating how two or more *independent variables jointly affect a *dependent variable.

For example, the following joint contingency table shows the suicide rate (dependent variable) of different age, sex, and racial groups (independent variables). Suicides are jointly affected by sex, age, and race; African Americans, women, and (somewhat less clearly) young persons are less likely to take their own lives.

Suicides per 100,000 in the United States, 1988 (approximate)

	Males		*Females*	
Age	*Blacks*	*Whites*	*Blacks*	*Whites*
10-14	1	2	1	1
15-19	10	20	2	5
20-24	20	27	3	4
25-34	22	26	4	6
35-44	16	24	4	7
45-54	12	23	4	9
55-64	11	27	3	8
65+	14	45	2	7
All ages	12	22	2	6

Joint Probability The probability of two or more *conditional events occurring together.

For example, the probability of drawing from a normal deck a card that is a club is 1 out of 4 (or .25). The chances of drawing a 7 are 1 out of 13 (or .0769). The probability of drawing a card that is both a club and a 7 is 1 out of 52 ($1/4 \times 1/13 = 1/52$) or .01923 ($.25 \times .0769$).

Judgment Sampling A procedure in which a researcher makes a judgment that a *convenience sample (e.g., volunteers) might be similar enough to a *random sample that it could make sense to use statistical procedures designed for use on random samples. Selecting a sample according to the researcher's judgment of its representativeness is recommended only when a *probability sample is impossible or highly impractical. See *purposive sample.

Just-Identified Model Another term for a *fully recursive, but not *over-identified, model. See *recursive model.

K The usual symbol for a *coefficient of alienation.

Kendall's Coefficient of Concordance A *nonparametric statistical test of the agreement among sets of rankings. Symbolized: "*W*." *W* can range from 0 (no agreement) to 1.0 (complete agreement). See *interrater reliability.

For example, if we wanted to see how much 7 wine tasters agreed (were in "concord") about their rankings of a dozen different wines, we could use Kendall's coefficient.

Kendall's (tau) Correlation One of three measures of *association (tau a, tau b, tau c) between two *ordinal variables. A form of *correlation between ordinal variables used when the ranks of the ordered categories are not treated as interval scales. Compare *Somers's *d*, *Spearman's rho.

Kim's *d* A measure of *association between two *ordinal variables used when the ranks of the ordered categories are not treated as *interval scales. Contrast *Spearman's rho.

K

Kolmogorov-Smirnov Tests *Nonparametric tests of whether *sample data are consistent with a specified *distribution function and whether two samples may reasonably be assumed to come from the same distribution.

KR20 and KR21 Abbreviations for *Kuder-Richardson formulas 20 and 21.

Kruskal-Wallis Test A *nonparametric test of *statistical significance used when testing more than two independent samples. It is an extension of the *Mann-Whitney *U* test, and of the Wilcoxon rank sum test, to three or more independent samples. Symbolized: *H*.

Kuder-Richardson Formulas (20 and 21) Measures of the internal consistency or *reliability of tests in which items have only two possible answers, such as agree/disagree or yes/no. Compare *split-half reliability, *Spearman-Brown formula.

Kurtosis The shape (degree of peakedness) of a curve that is a graphic representation of a (*unimodal) *frequency distribution. Kurtosis usually indicates the extent to which a distribution departs from the bell-shaped or *normal curve by being either pointier (leptokurtosis) or flatter (platykurtosis).

Kurtosis can be expressed numerically as well as graphically. Computer programs often provide such numbers. The basic rule for interpreting them is that negative numbers mean short tails and positive numbers mean long tails.

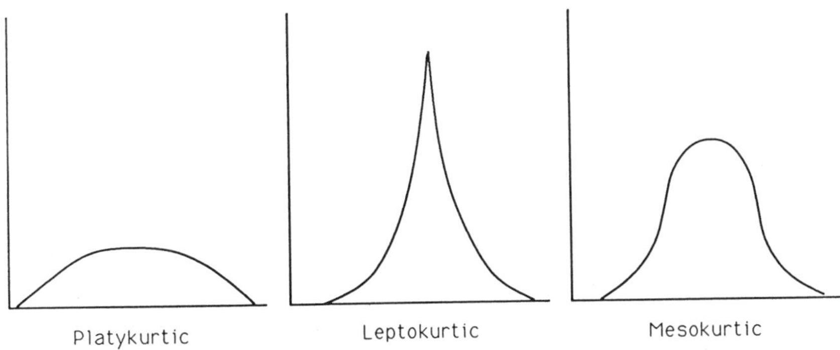

Kurtosis

Laboratory Research Any of several methods of isolating subjects so as to *control *extraneous variables. Often considered to be synonymous with *experimental research. The advantage of the laboratory method in the social and behavioral sciences is also its disadvantage. Subjects can be isolated from contexts that might influence their behavior; hence the researcher can focus only on those independent variables of interest. It may be difficult to generalize results to situations outside of the laboratory, however, because people seldom act in isolation from context. Otherwise put, in using laboratory research, one may sometimes trade a gain in *internal validity for a loss in *external validity.

Lagged Dependent Variable Said of a dependent variable whose value at a particular time is to some degree dependent on its value at a previous time.

For example, the amount of money families spend annually on vacations (the dependent variable) may tend to fluctuate with their income (an *independent variable). If income goes up, the amount spent on vacations may go up. But the amount families spend this year will tend also to be predictable by how much they spent in previous years. For instance, families that didn't spend much on vacations in the past might continue for some time to use increases in income for other things. When such is the case, one speaks of a lagged dependent variable. One of the predictors of the value of this year's dependent variable, then, is last year's. Last year's dependent variable becomes one of this year's independent variables.

Lambda More fully known as "Goodman and Kruskal's lambda." A *measure of association appropriate to use when the *variables being described are *categorical (*nominal or *discrete). Lambdas range from zero, when knowing one variable tells you nothing about another, to 1.0, when knowing one always enables you to predict the other. Lambda is an *asymmetric measure of association and is a *proportional reduction of error (PRE) measure.

For example, say that a statistics professor had 40 students in a class, 20 women and 20 men. The professor gave a pass/fail test; 22 students passed and 18 failed. If, of the 22 students who passed, 11 were men and 11 were women, there would be no association between the two variables; knowing the sex of students wouldn't help predict whether they passed or not. The lambda would be zero. But, suppose that 20 of the 22 who passed were female and 2 were male (and therefore that all of the 18 who failed were male). Then there would be a strong association between sex and success on the test. Knowing students' sex would most often enable you to tell whether they passed or failed. The lambda in this example is .89. This means that our prediction is 89% better when we know the students' sex.

Latent Class Analysis (LCA) A method similar to *factor analysis but used with *categorical data. While factor analysis is used to discover *latent *variables,* LCA is used to find latent *categories* or "classes" of variables, such as questionnaire items that have categorical, not continuous, answers.

Latent Factor See *latent variable.

Latent Function In *functionalism, a purpose or use of a social phenomenon that is not obvious (it is hidden or "latent") to social actors. Researchers hypothesize that it exists so as to explain otherwise mysterious phenomena. Researchers looking for latent functions are looking for *latent variables.

Men's neckties might be a good example. At one time, they were probably scarves meant to keep men warm. But today they are worn indoors in well-heated buildings and even on very hot days when it is uncomfortable to do so. Keeping warm cannot be the function they fill; it cannot explain their widespread use. Nor can neckties be wholly explained by their decorative functions because there are many ways for men to decorate themselves (e.g., wearing a brooch pinned to the collar). But all except neckties are considered socially inappropriate—for men, but not women, at least in some circumstances. So what is the latent function of necktie wearing? Latent functions are always speculative because, like all latent variables, they cannot be studied and measured directly. But one might hypothesize the following. By wearing a necktie, a man makes a statement: "I am a serious person, I recognize that this is an important social context [work, a formal social event], and, by dressing appropriately, I show you that I am the kind of person who can be trusted to do the right thing. Were I not wearing a tie, you might imagine that I was frivolous or rebellious."

Latent Structure A pattern of relations among variables that is not directly observable but is hypothesized to exist so as to explain variables that are observable. See *latent variable, *analysis of covariance structures.

Latent Variable An underlying characteristic that cannot be observed; it is hypothesized to exist so as to explain variables, such as behavior, that can be observed (*manifest variables). Latent variables are also often called *factors, especially in the context of *factor analysis. Compare *latent function, *LISREL.

For example, if we observed the votes of members of the House of Representatives on spending bills for the military, medicare, food stamps, education, law enforcement, and promoting business investment, we might find underlying patterns that could be explained by postulating latent variables (factors) such as conservatism and liberalism.

Latin Square A method of allocating subjects, in a *within-subjects experiment, to *treatment group orders. So called because the treatments are symbolized by Latin (not Greek) letters. The main goal of using Latin squares is to avoid *order effects by rotating the order of treatments. See *counterbalancing.

In the following example, A, B, C, and D are treatments. There are 4 subjects and 4 orders of treatment. Note that a Latin square must be square, that is, the number of rows and columns must be equal. Also, the number of subjects must equal or be a multiple of the number of treatments—in this example, 4, 8, 12, 16, and so on.

	Order			
	1st	*2nd*	*3rd*	*4th*
Subject 1	A	B	C	D
Subject 2	B	D	A	C
Subject 3	C	A	D	B
Subject 4	D	C	B	A

Law A statement about the relations among *variables that has been frequently confirmed and that seems to hold under all circumstances. While a law is generally thought to be more certain than a theory, the difference between "law" and "theory" is often little more than a matter of accidents of usage (e.g., the *law* of supply and demand; the *theory* of evolution).

L

Modern social and behavioral scientists rarely refer to their generalizations as laws; they use "theory" almost to the exclusion of "law" to refer to statements about regular relations among variables. (The next two entries in this dictionary are terms that originated long ago.)

Law of Averages The principle that *random errors in measurement will tend to balance one another out, that is, they will as often be above as below the true values. This means that the average (*mean) is the best estimate of the true value. Compare *law of large numbers, *central limit theorem.

Law of Large Numbers Created/discovered by Jacob Bernoulli, the law of large numbers states that, the larger the *sample, the more likely it is to represent the *population from which it was drawn—specifically, the more likely it is that the sample *mean will equal the population mean. Compare *central limit theorem.

Learning Curve The tendency to learn how to do something more efficiently the more often you do it. When graphed, this yields the kinds of curves illustrated on the next page. The concept is widely used in manufacture when the focus is on the unit cost of production, but it can be applied to other sorts of learning as well.

For example, suppose that six weeks ago you moved into a new apartment and bought a new computer. Two of your routine tasks over the past six weeks have been: (A) washing the kitchen floor; (B) booting up the new computer and loading the word processing software. The first time you do each task, each takes you 25 minutes. You get better as you repeat each task—but not at the same rate. A "steep" learning curve (curve B, the computer task, in the illustration) is one depicting fast learning. Curve A illustrates the slower progress on the kitchen floor.

Week	*1*	*2*	*3*	*4*	*5*	*6*
mop up (A)	25	20	19	18	17	17
boot up (B)	25	10	3	2	1	1

Least-Squares Criterion (or Principle) In *regression analysis, a criterion for calculating the *regression equation (or drawing the *regression line) that best summarizes or fits a distribution. A rule for choosing a statistic so that the *sum of the squared deviation scores (*errors) is minimized—or, looking at it the other way around, so that the prediction's accuracy is maximized. Also called *ordinary least squares. See *general linear model, *generalized least squares.

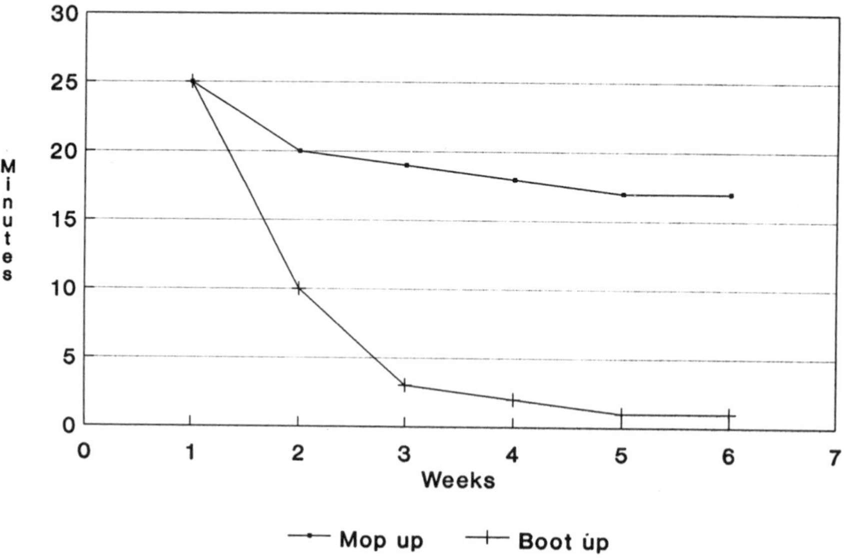

Learning Curve

Leptokurtic More peaked than a *normal curve. See *kurtosis for an illustration.

Level A *treatment or a *condition of an *independent variable in an experiment. "Level" implies amount or magnitude in ordinary language, and it is used that way in experiments too. If subjects were given 10 cc, 15 cc, and 20 cc of a medication, those amounts would be the three levels. But "level" is also used for *categorical variables, such as medications A, B, and C, where the three are different in kind, not different amounts of the same thing.

Level of Analysis (or Aggregation) If we were to study the United States, we could look at individuals, neighborhoods, counties, states, or regions. Individuals would be the lowest level of analysis or aggregation; regions would be the highest. The lower the level of analysis, the higher the level of specificity tends to be, and vice versa. See *level of generality.

L

Level of Generality The breadth of generalizations.

Take, for example, statements that apply to deviance, crime, and theft. Theft, a specific type of crime, is at the lowest level. Crime is a more general category than theft but is less broad than deviance, which includes crimes but can also be taken to mean any big departure from the ordinary.

Level of Generality	*Example*
Low	Theft
Middle	Crime
High	Deviance

Level of Measurement A term used to describe measurement scales in terms of how much information they convey about the differences among values—the higher the level, the more information.

There are four levels of measurement. Arranged in order of strength, from the highest to the lowest, they are *ratio, *interval, *ordinal, and *nominal. It is possible to describe data gathered at a higher level with a lower level of measurement; but the reverse is not true. For example, one can express income in dollars and cents (interval level) or with ordinal descriptions like upper class, middle class, and lower class.

It is important to be aware of the level of measurement you are using because statistical techniques appropriate at one level might produce ridiculous results at another. For example, in a study of religious affiliation, you might number your variables as follows: 1 = Catholic, 2 = Jewish, 3 = Protestant, 4 = Other, 5 = None. The religion variable is measured at the nominal level. The numbers are just convenient labels or names; you can't treat them as if they mean something at the interval level; you can't add up one Jewish person (2) and one Protestant person (3) to get an atheist (5).

Considerable controversy exists concerning which statistics can validly be used to analyze variables measured at different levels of measurement. The debates usually revolve around questions of how serious a distortion occurs when one violates particular *assumptions presumed by certain statistical techniques. As with constitutional law, there are strict and loose constructionists in the interpretation of adherence to assumptions.

Level of Significance More fully, the level of *statistical significance. The probability that a result would be produced by chance (*sampling error, *random error) alone.

The level of significance indicates the risk or *probability of committing an error (*Type I Error in *hypothesis testing). The level of significance is stated as a *probability, often abbreviated p, followed by a number, for example, $p \leq .05$ or $p < .01$. The smaller the number, the smaller the chance of Type I Error and the more statistically significant the finding. See also *alpha level, **p* value.

Note: The level of statistical significance says nothing about a finding's *substantive or *practical significance; there are no statistical tests for substantive or practical significance.

Level of Specificity See *level of analysis, *level of generality.

Liar's Paradox A paradox that arises from someone making a statement such as this one: "I am lying." If the statement is true, then it is false; and if it is false, then it is true.

Life Table A table showing life expectancy at various dates and/or for different groups.

Life Expectancy for Men and Women, 1950-1980

Year	*Men*	*Women*
1950	66	72
1960	68	74
1970	68	76
1980	71	78

Likelihood The *probability of observed results (in a *sample) given the estimates of the *population parameters. In other words, the *conditional probability of observed frequencies or values given expected frequencies or values. It is perhaps most widely used as a way to determine the *goodness of fit of a *logistic regression model. See *maximum likelihood estimation.

Likelihood Ratio (LR) As the name implies, the LR is a *ratio of two *likelihoods. It is widely used as a *test statistic, perhaps especially for relations among *categorical variables displayed in *contingency tables. The smaller the LR, the *stronger* the relationship. This is because (in comparison with the *chi-square method) with the LR we attempt to *accept* a particular *model, not reject a *null hypothesis.

L

Likert Scale A widely used questionnaire format developed by Rensis Likert. Respondents are given statements and asked to respond by saying whether they "strongly agree," "agree," "disagree," "strongly disagree." Wording varies considerably; for example, people might be asked if they "totally approve," "approve somewhat," and so on. See *summated scale.

Likert scales, and Likert-like scales, are the most widely used attitude scale type in the social sciences. They are comparatively easy to construct, can deal with attitudes of more than one dimension, and tend to have high reliabilities.

Limit (a) In mathematics, a theoretical end point that can be ever more closely approached but never quite reached. For example, if we added the following fractions ½ + ¼ + ⅛ + 1⁄16 + 1⁄32 . . . and so on, each time adding half of the previous fraction to the string, the more we added, the closer we would get to the limit of 1.0; but we would never reach it. Compare *asymptote.

(b) In *probability theory, the larger the number of *trials, the closer the *empirical probability gets to the limit or the *theoretical probability. The more times we flipped a fair coin, the closer the proportion of heads would get to the limit of .5, or the closer the ratio of heads to tails would get to 1:1.

Linear Dependency Said of a variable that depends on another in the sense that it can be directly derived from the other. See *function.

For example, when one *vector in a *matrix can be derived from another, it is in a state of linear dependency; it is simply the same vector in a different form; this means that the matrix contains redundant information.

Linear Equation An equation that can be plotted on a graph as a straight line; such an equation contains no *powers higher than 1.

For example, $x = 2a$ is linear, but $x = a^2$ is not.

Linear Function A *linear relation expressed as a *linear equation.

Linear Regression Analysis A method of describing the relationship between two or more variables by calculating a "best fitting" straight line (or plane) on a graph. The line averages or summarizes the relationship. The result is a *regression line, which can also be expressed in a *regression equation.

The generic term is *regression analysis, which, without further specification, means the linear variety. Compare *curvilinear relation, *polynomial regression analysis.

Linear Relation (or Correlation) A relationship that, when plotted on a graph, forms a straight line. It forms a straight line because the direction and the rate of change in one variable are constant with respect to changes in the other. Compare *curvilinear relation, *monotonic relation.

For example, if a baker notices that whenever he raises the price of a loaf of bread by a nickel, sales drop by exactly 2%, and every time he lowers the price by a nickel, sales go up 2%, the relationship between price and sales would be linear. (This is also an example of an *inverse—or negative—relation, because whenever one variable goes up the other goes down.)

Linear Transformation Changing a number, group of numbers, or an equation by adding, subtracting, multiplying, or dividing by a constant. The best known example is probably multiplying *proportions by 100 (the constant) to change ("transform") them into percentages. Called "linear" because, when you plot the old values against the new on a graph, the result is a straight line. Compare *nonlinear transformation and see that entry for an illustration.

LISREL Short for Linear Structural Relations. A highly versatile *computer program, developed by K. Jöreskog, now in its seventh version (LISREL VII) and recently available as part of the *SPSS package. It is used for analyzing *covariance structures or (what amounts to the same thing) *structural equation models. It can be used to analyze causal models with multiple indicators of *latent variables and structural relations among latent variables. It is more powerful than *path analysis, goes beyond the more typical *exploratory factor analysis, and allows the researcher to do *confirmatory factor analysis. The software brand name has become so well known that it is often used for the methods of analysis as well as for the technology for executing them.

Literature Review A systematic survey and interpretation of the research findings (the "literature") on a particular topic, usually designed to prepare for undertaking further research on the subject. The literature review is often done a second time to help one interpret unexpected results. In a *meta-analysis, the literature review is less preparatory and more the goal of the research.

LN Abbreviation for natural *logarithm, usually lowercase, ln.

Loading See *factor loading.

Log See *logarithm

Log$_e$ Symbol for natural *logarithm.

Logarithm An *exponent of a base number indicating the *power to which that number must be raised to produce another number.

For example, the log of 100 is 2, because 10^2 (10×10) equals 100; the log of 1,000 is 3, because 10^3 ($10 \times 10 \times 10$) equals 1,000. The log of 47 is 1.6721 because $47 = 10^{1.6721}$. The "antilog" (or inverse log) turns the relation around; for example, antilog 2 = 100; antilog 3 = 1,000; antilog 1.6721 = 47.

When "log" or "logarithm" is used without qualification, this means "*common* logarithm," that is, logarithm using base 10, as in the examples above. Statisticians also use the "*natural*" or ("Napierian") logarithm, where the base is the *universal constant, e (2.71828). See *logit, *log-linear analysis.

Logistic Model See *logit analysis/models.

Logistic Regression Analysis A kind of regression analysis used when the *dependant variable is *dichotomous and scored 0, 1. It is usually used for predicting whether something will happen or not, such as graduation, business failure, heart disease—anything that can be expressed as Event/Nonevent. Independent variables may be categorical or continuous in logistic regression analysis. It is based on transforming data by taking their natural *logarithms so as to reduce nonlinearity. Rather than using *OLS methods, logistic regression estimates parameters using *maximum likelihood estimation. It is an increasingly popular alternative to *discriminant analysis because it requires fewer assumptions. See *logit analysis/models.

Logit Short for "logistic probability unit" or the natural "log of the odds." A *logistic regression analysis yields a probability of an event; that probability is transformed into an odds; the natural log of that odds is taken to get the logit. See *logit analysis/models. Compare *probit analysis.

Logit Analysis/Models A type of *log-linear analysis similar to multiple *regression analysis; it is used when both the independent variables and the dependent variable are *dummy (*dichotomous) variables. It is used for predicting a categorical dependent variable on the basis of two or more independent variables. *Ordinary least squares can be used when the *independent variables are dichotomous but not when the dependent variable is.

Log-Linear Analysis/Models Methods for studying relations among *categorical (*nominal) variables in contingency tables. So called because it uses equations that are transformed, by taking their natural logs, to make them linear. Log-linear analysis uses *odds rather than *proportions as is done in the more familiar *chi-square tests. Log-linear models are capable of handling several nominal variables and their relations in a way that approximates analysis of *covariance structures. The results of a log-linear analysis can be analyzed either by the usual chi-square goodness-of-fit test or by the *likelihood ratio test.

Longitudinal Study A study over time of a variable or a group of subjects. See *panel study, *event history analysis.

The National Longitudinal Study of the Class of 1972 and the High School and Beyond Study are well-known longitudinal studies. The investigators began with large, national samples of high school seniors whom they surveyed extensively. Every few years, the same students were contacted again to find out whether and where they went to college, whether they graduated, what employment they had found, how much money they were making, and so on.

Lowspread The range of values in a *distribution between the *median and the lowest value. Compare *highspread, *boxplot.

LR *Likelihood ratio.

Lurking Variable A third variable that causes a *correlation between two others—sometimes, like the troll under the bridge, an unpleasant surprise when discovered. A lurking variable is a source of a *spurious correlation. See also *confound. Compare *covariate, *latent variable, *moderator variable.

For example, if researchers found a correlation between individuals' college grades and their income later in life, they might wonder whether doing well in school increased income. It might; but good grades and high income could both be caused by a third (lurking or hidden variable) such as tendency to work hard.

M Symbol sometimes used for the *mean (of a *sample).

Main Effect The simple effect of an *independent variable on a *dependent variable; the effect of an independent variable uninfluenced by other variables. Used in contrast with the *interaction effect of two or more independent variables on a dependent variable. There is some controversy about whether it is appropriate to try to interpret main effects in the presence of interaction effects.

MANCOVA *Multivariate analysis of covariance, an extension of *ANCOVA to problems with multiple *dependent variables.

Manifest Function The obvious, ostensible, or purported use or purpose of a social phenomenon—usually contrasted with its *latent function. See *functionalism.

For example, the manifest function of the death penalty might be deterrence. If you asked its supporters, this might be the reason (manifest function) they would offer for favoring it. But, because there is little convincing evidence that the death penalty deters crime, a functionalist might look for latent functions to explain the widespread support for capital punishment. Satisfying a primitive urge for revenge might be suggested as the latent function.

Manifest Variable An observed variable assumed to indicate the presence of a *latent variable. Also called an "indicator variable."

For example, we cannot observe intelligence directly; it is a latent variable. But we can look at indicators such as size of vocabulary, success in one's occupation, IQ test score, ability to play complicated games such as chess or bridge well, and so on.

Manipulated Variable Another term for *independent variable. Also called "treatment variable." Compare *predictor variable.

Mann-Whitney *U* Test A test of the *statistical significance of differences between two groups. It is used when the *data for two *samples are measured on an *ordinal scale (in rank order). It is a *nonparametric equivalent of the **t* test. Although ordinal measures are used with the Mann-Whitney test, an underlying continuous distribution is assumed. Compare *Wilcoxon test.

MANOVA *Multivariate analysis of variance.

Marginal Distribution See *marginal frequency distribution.

Marginal Frequencies See *marginal frequency distribution.

Marginal Frequency Distribution Frequency distributions of grouped data in *cross-tabulations. So called because they are found in the "margins" of the table (and/or printed in the margins of a *codebook). Often called "marginals" for short.

For example, suppose researchers polled a sample of city residents about whether they favored busing to achieve school desegregation. If they cross-tabulated the answers by the race of the *respondents, the results might be as follows. The totals are the marginal frequency distributions. The "row marginals" are 155 and 293; the "column marginals" are 187 and 261. These marginals might then be used to calculate the *expected frequencies to use in a *chi-square test of the *statistical significance of the findings.

	Race		
	Black	*White*	*Total*
Favor Busing			
Yes	103	52	155
No	84	209	293
Total	187	261	448

Marginally Significant Just barely or almost significant. Said of research results that fail to exceed the *critical value needed to be *statistically significant but that come close enough that the researcher wants to discuss them anyway.

Marginal Probability A probability calculation that depends only on the frequencies in the margins of a table. See *expected frequency, *marginal frequency distribution.

For example, suppose you randomly sampled 1,000 adults in a nearby large city and obtained from each of them their sex, height, and weight. Let's say your sample includes 600 men and 400 women. Using height and weight figures obtained from an insurance company, you calculate that 300 of your subjects are seriously overweight (obese); 700 are not. The marginal probabilities for sex would be .60/.40; for obesity, they would be .30/.70, as in the bold numbers in the following table. The *expected frequency for each of the cells, if sex had no relation to obesity, would be .18, .12, .42, and .28. If the actual, *observed frequencies departed significantly from those probabilities (expected frequencies), we could conclude that sex and obesity are related in the population sampled.

Obesity by Sex, Big City Sample

	Men	*Women*	***Total***
Obese	.18	.12	**.30**
Not Obese	.42	.28	**.70**
Total	**.60**	**.40**	

Marginals Short for *marginal frequencies.

Marginal Utility The additional benefit that comes from obtaining a small (marginal) increase in some good, given the amount that you already have.

For example, the benefit or utility of a glass of cold water on a hot summer day might be very great. The value to you of a second glass of water would probably be less great. After you drank the third or fourth glass of water, the marginal utility of one more would probably decline to almost nothing.

Markov Chain *Time-series model in which an event's *probability is dependent only upon the immediately preceding event in the series, and this dependence is the same at all stages. The general idea is that the state of a system in the future will be unaffected by its past, except its immediate past. Also called "Markov process," "Markovian principle," and "chain path model."

Matched Pairs A *research design in which subjects are matched on characteristics that might affect their reaction to a *treatment. After the pairs are determined, one member of each pair is assigned *at random* to the group receiving treatment (*experimental group); the other group (*control group) does not receive treatment. Without random assignment, matching is not considered good research practice. Also called "subject matching."

For example, if professors wanted to test the effectiveness of two different textbooks for an undergraduate statistics course, they might match the students on SAT quantitative scores before assigning them to classes using one or another of the texts. An alternative, if the professors had no control over class assignment, would be to treat SAT quantitative scores as a *covariate and control for it using an *ANCOVA design.

Matching See *matched pairs.

Materialism The philosophical position that physical matter is the only reality and that other sorts of phenomena, such as ideas and social values, are reducible to or are merely expressions of material reality. Compare *idealism, *empiricism.

Matrix Any rectangular array of data into rows and columns. See *correlation matrix, *matrix algebra, *vector.

Matrix Algebra Rules for adding, subtracting, multiplying, and dividing matrices. It is widely used in *regression analysis, because it greatly simplifies the calculations needed when there are more than two independent variables. *LISREL analyses are inconceivable without matrix algebra.

The following example shows how one adds two matrices, ***A*** + ***B***, to get a third, ***C***.

$$\underset{\boldsymbol{A}}{\begin{bmatrix} 4 & 8 \\ 9 & 6 \\ 1 & 2 \end{bmatrix}} + \underset{\boldsymbol{B}}{\begin{bmatrix} 4 & 3 \\ 2 & 4 \\ 8 & 6 \end{bmatrix}} = \underset{\boldsymbol{C}}{\begin{bmatrix} 8 & 11 \\ 11 & 10 \\ 9 & 8 \end{bmatrix}}$$

Maturation Effect A *threat to validity that occurs because of change in subjects over time.

For example, to study the effects of a college education on social and political attitudes, we might ask entering students to complete an attitude survey. Three and one-half years later, we could ask the same students (now seniors) to answer the same survey questions. Any changes might be due to the effects of college, but they also might be due to the fact that the students have gotten older (matured) since we first surveyed them.

Maximin Strategy In *game theory, a strategy in which players try to *maxi*mize their *mini*mum winnings. Compare *minimax strategy.

An example might be concentrating one's investments in low-yield, but very safe, government bonds.

Maximum Likelihood Chi Square A test of the *statistical significance of a *confirmatory factor analysis, a *LISREL model, and other statistical results that can be expressed as *likelihoods.

Maximum Likelihood Estimation (MLE) Statistical methods (usually alternatives to *OLS methods) for estimating the *population parameters most likely to have resulted in observed *sample data. MLE is an integral part of *LISREL analyses. It is also often used in *log-linear models to estimate *expected frequencies in a *contingency table.

OLS methods work by minimizing the sum of squared differences between observed and predicted scores; MLE chooses as the estimate of the parameter the value for which the probability of the observed scores is the highest. See *likelihood. The basic procedure in MLE is as follows: For each possible value a parameter might have, compute the probability that the particular sample statistic (observed value) would have occurred if it were the true value of the parameter. Then, for the estimate, pick the parameter for which the probability of the actual observation is greatest.

Maxplane A method of *oblique rotation of the axes in *factor analysis.

MCA *Multiple classification analysis.

MD A common abbreviation for *median and for *mean deviation.

Mean The average. To get the mean, you add up the values for each case and divide the total by the number of cases. Often symbolized as *M* or as $\bar{X}$ ("*X*-bar").

When used without specification, "mean" refers to the *arithmetic* mean. Much less commonly used in statistics are the *harmonic* mean and the *geometric* mean.

For an example of how to calculate an arithmetic mean, see *mode. The geometric mean is computed by taking the nth root of the product of n scores, for example, the square root of 2 scores, the cube root of 3, and so on. For example, to get the geometric mean of 5, 7, and 9, you multiply $5 \times 7 \times 9 = 315$ and take the cube root to get 6.8, which is somewhat smaller than the arithmetic mean for the same scores, 7.0.

Mean Deviation An infrequently used measure of *dispersion. It is calculated using the *absolute values of the *deviation scores—not the squares of the deviation scores as is done when computing the *variance and *standard deviation. Also called *average deviation.

Mean Square Residual (MSR) Another term for *variance of estimate.

Mean Squares (MS) What the *variance is called in an *ANOVA. An estimate of population variance calculated by adding together the squares of the deviation scores (*sum of squares) and dividing by the *degrees of freedom.

Measurement Error Inaccuracy due to flaws in a measuring instrument—as contrasted with other sorts of *error, or unexplained *variance. See *random error, *sampling error.

For example, if a research team were studying the effects of stress on blood pressure, and the pressure gauge were faulty, this would lead to measurement error.

Measure of Association See *association, measure of.

Median The middle score in a set of ranked scores. When the number of scores is even, there is no single middle score; in that case, the median is found by taking an average of the two middle scores. See the example at *mode.

Median Test A *nonparametric test performed on *samples drawn from two different *populations to see whether the two populations have the same median.

Mediating Variable Another term for *intervening variable, that is, a variable that "transmits" the effects of another variable. Compare *interaction effect, *moderator variable.

For example, parents transmit their social status to their children directly. But they also do so indirectly, through education, as in the following diagram, where education is the mediating variable. See *path diagram.

Parents' Status → Child's Education → Child's Status

Meta-Analysis Also spelled "metanalysis." Quantitative procedures for summarizing or integrating the findings obtained from a *literature review of a subject. Meta-analysis is, strictly speaking, more a kind of *synthesis than analysis. The meta-analyst uses the results of individual research projects on the same topic (perhaps studies testing the same *hypothesis) as *data points for a statistical study of the topic.

Metaphysical Explanation An explanation not subject to physical (or observational or behavioral) test. The term is most often used loosely by social and behavioral scientists to mean "unscientific," "hard to understand," and/or "highly unlikely."

Metatheory Theory about theory.

For example, a theoretical account of the *epistemological presuppositions of *conflict theory and *functionalism would be a metatheoretical work.

Methodological Individualism The *assumption that all generalizations about groups can be explained by (or reduced to) facts about individuals. Sometimes also called—more often by its opponents than its friends—*reductionism. Methodological individualism is often contrasted with *holism.

For example, take the statement "teachers' middle-class values often make them unable to respond to the needs of lower-class children." Methodological individualists would say that this statement makes no sense apart from the values of individual teachers and the needs of individual students; "middle class" and "lower class" are merely convenient generalizations, which, when valid, summarize what we know about individuals.

Methodology (a) The study of research methods, from general problems bordering on *epistemology to specific comparisons of the details of various techniques. See *research design. (b) Sometimes just a highfalutin way of saying "method," as in, "this article employs an interesting methodology."

Metric Any standard or scale of measurement: inches, seconds, minutes, dollars, test scores, kilograms, and so on. The term is most often used in statements such as this one: "Results are reported in the original metric"—meaning that they have not been *transformed or *standardized.

Metric Variable A variable that can be measured on an *interval or *ratio scale.

Micro-Data Data about variables within a behavioral unit, such as an individual or a corporation. Micro-data is often contrasted with *aggregate data, which is about groups of behavioral units such as individuals grouped by race, sex, or class or corporations grouped by economic sector.

Middle-Range Theory Robert K. Merton's term for theory describing relations at modest *levels of abstraction or middling *levels of generality—somewhere between an *empirical generalization and a *metatheory, or what C. Wright Mills once called "grand theory." Middle-range theories are, as Goldilocks put it, "just right," not too atheoretical like empirical generalizations but not too hard to test like grand theories.

Midspread Another term for *interquartile range, that is, scores that range from the 25th through the 75th percentile.

Milgram Experiments A series of studies of individuals' willingness to "just follow orders," even when doing so appeared to require hurting other people. The studies were controversial both because of their shocking findings about how many people would be willing to obey evil orders and because the methods used put the subjects of the study at risk of psychological harm.

Minimax Strategy In *game theory, a strategy in which players try to *mini*mize their *max*imum losses. Compare *maximin strategy.

An example of where this strategy could be applicable might be designing power plants to avoid nuclear accidents. It might be wise to reduce the odds of meltdown (maximum loss) to the lowest possible level, even if that had to come at the cost of raising the odds of occasionally spewing small amounts of radioactive particles into the air.

Minitab A popular *software package for *regression analysis.

Missing Data Information not available for a subject (or case) about whom other information is available—as when a *respondent fails to answer one of the questions in a survey.

Misspecification An error in *regression analysis made by constructing a *model that excludes a *variable that ought to have been included—or includes one that ought to have been excluded. Compare *identification problem.

Mixed Designs (a) *Factorial designs in which the number of *levels of the factors is not the same for all factors. (b) Factorial *multiple regression analyses that combine *repeated measures (for the within-subjects variables) and one-time measures (for the between-subjects) variables.

Mixed-Effects Model An ANOVA design combining the *random-effects model and the *fixed-effects model. Also called "Model III ANOVA."

MLE *Maximum likelihood estimate.

Mobility Table A table showing persons' social or occupational status at two different times. Most commonly, individuals are cross-classified according to a parent's occupation (origin) and their own first occupation (destination).

Suppose we sampled 2,000 of the adult men in a large city and asked them two questions: When you were growing up and going to high school, what was your father's occupation? What was your first full-time job? If we assigned levels to the occupations and entered the results in a mobility table, it might look something like the following. The bold numbers on the diagonal are nonmobile sons, that is, sons who have the same rank as their fathers. Cells to the lower left of the diagonal show the numbers of upwardly mobile sons, while those to the upper right of the diagonal show the downwardly mobile.

Father's Job by Son's First Job

			Son's First Job			
Father's Job	*Upper*	*Upper Mid*	*Mid*	*Lower Mid*	*Lower*	*Total*
Upper	**120**	75	45	60	3	303
Upper middle	80	**50**	55	65	5	255
Middle	80	65	**90**	170	10	415
Lower middle	70	90	90	**300**	45	595
Lower	20	30	25	167	**190**	432
Total	370	310	305	762	253	2000

Mode The most common (most frequent) score in a set of scores.

For example, if students' scores on a midterm were distributed as in the following list, the mode would be 90, the *median 81, and the *mean 74.

Students' Midterm Scores: Mean, Median, and Mode

Student 1	94	
Student 2	90}	
Student 3	90}	→ the most common score (**mode**)
Student 4	90}	
Student 5	81	→ the middle score (**median**)
Student 6	70	
Student 7	65	
Student 8	56	
Student 9	30	
Total	666	666 divided by 9 = 74 (**mean**)

Model A representation or description of something (a phenomenon or set of relationships) that aids in understanding or studying it; a set of assumptions about relationships used to study their interactions, as a computer simulation might model economic developments or as role-playing might model social interaction. Compare *ideal type, *paradigm, *theory.

Usually the purpose of constructing a model is to test it. For an example of a graphic causal model, see *path diagram. Perhaps the most common form of model is an *equation, which is a model that states a theory in formal, symbolic language, as in a *regression equation.

Model I ANOVA See *fixed-effects model.

Model II ANOVA See *random-effects model.

Model III ANOVA See *mixed-effects model.

Modeling A term sometimes used to describe building a *model.

Moderating Effect Another term for *interaction effect. Also called "conditioning" effect and "contingency" effect.

Moderating Variable See *moderator variable.

Moderator (Variable) A variable that influences ("moderates") the relation between two other variables and thus produces an *interaction effect. Compare *mediating variable.

Modus Ponens A rule of inference in the form: If A exists, then so does B; A exists; therefore B exists also. From the Latin meaning "method of affirming."

Modus Tolens A rule of inference in the form: If A exists, then so does B; B doesn't; therefore neither does A. From the Latin meaning "method of denying."

Molar Loosely, "big." Said of research concerned with whole systems or categories of subjects (large units of analysis) rather with than the characteristics of the individuals making up the categories or systems. Usually contrasted with *molecular.

Molecular Loosely, "little." Having to do with parts rather than wholes, with simple rather than complex systems, with small rather than large units of analysis. Compare *molar. Molar and molecular are used more often in psychology than in sociology or economics. In the latter two disciplines, a similar concept is captured by the macro-micro distinction.

Moment In statistics, the expected power of a variable over all the cases in a *distribution; the mean of the expected values of a variable raised to a particular power. Moments can be used for computing measures that describe a distribution; the first moment is used to calculate the *mean; the second, the *variance; the third, *skewness; and the fourth, the *kurtosis of a distribution.

Monotonic Relation Said of a relation between two variables in which an increase in one always ("monotonously") produces an increase (or decrease) in another. A monotonic relation is often, but not necessarily, a *linear relation; increases interrupted by periods of no change will still be monotonic as long as there is no reversal of direction. Compare *curvilinear relation, *nonmonotonic linear relation. In the following example, the lower line is sometimes called "strictly monotonic."

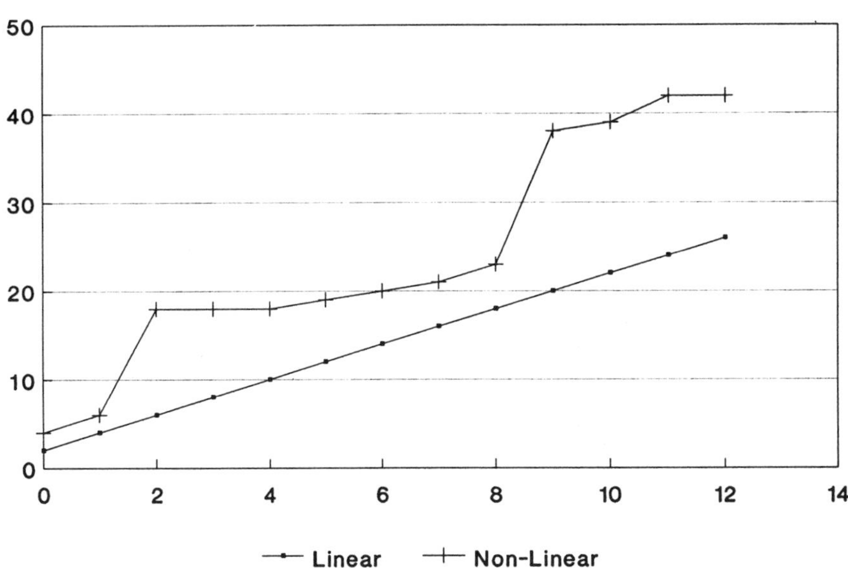

Monotonic Relation

Monte Carlo Methods Any generating of *random values (most often with a computer) to study statistical *models.

For example, statisticians who develop a new theory want to test it on data. They could collect real data, but it is much more cost efficient, initially at least, to test the theory on sets of data generated by a Monte Carlo computer program.

Mortality Another term for *attrition, or losing subjects in the course of a study, as in a *panel study when the researcher cannot find members of the panel to reinterview.

Moving Average In *time-series analysis, a method of *smoothing the curve representing the data. Individual observations are replaced by a *mean of each observation and the observations on either side of it. By

M

reducing random *fluctuations, smoothing makes long-term *trends clearer. The two most common kinds of moving average are the three-year moving average (used in the following example) and the five-year weighted moving average. See also *ARIMA, which is among the most advanced of smoothing techniques.

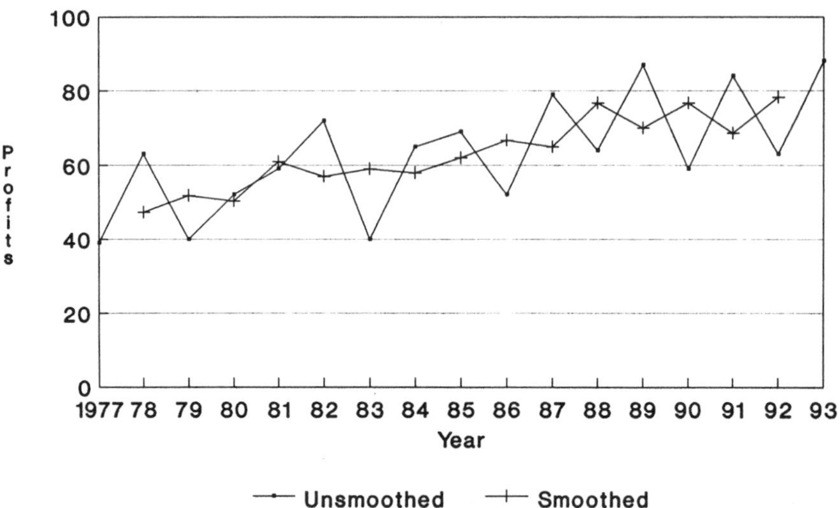

Moving Average

MRA *Multiple regression analysis.

MS Short for *mean squares.

MSR Mean square residual. See *variance of estimate.

Multicollinearity In *multiple regression analysis, multicollinearity exists when two or more *independent variables are highly *correlated; this makes it difficult if not impossible to determine their separate effects on the *dependent variable. See *intercorrelation.

Multidimensionality Having more than one aspect or dimension. Often used to describe attitudes.

For example, say a survey asked respondents for their overall attitude toward a presidential candidate. Any answers they give would likely

M

mask the fact that their overall assessment was a composite of many dimensions, for example, attitude about the candidate's positions on foreign policy, welfare, and so on as well as attitudes about his or her personal integrity, leadership qualities, and so on. In one sense, it is unrealistic to treat a complicated cluster of attitudes, some of which might be positive and others negative, as though it had only one dimension. In another sense, however, we often have to treat an "attitude object" on the basis of an overall attitude. In the case of a presidential candidate, this is especially clear. One must ultimately vote for or against—or not vote. The same kind of problem—a multidimensional attitude requiring a monodimensional decision—can apply to many choices, such as whether to go back to school, to accept a job offer, and so on.

Multidimensional Scaling (MDS) A method of using space on a graph to indicate statistical similarity and difference. Pairs of variables with the highest correlations are plotted closest together; those with the lowest correlations are furthest apart. MDS involves treating social or psychological distance as physical, graphic distance to draw a map of how individuals' attitudes or characteristics cluster.

Multimethod-Multitrait Models A version of *confirmatory factor analysis in which each factor (trait) is measured in several ways (methods) to reduce the distortion that any single measure always contains.

Multinomial Distribution A *probability distribution used to calculate the probabilities of entire frequency distributions.

Suppose, for example, that at a certain college 40% of the students were freshmen, 30% sophomores, 20% juniors, and 10% seniors. Say we drew a random sample of 10 students (with replacement) and got 2 freshmen, 3 sophomores, 5 juniors, and 0 seniors. The multinomial distribution could give us the probability of getting *exactly* that *sample distribution. That probability is, by the way, .0035.

Multioperationalize To *operationalize a *construct in more than one way, that is, to measure a construct in more than one way.

For example, academic success of college students (the construct) could be measured by (operationalized as) grade point average, graduation, and/or rank in graduating class.

Multiple Classification Analysis (MCA) A technique used when the *independent (or *predictor) variables are "classificatory" (i.e., *nominal, *categorical, or *discrete) and the *dependent variable is measured on an *interval or *ratio scale. MCA results in *coefficients (etas and betas) that are *weighted according to the number of cases in each category of the independent variables. MCA is an alternative to *dummy variable methods and is often used to handle ANOVA designs in which there is an unequal number of cases in the cells.

Multiple Comparisons Usually called *post hoc comparisons. Looking among the possible comparisons, in a *factorial or *ANOVA design, trying to find some significant difference. Considered poor practice in most circumstances. See *fishing expedition, *exploratory data analysis, *Tukey's HSD Test.

Multiple Correlation A correlation with more than two *variables, one of which is *dependent, the others *independent. The object is to measure the combined influence of two or more independent variables on a dependent variable. R is the symbol for a multiple correlation coefficient. R^2 gives the proportion of the variance in the dependent variable that can be explained by the action of all of the independent variables taken together.

For example, researchers could use multiple correlations to measure the combined effects of age, years of education, and ethnicity on individuals' incomes.

Multiple Discriminant Analysis See *discriminant analysis.

Multiple Linear Regression A method of *regression analysis that uses more than one *predictor variable (or *independent variable) to predict a single *criterion variable (or *dependent variable). The *coefficient for any particular predictor variable is an estimate of the effect of that variable while *holding constant the effects of the other predictor variables.

The generic term is "regression analysis," which when used without qualification is "*linear." "Multiple" means two or more independent variables, and most regression analyses are in fact multiple.

Multiple Regression Analysis (MRA) Any of several related statistical methods for evaluating the effects of more than one *independent variable on a *dependent variable. Because MRA can handle all ANOVA problems (but the reverse is not true), some researchers prefer to use MRA exclusively. See *regression analysis.

Multiplicative Relations Another term for *interaction effects; it is most often used when the research is *nonexperimental.

Multistage Sampling Any sampling design that requires two or more successive steps or stages. Often used with *cluster sampling and *area sampling. Each stage increases the probability of *sampling error.

For example, suppose we wanted a sample of third-grade students in U.S. schools. Because we do not have a list of all third graders from which to draw our sample, we might do something like the following. First, stage one, we would take a (perhaps *stratified) sample of the roughly 15,000 school districts in the United States. Then, stage two, we could sample elementary schools within the districts; then, third-grade classes within the schools; then, students within the sampled classes. This would be a four-stage cluster sample.

Multitrait-Multimethod Matrix (MTMM) A *correlation matrix used to examine the *convergent and *discriminant validity of a *construct. The matrix contains correlations among two or more constructs (traits) measured in two or more ways (methods).

Multivariate Analysis Any of several methods for examining multiple *variables at the same time. Usage varies. (a) Stricter usage reserves the term for *designs with two or more *independent variables and two or more *dependent variables. (b) More loosely, multivariate analysis applies to designs with more than one independent variable or more than one dependent variable or both. Whichever usage you prefer, either allows researchers to examine the relation between two variables while simultaneously *controlling for how each of these may be influenced by other variables. Examples include *path analysis, *factor analysis, *multiple regression analysis, *MANOVA, *LISREL, *canonical correlations, and *discriminant analysis.

Multivariate Analysis of Covariance (MANCOVA) An extension of *ANCOVA to research problems with multiple *dependent variables.

Multivariate Analysis of Variance (MANOVA) The extension of *ANOVA techniques to studies with multiple *dependent variables. MANOVA allows the simultaneous study of two or more *related* *dependent variables while controlling for the correlations among them. If the dependent variables are not related, there is no point in doing a MANOVA; rather, separate ANOVAs for each (unrelated) dependent variable would be appropriate.

For example, to study the effects of exercise on at-rest heart rate, you could use ANOVA to test the (null) hypothesis that there is no difference in the average heart rate of three groups: women who never exercise, who exercise sometimes, and who exercise frequently. MANOVA makes it possible to add related dependent variables to the design, such as mean blood pressure and respiratory rates of the three groups.

Mutually Exclusive Said of two events, conditions, or variables when both cannot occur at once.

For example, subjects in a study cannot be both female and male, nor can they be both Protestant and Catholic, for those are mutually exclusive categories. They could, however, be both female and Protestant because those are not mutually exclusive groups.

N

N Number. Usage varies; among the most common meanings of the uppercase *N* are (a) number of subjects or cases in a particular study, (b) number of individuals in a population, (c) number of variables in a study.

n Number. Usage varies; among the most common meanings of the lowercase *n* are (a) number in a sample, as opposed to in a population, (b) number of cases in a subgroup.

For example, consider the following from a research report: "We interviewed a random sample of college graduates ($N = 520$) to get their opinions on several issues; males were 45% ($n = 234$) of the sample." This means that a total of 520 graduates were interviewed; 234 of them were in the male subgroup.

***N*!** *N* *factorial. For example, 5! (5 factorial) means $5 \times 4 \times 3 \times 2 \times 1 = 120$.

NA Common abbreviation in questionnaires for "Not Applicable" or "No Answer."

n-Ach Abbreviation for "need for achievement" or motivation to achieve. A personality measure created by McClelland and used widely by others.

Napierian Log Another term for "natural log." See *logarithm.

National Election Study (NES) A series of more than 20 national surveys of representative samples of the U.S. population studying personal characteristics, attitudes, and political behavior of *respondents. Often used in *secondary analysis.

Natural Experiment A situation happening naturally, that is, without the researcher's manipulation, that approximates an experiment; variables occur naturally in such a way that they have some of the characteristics of *control and *experimental groups. The opposite of a natural experiment would be an "artificial experiment." Although this term is rarely used, it does capture the essence of the laboratory: an environment artificially purified of variables in which the researcher is not interested. Compare *natural setting, *observational research, *correlational research, *quasi-experiment.

For example, a solar eclipse provides astronomers opportunities to observe the sun that they cannot provide for themselves by experimental manipulation. Or, the comparison has been made between the number of dental cavities in a city with naturally occurring fluoridated water and a similar city without fluoridation. Or, comparisons between children's vocabulary growth during the school year versus during the summer months allow researchers to separate the effects of schooling from those of the children's backgrounds.

Natural Logarithm See *logarithm.

Natural Setting A research environment that would have existed had researchers never studied it. Used also to refer to behaviors and events that occur in those settings. See *natural experiment.

Among examples of social phenomena that seem to demand study by social scientists but that are not easy to put in a laboratory or otherwise manipulate are elections, unemployment, monetary inflation, riots, wars, poverty, kinship structures, marriage practices, and so on.

***N*-by-*M* Design** Said of a *factorial research design in which each of the factors has more than two *levels. *N* and *M* stand for the number of levels of each factor.

NCE Abbreviation for normal curve equivalent.

N*-Choose-*K Short for the number of *samples of a particular size (*K*) that can be chosen from a given number (*N*) or *population of items. The terminology is often used in the explanation of *sampling distributions.

Necessary Condition In causal analysis, a *variable or event that must (necessarily) be present for another variable or event to occur. See *cause.

A necessary condition may or may not be *sufficient to produce an effect. For example, for it to snow, it is necessary that the air temperature be 32 degrees Fahrenheit or colder, but that is not sufficient; cold air is just one of the necessary conditions.

Negative Binomial Distribution In *probability theory, the *distribution of the number of *failures prior to the first *success (or other specific number of successes) in a sequence of *Bernoulli trials. Compare *Pascal distribution.

Negative Case Analysis A procedure used in qualitative research for revising hypotheses. One begins with a hypothesis (about, say, the causes of urban riots) and systematically studies examples looking for disconfirming instances. As these are found, one revises the hypothesis in light of the negative evidence, resumes the search, and continues until no further disconfirming cases are found.

Negative Number A number that is less than zero; it is indicated by a minus sign in front of it; "–8" is minus or negative 8, as in 8 degrees below zero.

Negative Relation (or Correlation) Another term for *inverse relation, a relation between two *variables such that, whenever one increases, the other decreases, and vice versa. Compare *positive or direct relationship.

Nested Design Said of a *factorial design in which *levels of one factor appear within only a single level of another factor. The opposite of such "nested factors" are *crossed factors.

In the following examples, the speed of solving problems (*dependent variable) is studied as it is influenced by two factors: Levels of Difficulty (A) and Types of Reward (B). In both the crossed and the nested designs, there are three levels of difficulty; in the crossed design, there are two types of reward; in the nested, six. In the nested design, levels of reward B_1 and B_2 appear only in (are nested in) level A_1. In the crossed design, on the other hand, B_1 and B_2 appear at all three levels of A, but B_3 through B_6 do not appear in the experiment.

Nested Design

Difficulty	A_1		A_2		A_3	
Reward	B_1	B_2	B_3	B_4	B_5	B_6

Crossed Design

Difficulty	A_1		A_2		A_3	
Reward	B_1	B_2	B_1	B_2	B_1	B_2

Nested Variables Said of variables located inside other variables—such as city, state, and national murder rates.

Net Remaining after deductions. Net income, for example, is income after expenses have been deducted. Compare *gross.

Net of After having *controlled for the effect(s) of some variable(s). Also called "net relationship."

For example, phrases such as the following often occur in research reports: "the influence of education level on political attitudes, net of the effects of age and region of residence . . ." This means the influence of education on attitudes, having subtracted (*controlled for) any effects of respondents' age and where they live.

Noise In *information theory, any random disturbances to communication. The term originated from the analogy with static interfering with a radio transmission. This popular term is used broadly to refer to any *random error, such as *fluctuations around a *trend line in a *time series.

Nominalism A philosophical doctrine to the effect that abstract *concepts (such as justice, virtue, or nothingness) are simply convenient labels or names; they do not refer to real entities. Compare *realism, *methodological individualism, *holism.

Nominal Scale (or Level of Measurement) A scale of measurement in which numbers stand for names but have no order or value. See *categorical variable.

For example, coding female = 1 and male = 2 would be a nominal scale; females do not come first; two females do not add up to a male; and so on. The numbers are merely labels.

Nominal Variable Another term for a *categorical (or a discrete or a qualitative) variable. See *nominal scale.

Nomological Net When a *concept or *construct is defined in terms of other concepts or constructs, those other concepts or constructs are its nomological net; they allow one to name it.

Nomothetic Said of research that attempts to establish general, universal, abstract principles or *laws. Also used to describe relations among variables as well as the research that tries to discover them. Nomothetic is often contrasted with *idiographic. Compare *etic, *emic.

Nonadditive Said of a relation such that its total effect cannot be obtained by adding up its separate effects. See *additive. When there is an *interac-

N

tion effect among the *independent variables in a study, the relation among those variables and with the *dependent variable is nonadditive.

Nondetermination, Coefficient of That part of the *variance that cannot be explained by or accounted for by the measured effects of the *independent variable(s). Symbolized: $1 - R^2$. Compare coefficient of *alienation, coefficient of *determination, *error term.

Nonexperimental Design A research design in which the researcher observes or measures subjects without altering or controlling their situation. In experimental research, the investigator controls the *independent variables but cannot do so in nonexperimental research. Compare *experiment, *descriptive research, *quasi-experiment.

Nonlinear Regression A regression problem in which the *parameters are nonlinear, which prevents the use of the *least-squares criterion.

Nonlinear Relationship A relation between two variables, which, when plotted on a graph, does not form a straight line. See *curvilinear relationship.

Nonlinear Transformation A *transformation of data such that, when the original and the transformed data are plotted against one another on a graph, this does not result in a straight line. See *linear transformation.

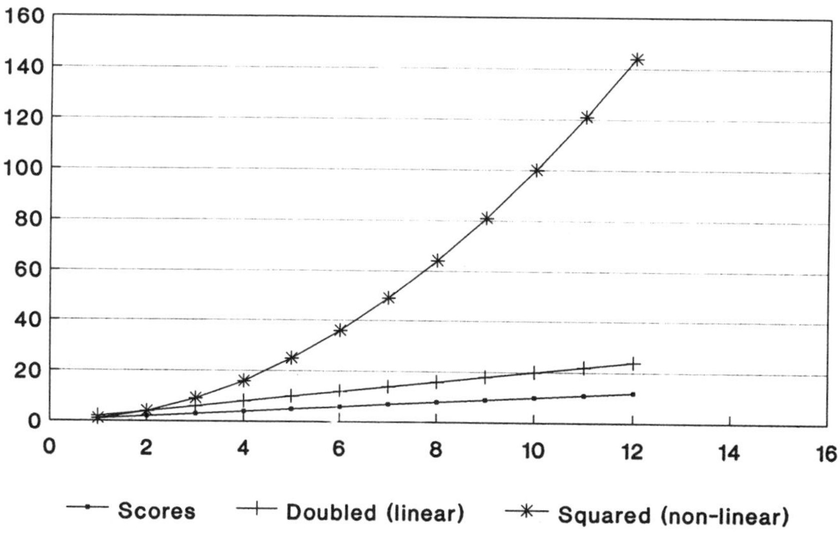

Nonlinear Transformation

N

The most common nonlinear transformations are done with logs, roots, and powers. These transformations change the relative distances between the data points in the original data.

The following graph shows a series of scores (1, 2, 3, 4, and so on) that have been transformed in two ways. When they are doubled (2, 4, 6, 8, and so on) and plotted on the graph, this results in a straight line. When the original scores are squared (1, 4, 9, 16, and so on) and the results of that transformation are entered on the graph, you get the curved line shown on the previous page.

Nonmonotonic Linear Relation A relation in which increases (or decreases) in one variable are always accompanied by increases (or decreases) in another, but the changes are not uniform. The direction of change is always the same (so the relation is linear), but the rate of change increases or decreases (so the relation is nonmonotonic). See *monotonic and *linear relations.

Usage varies importantly here. Many would consider "nonmonotonic linear" a contradiction in terms. Indeed, the kind of relation graphed here as "linear" is called "nonlinear" in the entry for *monotonic relation.

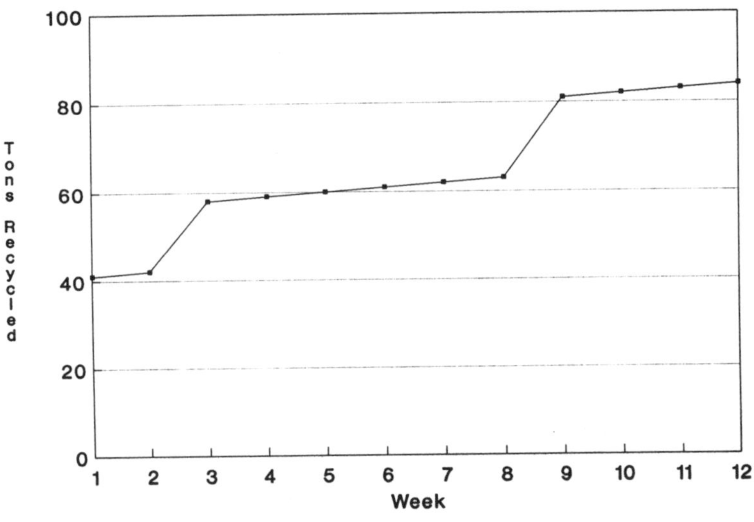

Nonmonotonic Linear Relation

Nonorthogonal Designs *Factorial designs are said to be nonorthogonal when the *cells, or *treatment groups, have unequal numbers. Also called "unbalanced" designs.

Nonparametric Statistics Statistical techniques designed to be used when the *data being analyzed depart from the distributions that can be analyzed with *parametric statistics. The *chi-square test is probably the best known example. Also called *distribution-free statistics. See *parametric statistics.

Nonrecursive Model A causal model that postulates that a variable can be both cause and effect, that there is a reciprocal relationship between two or more variables. See *recursive model.

For example, if you believed that education increases knowledge and that knowledge increases individuals' tendency to seek more education, you would be postulating a nonrecursive causal model.

NORC National Opinion Research Center. Located at the University of Chicago, the organization is best known for conducting the annual *General Social Survey (GSS).

Norm A standard of performance. In a *standardized test, the norm is determined by recording the scores of a large group, such as a sample of elementary school students. When subsequent students take the test, the norms (or standards) for them will be those of the larger group (i.e., the group on which the test was "standardized"). Thus, for example, the expected *mean for subsequent students taking the test is the mean achieved by the original large sample of elementary students.

Normal Curve See *normal distribution.

Normal Curve Equivalent (NCE) A *standardized scale of scores developed by the U.S. Department of Education. Test takers scoring at the *mean get an NCE of 50; persons scoring in the 1st *percentile get a score of 1; those in the 99th percentile, a score of 99. The *standard deviation for the NCE is 21.06. Compare *z-score.

Normal Distribution A purely theoretical continuous probability distribution in which the horizontal axis represents all possible values of a variable and the vertical axis represents the probability of those values occurring. The scores on the variable (often expressed as *z-scores) are clustered around the *mean in a symmetrical, unimodal pattern known as the bell-shaped curve or normal curve (see diagram). In a normal distribution, the *mean, *median, and *mode are all the same. There are many different normal distributions, one for every possible combination of *mean and *standard deviation. Also sometimes called the "Gaussian distribution."

Because the *sampling distribution of a statistic tends to be a normal distribution, the normal distribution is widely used in *statistical inference. For small samples, the *Student's t distribution (which is also "bell shaped" but not "normal") is used.

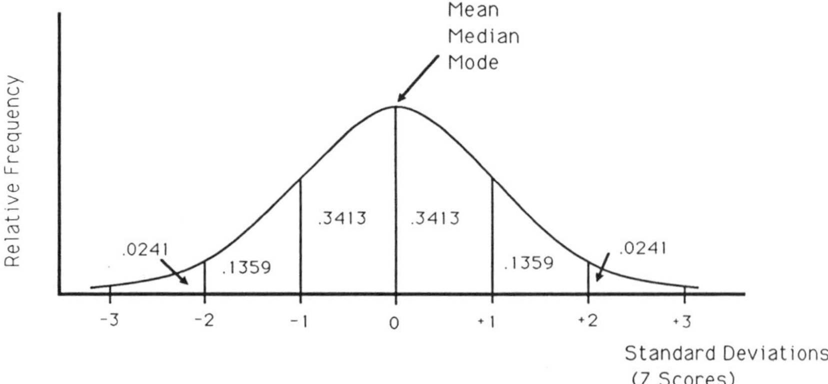

Normal Distribution

Normative Pertaining to norms or standards. It is often used to refer to *prescribing* norms, standards, or values—as opposed to describing them.

Normative-Empirical Research Research undertaken with the goal of learning how to improve what is being studied. Compare *action research.

Normative Scale Generally any evaluative scale. Often used in contrast with *ipsative scale; see that entry for an illustration.

Norm-Referenced Test A test in which the scores are calculated on the basis of how subjects did in comparison with (relative to) others taking the test (others' scores provide the norm or standard). The alternative is some absolute standard or criterion. Compare *criterion-referenced test, *norm.

NS Not (statistically) significant.

For example, the finding: "F = 2.38, ns" means that the F ratio for that particular result was not large enough to be statistically significant.

Null Hypothesis (H_0) The hypothesis that two or more variables are *not* related or that two or more *statistics (e.g., means for two different groups) are not the same. In accumulating evidence that the null hypothesis is *false,* the researcher indirectly demonstrates that the variables *are* related or that the statistics are different. The null hypothesis is the core idea in *hypothesis testing. Compare *falsificationism.

Null Set In *set theory, an *empty set.

Numerator In a fraction, the number above the line; the number into which the *denominator is divided.

O

Objective Said of a type of research or a finding that resembles an object in that it exists independently of the beliefs and desires of researchers or subjects. "Objective" is often used to refer to matters of fact rather than opinion. For example, people might disagree about whether a judge's ruling was fair, but they would be more likely to agree about the "objective fact" that she ruled against the plaintiff.

There should in principle be a high level of agreement about objective phenomena. But such consensus is fairly rare in the social sciences, largely because people often disagree over whether a particular sort of research or phenomenon is "really" objective. In practice, objectivity boils down to the level of consensus. If nearly everyone agrees that something is an objective fact, it becomes one more or less by definition; on the other hand, if there is much disagreement, it is hard to maintain that something is objectively true. This has led some writers to cease using the word "objectivity" and to replace it with *"intersubjectivity," that is, consensus. Compare *subjective.

Oblique Not at right angles; an angle greater or less than 90 degrees. Used in *factor analysis and other research designs to refer to variables that are *correlated or not independent of one another. Compare *orthogonal.

Observational Research Any of several research designs in which the investigator observes subjects but does not interact with them in his or her role as a researcher, as he or she would have to, for example, in an interview. Compare, however, *participant observation.

Usage varies. Some call almost any *nonexperimental research "observational"; others reserve the term for investigators who observe in a *natural setting, do not identify themselves as researchers, and do not participate in what they are observing.

Observed Frequencies When conducting a *chi-square test, the term "observed frequencies" is used to describe the actual data in the *cross-tabulation. Observed frequencies are compared with the *expected frequencies, that is, the frequencies you would expect if the *independent variable had no effect. Differences between the observed and expected frequencies suggest a relation between the *variables being studied.

Observer Drift The tendency, especially in lengthy research studies, for observers to become inconsistent in the criteria they use to make and record their observations. This results in a decline in the *reliability of the data they collect.

Ockham's Razor A philosophical doctrine to the effect that theories and explanations should be as streamlined as possible. All other things equal, the simplest theory (e.g., the explanation with the fewest predictors) is the best. Named after William of Ockham (1285-1349). More often called *parsimony today.

OCLC Online Computer Library Center. A national bibliographic center for library materials containing, among other things, information about which libraries own which books. A kind of computerized national "card catalogue."

Odds The *ratio of *success to *failure in *probability calculations.

For example, the odds of drawing, at random, a heart (success) from an ordinary deck of cards are 13 to 39, or 1 *to* 3. By contrast, the *probability (likelihood of success) of drawing a heart is .25, or 1 *out of* 4.

Odds Ratio A *ratio of one *odds to another. The odds ratio is a *measure of association, but, unlike other measures of association, "1.0" means that there is no relationship between the variables. The size of any relationship is measured by the difference (in either direction) from 1.0. An odds ratio less than 1.0 indicates an *inverse or negative relation; an odds ratio greater than 1.0 indicates a *direct or positive relation. Also called "cross-product ratio."

Ogive A graph of a *cumulative frequency distribution, so called because it resembles an architectural arch of the same name. The term is rarely used today.

OLS *Ordinary least squares.

Omega Squared A measure of *strength of association, that is, of the proportion of the *variability in the *dependent variable associated with the variability in the *independent variable. Omega squared ranges from 0 to 1. When it is 0, knowing *X* (the *independent variable) tells us nothing at all about *Y* (the *dependent variable). When it is 1.0, knowing *X* lets us predict *Y* exactly. The omega squared for a particular study will yield an estimate smaller than either *eta squared or *R^2, which tend to overestimate the strength of association.

Omnibus Test An overall test to determine whether there are any *statistically significant differences among three or more *treatment groups—such as the *F* ratio used to test the results of an analysis of variance. Omnibus tests are general; because they average all pairs of comparisons, they cannot specify what kinds of differences exist among which groups. See *planned comparisons, *post hoc comparisons.

One-Tailed Test of Significance A *hypothesis test stated so that the chances of making a *Type I (or alpha) Error are located entirely in one tail of a *probability distribution. See *significance testing, *two-tailed test.

For example, suppose that, in an experiment on speed of vocabulary learning, the *null hypothesis is that there is no difference between males and females. A one-tailed hypothesis would be that one or the other sex learns faster. A two-tailed test would determine whether there was a statistically significant difference between the males and females studied, but it would not specify in advance what that difference was.

One-Way ANOVA *Analysis of variance with only one *independent variable. Compare *factorial designs.

Open Question Format A survey or interview format that allows respondents to answer questions as they choose. Unlike a *closed question format, it does not provide a limited set of predefined answers.

Operational Definition (a) A description of the way researchers will observe and measure a *variable. (b) The criteria used to identify a variable or condition. Operational definitions are essential. They make *intersubjectivity (objectivity) possible because they can be replicated, but they are always imperfect. See *operations, *operationalize, *construct.

For example, the operational definition of an obese person could be one who weighs more than 120% of his or her "ideal weight" as defined by an insurance company chart.

Operationalize To define a *concept or *variable in such a way that it can be measured or identified (or "operated on"). When you operationalize a variable, you answer the questions: How will I know it when I see it? How will I record or measure it?

For example, in a study of the academic achievement of poor schoolchildren, "poor" could be operationalized as eligibility for a subsidized lunch program, and "achievement" as grade point average.

Operations Variables defined in such a way that they can be manipulated and measured. Such operations are ways to study more general *constructs or *theories. Also called *operational definitions or "operationalizations."

For example, one of the ways the general construct of "job satisfaction" could be studied would be to use the absenteeism rate as a *proxy measure or operation. See *construct, *operational definition, *operationalize.

Operations Research (OR) A general approach to the scientific study of the activities (operations) of complex systems such as large corporations. Quantitative criteria are often used to make decisions about ways to increase efficiency. See *decision tree, *evaluation research.

Opportunity Cost What one has to give up or forgo in order to do something else.

For example, deciding to use all your spare time to practice the piano means that you will not have any left to practice the violin. Or, going on for your master's degree might involve giving up an opportunity to take a good job.

Order Effects In experiments where subjects receive more than one *treatment (a *within-subjects design), the influence of the order in which they receive those treatments. Order effects may *confound (make it difficult to distinguish) the treatment effects. To avoid this problem, experimenters often use *counterbalancing. See that entry for an example.

Ordinal Interaction Said of an *interaction effect that, when plotted on a graph, produces lines that do not intersect. Because the lines of any interaction effect are not parallel, those of an ordinal interaction *would* intersect if they were extended far enough, perhaps beyond the range of values of interest to the researcher. See *interaction effect and *disordinal interaction for a fuller definition and illustrations.

Ordinal Sampling Another term for *systematic sampling.

Ordinal Scale (or Level of Measurement) A scale of measurement that *ranks* subjects (puts them in an order) on some variable. The differences between the ranks need not be equal (as they are in an *interval scale).

Team standings or scores on an attitude scale (highly concerned, very concerned, concerned, and so on) are examples.

Ordinary Least Squares (OLS) A statistical method of determining a *regression equation, that is, the equation that best represents the relationship among the *variables. See *least-squares criterion. Compare *generalized least squares.

Ordinate The vertical axis (or *y* axis) on a graph. Compare *abscissa.

ordinate →

Organismic Variables A term sometimes used to refer to *background variables.

Orthogonal (a) Intersecting or lying at right angles. (b) Uncorrelated *variables are said to be orthogonal because, when plotted on a graph, they form right angles to one of the *axes. (c) In *factor analysis, said of a *rotation when the axes are kept at right angles, that is, when it is assumed that the factors are not correlated. Compare *oblique.

Orthogonal Coding A method of coding variables in a *regression analysis to make *planned comparisons and test *hypotheses about the effects of *treatments on group *means. Also called "contrast coding." Compare *effect and *dummy coding.

Outcome Variable Another term for *dependent variable, used mainly in *nonexperimental research to refer to the presumed effect. Compare *criterion variable.

Outlier A subject or other unit of analysis that has extreme values on a *variable. Outliers are important because they can distort the interpretation of *data or make misleading a statistic that summarizes values (such as a *mean). See *trimmed mean.

For example, you might want to get the average (mean) income of households in your neighborhood so that you could argue that yours was not a rich neighborhood and it should not be subject to a tax hike. Your results might be something like those in the following table. The outlier is Household 9. It raises the mean to $86,000, even though most households in the neighborhood do not earn even half that amount. To make your best case, you could either recompute the mean excluding Household 9 (which would give you a figure of $36,250). Or you could use the *median income ($38,000). Because the median is more *resistant to the effects of outliers, it would be a less misleading measure of *central tendency for your neighborhood.

Household Income in Our Neighborhood

Household 1	$22,000	
Household 2	$27,500	
Household 3	$28,000	
Household 4	$35,000	
Household 5	$38,000 (median)	
Household 6	$40,000	
Household 7	$49,000	
Household 8	$50,500	
Household 9	$484,000	
Total	$774,000	774,000/9 = $86,000 (mean)

Outlying Case Another term for *outlier.

Overall Regression Equation A *regression equation in which terms for *interaction effects are included, that is, in which *product variables are calculated and product terms included.

Overidentified Model In *regression analysis, a model containing more information than necessary to estimate regression coefficients. Compare *underidentified model and *just-identified model.

Oversampling A procedure of *stratified sampling in which the researcher selects a disproportionately large number of subjects from a particular group (stratum). Most often, researchers oversample in a stratum that has a large *variance or in a stratum that would yield too few subjects if a simple *random sample were used.

P

P (upper- and lowercase *P*, usage varies considerably) (a) Symbol for sample proportion, that is, the frequency of a particular event divided by the size of the sample. For example, if the sample were 20 coin flips, 9 of which came up heads, the sample proportion for heads would be .45 (9 heads/20 flips).

(b) In path analysis, the symbol for a path, usually written with subscripts indicating the particular path and the direction of causal influence. For example, p_{32} means the effect of variable 2 on variable 3.

(c) *Probability value, or *p* value. Usually found in an expression such as $p < .05$. This expression means: "The probability (p) that this result could have been produced by chance (or *random error) is less than (<) five percent (.05)." Thus, the smaller the number, the greater the likelihood that the result expressed was not merely due to chance. For example, $p < .001$ means that the odds are a thousand to one (one tenth of 1%) against the result being a fluke. What is being reported (.05, .001, and so on) is an *alpha level or *significance level. The *p* value is the actual probability associated with an obtained statistical result; this is then compared with the alpha level to see whether that value is (statistically) significant.

Pairs When referring to all possible pairs of observations in a *sample, a way of arranging the *data so as to be able to use one of several *measures of association for *ordinal variables.

Pairwise Comparison Comparing the difference between two *treatment group means. Compare *omnibus test.

Pairwise Deletion Removing a case from the calculation of a *correlation coefficient when it has missing values for one of the *variables.

P

PAIS Public Affairs Information Service. An indexing service providing information about journal articles and other research reports in areas of public policy, such as political science, economics, and law.

Panel Study A *longitudinal study of the same group (or "panel") of subjects. Compare *cohort analysis, *cross-sectional study.

For example, the High School and Beyond study has followed the same group of high school sophomores for several years gathering information about their subsequent schooling and employment.

Paradigm A scientific discipline's general orientation or way of seeing its subject matter. This meaning, today the most common in the social and behavioral sciences, was introduced by Thomas Kuhn. Originally "paradigm" referred to an example in grammar showing a pattern in a conjugation or declension (e.g., ring, rang, rung; sing, sang, sung). Compare *schema, *model.

Physics around the time of Einstein is said to have undergone a "paradigm shift"—from one understanding of the discipline and the world it studied to a radically different one. Fields such as political science and sociology are sometimes referred to as "multiparadigm" disciplines, because there are several competing ways of understanding those disciplines and their problems.

Paradox of Inquiry A puzzle in research that can arise when one wants to study an unknown subject. In the *Meno*, Socrates is asked (roughly): How can we seek something if we don't know what it looks like, and, if we already know it, why would we seek it?

This paradox has important parallels with analytical problems in the social and behavioral sciences, most clearly with *specification error in *regression and *path analysis. If you do not have the "right" model, you cannot measure the effects of variables, but there is no way to know if you have the right model apart from the measured effects of variables.

Parameter Most broadly, a parameter is either (a) a limit or boundary or (b) a characteristic or an element. The word has many general and technical uses.

In statistics, the most common use of "parameter" is for a characteristic of a *population, or of a distribution of scores, described by a *statistic such as a *mean or a *standard deviation. For example, the mean (average) score on the midterm exam in Psychology 201 is a parameter. It describes the population composed of all those who took the exam. Population parameters are symbolized by Greek letters, such as sigma.

In computers, the most common use of "parameter" is as an instruction limiting or specifying what you want the computer to do. For example, if you typed the following into your computer: "delete files 4, 7, & 9," "delete" would be the command; "files 4, 7, & 9" would be the parameters.

Parametric Statistics Statistical techniques designed for use when *data have certain characteristics—usually when they approximate a *normal distribution and are measurable with *interval or *ratio scales. Also, statistics used to test hypotheses about *population parameters. Compare *nonparametric statistics.

Parsimony Generally, frugality or thriftiness. Used in methodological writing to mean a principle for choosing among explanations, theories, models, or equations: the simpler the better; less is more. Of course, applying this standard makes most sense when the explanations one is choosing among are about equally good except for their degree of simplicity. See *Ockham's razor.

For example, the smaller the number of predictor variables used to predict an outcome variable, the more economical or parsimonious the prediction.

Part Correlation Another term for *semipartial correlation, that is, a multiple correlation in which a variable is partialed out but only from one of the other variables. Not to be confused with *partial correlation.

Partial Correlation Called "partial" for short. A correlation between two *variables after the researcher statistically subtracts or removes (*controls for, *holds constant, or "partials out") the linear effect of one or more other variables. The opposite of a partial relation is not a "whole" relation but a simple relation, that is, one uncomplicated by considering other variables. See *covariate, *control variable, *semipartial correlation.

Symbolized "r" with subscripts. For example, $r_{12.3}$ means the correlation between variables 1 and 2 when variable 3 is controlled; $r_{13.2}$ means the correlation between 1 and 3 when 2 is controlled.

Partial Out To *control for or *hold constant. See *partial correlation.

Partial Regression Coefficient A *regression coefficient in a *multiple regression equation. So called because each regression coefficient in a multiple regression equation shows the part of the variance in the dependent variable associated with one of several independent variables. The partial regression coefficient estimates the difference in the dependent variable associated with a 1-unit difference in an independent variable—when "partialing out" (*controlling for) the effects of the other independent variables.

P

Partial Relations Called "partials" for short. Relations among variables discovered by dividing a sample into "parts" or subsets to test for (or *control for) the effects of additional variables.

For example, let's say we did a survey and found that young adults (aged 20-39) were less likely to be racially prejudiced than older adults (aged 40-59). We thought the differences might be due not only to age but also to the fact that older adults tended to be less educated than younger adults. We could see if that were true by "partialing"; that is, we could divide the total sample into a more educated group (13+ years of schooling) and a less educated group (12 or fewer). We could then recompute the level of prejudice and the effects of age in each of the two parts of the sample. By comparing the *partial tables produced in this way, we could get a better understanding of the partial relationships between education and prejudice and between age and prejudice.

Partials Short for *partial relations and *partial correlations.

Partial Table A subtable of *cross-tabulations for two *variables formed on the basis of the outcomes on a third (*control) variable. See *partial relations.

For example, if we computed a cross-tabulation table for coffee drinking and heart disease, we might want to *control for sex by constructing separate sub- or partial tables for men and women.

Participant Observation A kind of investigation in which a researcher participates as a member of the group she or he is studying. Sometimes the researcher informs the group that she or he is an observer as well as a participant, and sometimes the researcher pretends to be an ordinary member. Ethical dilemmas most often arise in the latter case, that is, when one is researching "under cover." See *ethnographic research.

Partition (a) *noun*: Two or more subdivisions or categories of a *factor. For example, if class is the factor, upper, middle, and lower could be partitions. (b) *verb*: In *set theory, to divide a *universal set into subsets that do not intersect and that exhaust all the elements in the universal set. (c) *verb*: In *analysis of variance, to break the total *variance of observations into parts for purposes of *analysis. The variance is partitioned into two parts: an *explained* part, which is due to *regression or to differences between groups, and an *unexplained* part (called *error or *residual variance), which comes from differences among subjects within groups. (d) *verb*: In *multiple regression, to divide the explained variance (R^2) into parts accounted for by different independent variables or groups of independent variables.

Pascal A programming language. Like *BASIC, *C, *COBOL, *FORTRAN, and others, it is used to write computer programs.

Pascal Distribution A *probability distribution used to calculate the number of *trials necessary to get a particular number of *successes. Compare *binomial distribution, *geometric distribution.

For example, we would use a Pascal distribution if we were interested in the number of flips of a fair coin (trials) it would take to get a total of 10 heads. The probability of getting 10 heads in just 10 or 11 flips would be very small, so would the probability of needing 40 or more flips to get 10 heads.

P

Path Analysis A kind of *multivariate analysis in which causal relations among several *variables are represented by graphs (*path diagrams) showing the "paths" along which causal influences travel. The causal relationships must be stipulated by the researcher. They cannot be calculated by a computer; the computer is used to calculate *path coefficients, which provide estimates of the strength of the relationships in the researcher's hypothesized causal system.

In path analysis, researchers use data to examine the accuracy of causal models. A big advantage of path analysis is that the researcher can calculate direct and indirect effects of independent variables; this cannot be done using ordinary *multiple regression analysis.

Path Coefficient A numerical representation of the strength of the relations between pairs of *variables in a *path analysis when all the other variables are held constant. Path coefficients are *standardized regression coefficients (*beta weights); these are regression coefficients expressed as *z-scores. Unstandardized path coefficients are usually called *path *regression* coefficients. See *path diagram.

Path Diagram A graphic representation of a hypothesized causal model.

For example, the path diagram on the following page shows the effects of educational and other *background variables on occupational achievement. Subjects' job status, the *dependent variable, is determined by three variables (parents' education, parents' job status, and the subjects' own education).

How to Read a Path Diagram

1. We can see that parents' education and job status affect their children's job status directly; they also do so indirectly, by way of their influence on children's education.

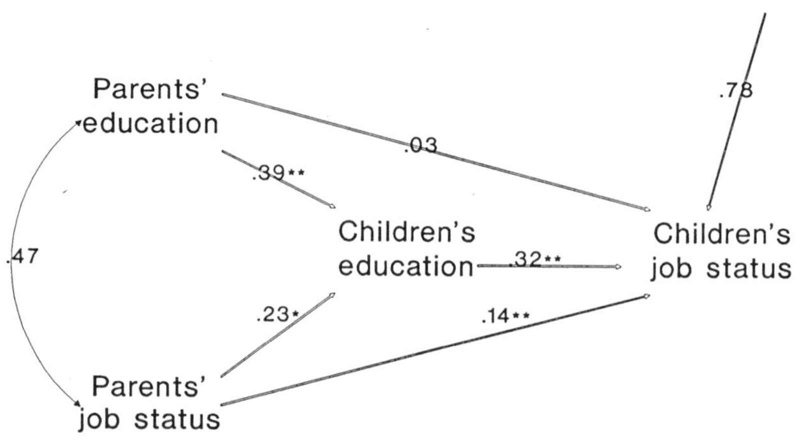

*$p \leq .05$; **$p \leq .01$

Path Diagram

2. The curved, two-headed line indicates that, while there is a relation between parents' job status and parents' education (.47), no causal assumptions are made about it.
3. The numbers on the lines are beta weights (*path coefficients). These are expressed in *z-scores (standard deviation units). For example, the .32 on the line between subjects' education and job status means that every 1.0 standard deviation increase in education level leads to a .32 standard deviation increase in child's job status. If the path coefficients were negative (none are in this diagram), that would indicate an *inverse (or *negative) relation.
4. The figure .78, on the line coming from outside the system, is the *residual (often abbreviated "*e*" or "*u*"). It is the part of the *dependent variable not explained by the *independent variables. To find out the percentage unexplained by the total model, you need to square the residual coefficient: $.78 \times .78 = .608$, which means 60.8% of the total variance is unexplained by the model pictured in this diagram.
5. Indirect effects can be computed by multiplying path coefficients. For example, to get the indirect effect of parents' education on children's jobs, you multiply the effect of parents' education on children's educations (.39) times the effect of children's educations on children's job status (.32). This gives you an indirect effect of .12 ($.39 \times .32 = .1248$), which is considerably bigger than the direct effect (.03) of parents' education on subjects' job status.
6. The asterisks (*, **) indicate the *statistical significance of the path coefficients. For example, .23* means that coefficient is significant at the .05 level, whereas the .39** is significant at the .01 level.

Path Regression Coefficient Another term for an *unstandardized* regression coefficient in a *path analysis. See *path coefficient.

Pattern Variable A *nominal or *categorical variable whose categories are made of combinations ("patterns") of other nominal variables. Pattern variables are often used to study *interaction effects. See *contingency table.

For example, if we know the employment status (employed/unemployed) and the sex (male/female) of a group of subjects, we could have four pattern variables: employed women, unemployed women, employed men, unemployed men.

PC Percent correct. Not to be confused with politically correct (or private corporation or prince consort).

PDI *Percentage difference index.

Pearson's Chi-Square Statistic See *chi-square test.

Pearson's Contingency Coefficient A measure of association that can be used when both the *dependent and the *independent variables are *categorical. Symbolized: "*C*."

Pearson's Correlation Coefficient More fully, the Pearson's product-moment correlation coefficient. More briefly, Pearson's *r*. A statistic, usually symbolized as *r*, showing the degree of *linear relationship between two *variables that have been measured on *interval or *ratio scales, such as the relationship between height in inches and weight in pounds. It is called "product-moment" because it is calculated by multiplying the *z-scores of two variables by one another to get their "product" and then calculating the average (mean value), which is called a "moment," of these products. Note: The Pearson's *r* is rarely computed this way; the preceding is known as the "definitional," not the "computational," formula. See *correlation coefficient.

Pearson's correlation is so frequently used that it is often assumed that the word "correlation" by itself refers to it; other kinds of correlation, such as *Kendall's and *Spearman's, have to be specified by name.

Pearson's *r* See Pearson's correlation coefficient.

Percent Per hundred; one part in one hundred; one part of a whole that has been divided into one hundred parts. If you multiply a *proportion times 100, you get a percentage.

Percentage Difference Index (PDI) An index calculated by subtracting one percentage from another.

For example, if 30% of the voters in your town wanted to replace the property tax with a sales tax and 70% were opposed, the PDI would be −40 (30 − 70 = −40).

Percentage Frequency Distribution A *frequency distribution that shows the percentage (not the number) of cases having each of the *attributes of a particular *variable. See *relative frequency distribution.

For example, say that, in Social Problems class, 22% of the students got As, 36% Bs, 29% Cs, 11% Ds, and 2% Es. The variable is grade; the attributes are A, B, C, D, and E; and the frequencies are 22%, 36%, 29%, 11%, and 2%.

Percentaging Rule This rule says that, in cross-tabulations, percentages should be calculated within the categories of the *independent (not the *dependent) variable.

Percentile Rank A number or score indicating rank by telling what percentage of those being measured fell below that particular score.

For example, if you scored in the 74th percentile on some part of the Graduate Record Examination, this means that your score cuts off the bottom 74% of the distribution; your score exceeded that of 74% of the others who took the test (or, sometimes, 74% of those upon whom the test was *standardized).

Period Effects Influences on people of a particular era or time (period). Compare *age effects, *cohort effects.

For example, living in a period in which the presidency has been held by political conservatives for two decades may have influenced Americans' attitudes toward their government.

Periodicity Said of something that recurs regularly, that is, that has periods.

Permutation (a) The process of changing the order of an ordered set of objects. (b) An ordered sequence of *elements from a *set.

A permutation is often contrasted with a *combination. AB and BA are two different permutations of A and B, but they are the same combination. The mixed doubles team of Jane and Dick is the same team (combination) as Dick and Jane. But, if Jane is first in a contest and Dick is second, that is a different result (permutation) than if Dick is first and Jane is second. Note that, for any set of two or more objects, the number of permutations is greater than the number of combinations because many permutations are just reorderings of a single combination.

Phi Coefficient A type of *correlation between two *variables when both are *dichotomous; a measure of *association for 2 × 2 *cross-tabulations. Phi is a *symmetric measure and is equivalent to *Pearson's correlation coefficient.

For example, to compute the correlation between sex (male/female) and employment status (employed/unemployed), you could use a phi coefficient. You couldn't use it for age and income, because these are not dichotomous variables.

Pie Chart A circle with areas ("slices") marked to represent the proportion of total units in each category.

The following two pie charts show each continent's percentage of the world's total land area and population.

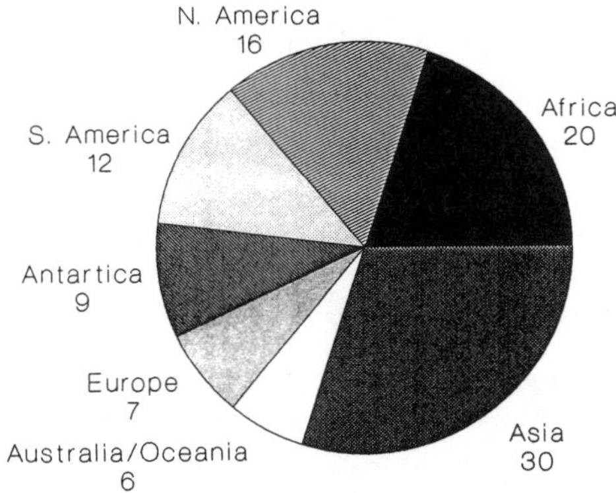

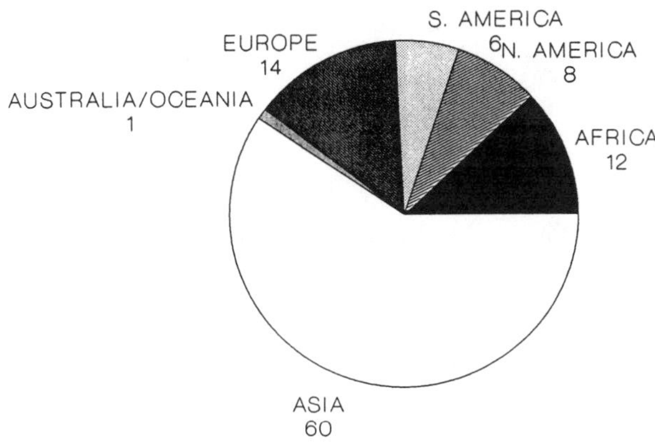

Pie Charts

Pillais Criterion A *test statistic that is very *robust and not highly linked to *assumptions about the *normality of the *distribution.

Pilot A preliminary test or study to try out procedures and discover problems before the main study begins. This enables researchers to make last-minute corrections and adjustments. It is a research project's "dress rehearsal."

In a pilot, the entire study with all its instruments and procedures is conducted in miniature (e.g., on a small sample). By contrast, a *pretest, definition b, is used to assess some part of an instrument or procedure.

Placebo (a) In experimental research, a *treatment given to a *control group that is meant to have no effect; it is used in comparison with the treatment (*independent variable) that is being tested. (b) A treatment given to a patient for its psychologically soothing effect rather than for its physiological benefits. See *double-blind procedure.

For example, in an experiment on the benefits of a drug, the control group could be given a sugar pill (the placebo), while the experimental group would be given the drug.

Placebo Effect Improvement in the condition of sick persons that cannot be attributed to the physiological effect of the treatment that was used but is due, rather, to their (mistaken) belief that they received an effective treatment (e.g., the medicine rather than the sugar pill).

Planned Comparisons Comparisons between the *means of *experimental and *control groups in *regression analysis or *analysis of variance. So called because they are specified at the outset of the research, before the *data are gathered. Also called "a priori comparisons." Compare *omnibus test, *post hoc comparisons.

Platykurtic Flatter than the *normal curve. See *kurtosis.

Point Biserial Correlation A type of correlation to measure the *association between two *variables, one of which is *dichotomous and the other *continuous.

Point Estimate An estimate made by computing a *statistic that describes a *sample; this is then used to estimate a *population *parameter. Compare *interval estimate.

For example, you could survey a sample of students in your department to get their opinion about the statistics requirement. Say that, on a scale of 1 to 10, the *mean score the sample of students gave the statistics requirement was 3.9. You could then conclude that 3.9 would be the best estimate of the mean score of the population; that is, it is your best (point) estimate of what the mean score would have been had all the students been polled.

Poisson Distribution A *probability distribution used when the number (N) of cases is very large and the probability (p) is very small.

For example, suppose the murder rate in U.S. cities is .0001, or 100 murders per million residents. Say that Our Town, a city of 500,000 people, had 80 murders last year. A simple calculation shows that Our Town's rate is higher than the typical rate (80/500,000 = .00016, or 160 murders per million). But, a more interesting question perhaps is whether 80 murders is higher than what could be expected by chance if ours is a typical town. We could use the Poisson distribution formula to find out. If Our Town is typical, then a total of 80 murders in a year has a probability of about .24. We might conclude that 30 murders more than the average rate could be expected by chance and that there was nothing atypical about our town. If the number of murders had been 120 instead of 80, however, we would probably come to a different conclusion, because the probability of 120 murders in a typical city of 500,000 is only .04.

Policy Analysis (Research) The study of social, political, economic, educational, and other policies. The goal is to discover alternative policies and/or problems that require action. Policy analysts are often closely allied with *evaluation researchers. Compare *applied research.

The following chart shows one way to divide up the nonbasic research domain. Compare *basic research.

Type of Research	*Typical Question Asked*
Policy	What should we do?
Applied	How should we do it?
Evaluation	How well did we do it?

Polygon (from the Greek for "many sided") A line graph constructed by connecting the midpoints of the bars of a *histogram. Also known as a *frequency polygon; see that entry for an illustration.

Polynomial Equation An equation in which one of the terms is raised to a *power greater than 1. See *linear equation, *polynomial regression analysis.

For example, the regression equation $Y = a + bX + bX^2 + bX^3$ is a polynomial because X is raised to the second and third powers. The highest power of a term gives the equation its "degree" or "order." The example equation is thus a third-order (or degree) polynomial equation.

P

Polynomial Regression Analysis *Curvilinear regression analysis, that is, regression analysis for relations that are or are suspected to be nonlinear. So called because the regression equation for a curvilinear (nonlinear) relation is a *polynomial equation. The more turns in the regression line, the higher the power of the terms in the equation must be. The following chart summarizes some of the terminology.

Turns of Regression Line	*Order or Degree*	*Number of Terms*	*Type of Analysis*
0	first	1	linear
1	second	2	quadratic
2	third	3	cubic
3	fourth	4	quartic
4	fifth	5	quintic

Polytomous Variable A *categorical variable with more than two categories—as in Marital Status: single, married, divorced, widowed.

Pooled Cross-Sectional Analysis A type of analysis conducted by combining (pooling) two or more *cross-sectional studies. This pooling is most often done for one of two reasons: to increase overall sample size beyond what is available in any single cross-sectional sample; or, to study the effects of the passage of time by comparing samples drawn in different years.

Population A group of persons (or institutions, events, or other subjects of study) that one wishes to describe or about which one wishes to generalize. To generalize about a population, one often studies a *sample that is meant to be representative of the population. Also called "universe."

Population Parameter A characteristic of a population described by a statistic, such as a *mean or a *correlation. Population parameters are usually symbolized by Greek letters; the Roman (English) alphabet is often used for *sample statistics. Consistency is not perfect here, however, as Greek letters are sometimes used for both statistics and parameters.

Population Validity A type of *external validity or representativeness; usually used to describe research in which criteria for validity are not met. Compare *ecological validity.

For example, studies in which the samples are composed solely of college sophomores might not be validly generalizable to the population of all adults.

Positive Number A number greater than zero.

Positive Relation (or Correlation) Another term for a *direct relationship, that is, one in which an increase in one *variable is always accompanied by an increase in another. Compare *inverse relationship, *negative relation.

Positive Skew Said of a graph on which the smaller frequencies are found on the positive (or high or right) end of the *x axis. Also called "right skew." For an illustration, see *skewed distribution.

Positivism A term introduced by Auguste Comte to refer to the *empirical study of phenomena, especially human phenomena. Comte contrasted the "positive knowledge" gained in this way with the less scientific knowledge obtained by *metaphysics and religion. Compare *scientism.

The term has had several meanings since it was introduced in the early nineteenth century, and it has always been the object of debate. Most commonly and loosely today, positivism refers to a belief, held by some people, that one can study scientifically and/or quantitatively things that other people believe cannot be studied in this way, such as religion, emotions, ideas, art, and morality.

Posterior Probability In *Bayesian inference, said of an investigator's opinion, expressed as a probability, after research has been done assessing the investigator's *prior probability opinions.

Post Hoc Comparison A test of the *statistical significance of differences between group *means calculated after ("post") having done an *analysis of variance (ANOVA) or a *regression analysis (RA) that shows an overall difference. See *planned comparison, *omnibus test, *fishing expedition.

The *F ratio of the ANOVA (or the R^2 of an RA) tells you that some sort of statistically significant differences exist somewhere among the groups being studied. Subsequent, post hoc, analyses are meant to specify what kind and where. Because these comparisons are not part of the original study design (otherwise they would be *planned comparisons), many researchers consider them of dubious validity. Such comparisons are easiest to justify for *exploratory research; they should not be used to test *hypotheses.

Post hoc comparison is a generic term for several kinds of analyses. *Tukey's HSD and the *Scheffé test are the two best known. Tukey's is more often associated with ANOVA, Scheffé's with RA. In either case, the general procedure is the same: After you get a significant overall or omnibus test result, you look for differences among groups to explain it.

Posttest A test given or measurement taken after an experimental *treatment. Compare *pretest.

Postulate A conjecture or other statement considered to be an essential starting point in a chain of logical reasoning. While there can be subtle distinctions, it is generally accurate to say that *assumption, *axiom, and postulate refer to the same basic concept.

P

Power The number of times a number is multiplied by itself, usually written as an *exponent. See *polynomial equation.

For example, 8^2 is 8 to the second power and means $8 \times 8 = 64$; 8^3 is 8 to the third power and means $8 \times 8 \times 8 = 512$.

Power of a Test Broadly, the ability of a technique, such as a statistical test, to detect relationships. Specifically, the probability of rejecting a *null hypothesis when it is false—and therefore should be rejected. The power of a test is calculated by subtracting the probability of a *Type II Error from 1.0. The maximum total power a test can have is 1.0; the minimum is zero. Also called "statistical power."

PR An abbreviation for *probability.

Practical Significance See *substantive significance.

PRE Proportional reduction of error. A type of *measure of association that calculates how much you can reduce your error in the prediction of a *variable by knowing the value of another variable. How much better can you estimate *Y* if you know *X* than if you do not? The answer is a PRE statistic. *Lambda is an example of a PRE measure.

Predetermined Variable A *variable in a *path analysis the cause or causes of which are not specified. Such variables are usually connected to other predetermined variables with curved, two-headed path lines. See *path diagram for an illustration.

Prediction Equation Another term for a *regression equation, that is, an equation that predicts the value of one variable on the basis of knowing the value of another. A prediction equation is a regression equation that does not include an *error term.

Predictive Research Said of an investigation whose goal is to forecast (predict, but not explain) the values of one variable by using the values of one or more other variables. Usually contrasted with *explanatory research in which the goal is to understand the *causes behind relations. The distinction between explanatory and predictive research usually amounts to little more than the dichotomy between *experimental research (which can be explanatory) and other kinds, especially *correlational research (which cannot). The debate over whether only experimentalists can make valid causal generalizations is sometimes quite heated.

Predictive Validity The ability of an *operation to make accurate predictions; the extent to which a test, scale, or other measurement given at one time predicts subsequent performance or behavior. Also called *criterion-related validity.

Predictor Variable Loosely, another name for *independent variable or *cause. The term is often used when discussing *nonexperimental research designs such as *correlational studies. Compare *criterion variable.

Pretest (a) A test given or measurement taken before an experimental *treatment begins. By contrasting the results of the pretest with those of the *posttest, researchers gain evidence about the effects of the treatment. (b) A trial run used to assess some part of an *instrument or procedure. Compare *pilot.

Pretest Sensitizing Unintentionally influencing the results of the *posttest by giving a pretest. Compare *order effects.

For example, the pretest could influence the posttest results if subjects have been alerted to what the researcher is interested in or if they learn skills on the pretest that they can later use on the posttest.

Primary Analysis Original analysis of the data in a research study. Compare *secondary analysis (reanalysis of data gathered by others) and *meta-analysis (analysis of analyses).

Primary Source An original source of *data; one that puts as few intermediaries as possible between the production and the study of data. Compare *secondary source.

For example, the primary sources for the study of the use of metaphor in Shakespeare would be works written *by* Shakespeare; secondary sources would be books *about* Shakespeare.

Principal Components Analysis Methods for undertaking a *linear transformation of a large set of correlated variables into a smaller group of uncorrelated variables. This makes analysis easier by grouping data into more manageable units and eliminating problems of *multicollinearity. Principal components analysis is similar in aim to *factor analysis, but it is an independent technique and is often used as a first step in factor analysis. See *discriminant analysis, *canonical correlations, *cluster analysis.

Prior Probability In *Bayesian inference, the opinion of an investigator who states his or her opinion as a probability before (prior to) a research study. On the basis of the study, he or she revises the opinion in light of the data collected to arrive at a new *posterior probability. Also called "priors."

Priors Short for *prior probability or prior distribution in *Bayesian inference.

Probabilistic Said of a causal relationship in which change in one *variable increases the *probability of change in another variable but does not invariably produce the change. Compare *necessary condition, *sufficient condition.

For example, marriage and sexual intercourse increase the probability of parenthood, but they do not invariably cause it.

Probability Probability, like "cause," is a highly controversial concept. The definitions that follow are intentionally loose. (a) The likelihood that a particular event or relationship will occur; the *proportion of tries that are *successes. More formally, out of all possible outcomes, the proportionate expectation of a given outcome. Values for statistical probability range from 1.0 (always) to 0 (never). Probability statistics cannot be negative numbers because something cannot be less than totally unlikely. See **p* value, *likelihood ratio, *Bayesian inference. (b) The field of mathematics devoted to the study of probability as defined in definition a.

For example, the probability that a person drawing a card at random from a deck of 52 playing cards will select a red card is 26/52, or .5. The probability of drawing a heart is 13/52, or .25; for an ace, it is 4/52, or .077.

Probability, Conditional Said of situations in which the probability of one event (A) depends on (is conditional on) another event (B). Symbolized: $p(A|B)$. Contrast *independence.

For example, the probability of contracting the AIDS virus is conditional upon contact with an infected person—$p(\text{AIDS}|\text{CONTACT})$. The greater the number of such contacts, the greater the probability of getting the disease.

Probability, Empirical An actual count of the number of events of a particular type divided by the total number of possible events. Usually contrasted with *theoretical probability.

For example, if we had a perfectly balanced coin, the theoretical probability of tossing the coin and getting tails is .50, that is, 1 out of 2

(1/2). But, if we actually flipped the coin, say, 200 times, we might get 96 tails and 104 heads. The empirical probability—describing what actually happened—would be .48 for tails, that is, 96 out of 200 (96/200 = .48). As we increase the number of trials (coin flips), the empirical probability tends to approach the theoretical probability.

Probability, Joint The probability of two or more events occurring together.

For example, the probability of drawing a spade from an ordinary deck of 52 playing cards is 13 out of 52, or .25. The probability of drawing a jack is 4 out of 52, or .0769. The *joint* probability of drawing a card that is both a jack and a spade is calculated by multiplying the probability of a spade (.25) times the probability of a jack (.0769). The product, .01923 (.25 × .0769), is the joint probability of the jack of spades.

Probability, Subjective A guess or feeling about some probability that is not based on any precise computation. But it may be a reasonable, if not computational, assessment by a knowledgeable person. See *Bayesian inference.

For example, an experienced member of a parole board might say, "I really believe that, on the basis of his attitude, the prisoner is a good risk; we should give him a chance."

Probability, Theoretical The expected or predicted likelihood that a particular event will occur. See *probability, empirical.

Probability Distribution (a) All of the outcomes in a distribution of research results and each of their probabilities (*empirical probability distribution). (b) The number of times we would expect to get a particular number of *successes in a large number of trials (theoretical probability distribution). The most important of the theoretical probability distributions are the *binomial, *normal, *Student's *t*, *chi-square, and **F* distributions. Theoretical distributions are compared with observed, empirical distributions to judge the probability that the latter could be due to chance alone.

For a *continuous variable, an empirical probability distribution is based on intervals. For example, a probability distribution for income could be the percentage of households whose incomes fell in each of the following intervals: less than $25,000 per year; $25,001 to $50,000; $50,001 to $75,000; and $75,000 and above. For *discrete variables, the probabilities are *relative frequencies. See *binomial distribution for an example.

P

Probability Level The *p value below which the *null hypothesis is rejected; this value or level is the chance of making a *Type I (or *alpha) Error.

Probability Sample A *sample in which each subject chosen has a *known* probability of being included. Usually a *random sample.

Probability Theory A branch of mathematics dealing with the odds or the chances that events will occur.

Probability Value The likelihood that a statistical result would have been obtained by chance alone. This actual probability value (p value) is compared by a researcher with an *alpha level to determine whether the result has *statistical significance. If the p value is smaller, the result is significant.

Probit Analysis A technique used in *regression analysis when the *dependent variable is a *dummy (or *dichotomous) variable. *Ordinary least squares, the more usual method in regression analysis, can be used when *independent variables are dichotomous, but not when the dependent variable is. Probit is short for "probability unit." See *logit.

Product The result of multiplying. For example, in the equation, $9 \times 6 = 54$, 54 is the product.

Product-Moment Correlation See *Pearson's correlation coefficient.

Product Variable A variable obtained by multiplying the values of two other variables. Product variables are most often used to study *interaction effects. See *product vector.

Product Vector The result of multiplying two *vectors of scores on variables. It is a step on the way to calculating the *covariance of two variables. "*Cross-product vector" is another term for the same operation.

For example, in the following table, Vector 1 is multiplied by Vector 2 to get Vector 3, which is the product vector.

Case	*Vector 1*	*Vector 2*	*Vector 3*
1	2	4	8
2	3	2	6
3	5	6	30
4	7	8	56

Program A set of instructions, written in a *programming language, that tells a computer how to handle *data according to certain rules. Unless it is programmed, a computer cannot perform operations. Also called *software.

Program Evaluation See *evaluation research.

Programming Writing a set of instructions to solve a problem with a computer.

Programming Language A *software program used to write other programs. Examples include *FORTRAN, *BASIC, and *C.

Projective Tests Psychological tests in which subjects are asked to describe what they see in pictures that can be interpreted in many ways. The idea is that subjects' interpretations will "project" their inner states. The Rorschach ("inkblot") test is a well-known, if not widely used, example.

Promax A method of *oblique rotation of the axes in a *factor analysis.

Proportion A number, ranging between 0 and 1.0, calculated by dividing the number of subjects having a certain characteristic by the total number of subjects. To get a percentage, you multiply the proportion by 100. See *relative frequency, *probability.

For example, if the graduating class had a total of 948 students and 237 of those were business majors, the proportion of business majors would be .25 (237/948). Twenty-five percent ($.25 \times 100 = 25\%$) would be business majors.

Proportional Reduction of Error (or PRE) A type of *measure of association that indicates how much you can reduce the error in the prediction of a *dependent variable by knowing the value of an *independent variable. How much better can you guess *Y* if you know *X* than if you do not? The answer is the proportional reduction of error. *Gamma and *lambda are examples of PRE measures of association.

Proportional Stratified Random Sample A *stratified random sample in which the proportion of subjects in each category (stratum) is the same as in the *population. Compare *quota sample.

Proposition A formal statement about the relationship among abstract concepts. Propositions usually occur early in an article or other research report. Subsequent parts of the report generally try to maintain or demonstrate the proposition. A *theory is a set of related propositions.

For example, "cognitive sophistication fosters social tolerance" is a proposition.

P

Proxy Variable (or Measure) An indirect measure of the variable a researcher wants to study; it is used when the object of inquiry is difficult to measure or observe directly. See *operation.

For example, in a classic study, Durkheim wanted to study the historical evolution of moral values in European societies. Because there was little directly available objective evidence about moral values, he studied the history of law. Laws, he believed, reflect moral values, and laws are easily accessible to the researcher.

Psychometric Research Research on how psychological *variables are *operationalized for purposes of measurement.

Public Use Microdata Samples (PUMS) Large samples of data from the U.S. Census Bureau decennial censuses. They are available to any researcher and are designed for doing *secondary analyses with a personal (micro) computer. Names, addresses, and other identifying data are deleted before the PUMS are made available to researchers.

PUMS *Public Use Microdata Samples.

Purposive Sample A *sample composed of subjects selected deliberately (on purpose) by the researcher, usually because he or she thinks certain characteristics are typical or *representative of the *population. Compare *quota sample.

This is generally an unwise procedure; it assumes the researcher knows in advance what the relevant characteristics are, and it runs the risk (because it is not *random) of introducing unknown *bias. Inferences about a population cannot legitimately be made using a purposive sample. A frequent compromise between *random sampling and purposive sampling is *stratified random sampling.

PUS Public Use Samples. See *Public Use Microdata Samples.

***p* Value** Short for *probability value.

Pygmalion Effect Changes in subjects' behaviors brought about by researchers' expectations. See *self-fulfilling prophecy.

The term originally comes from Greek mythology; it was popularized in a play by G. B. Shaw; it is perhaps best known to researchers in the form of a controversial study (by Rosenthal and Jackson) in which teachers were told to expect some of their students' intelligence test scores to increase. They increased, apparently solely because of teachers' expectations.

Q

Q (a) Abbreviation for *quartile. Q_1 is the first quartile, Q_2 the second, and so on. (b) A measure of *goodness of fit for an *overidentified *path model. It ranges from 0 to 1, with 1 indicating a perfect fit. (c) *Yule's *Q*.

Q Methodology A way of ordering or sorting the parts of objects of study. The most recognizable feature of Q Methodology is that "subjects" sort cards (a Q sort) into a number of piles that represent points on a continuum. The sorters are most often not the subjects of the research.

For example, one might ask known conservatives and liberals to sort a group of cards on which are written the names of governmental policies. They would rank the policies on a scale ranging from most to least favorable. The researcher could use their rankings to test a theory of the components of liberalism and conservatism by seeing how the two groups of sorters differed.

Q Sort See *Q Methodology.

Quadratic Relation Said of a relation in a *regression analysis when one of the *independent variables has been raised to a power of 2 (X^2) and doing so produces a significant *regression coefficient. A quadratic relation indicates that there has been one departure from *linearity, that is, one turn or change of direction in the regression line. See *curvilinear relation, *polynomial regression analysis.

Qualitative (a) When referring to *variables, "qualitative" is another term for *categorical or *nominal. (b) When speaking of kinds of research, "qualitative" refers to studies of subjects that are hard to quantify, such as art history. Qualitative research tends to be a residual category for almost any kind of nonquantitative research.

The qualitative/quantitative distinction is often overdrawn. It is difficult to avoid *quantitative elements in the most qualitative subject matter. For example, "The painter entered his 'blue period' in the 1890s." And qualitative components are crucial to most good quantitative research, which begins with *theories, *concepts, and *constructs.

Quantile Any of several ways of dividing the total number of cases or observations in a study into equally sized groups—into groups having the same *quan*tity.

*Quartiles, *quintiles, *deciles, and *percentiles are examples of quantiles.

Quantitative Said of variables or research that can be handled numerically. Usually (too sharply) contrasted with *qualitative variables and research.

Quartile Deviation Half of the range covered by the middle half of the scores in a *distribution; half of the distance between the first and third *quartiles. The advantage of the quartile deviation, in comparison with other measures of *dispersion, is that it is less influenced by *outliers (extreme values), certainly less so than is the ordinary *range. Also called "semi-interquartile range."

Quartiles Divisions of the total cases or observations in a study into four groups of equal size. Compare *quantile, *quintile, *decile.

Quasi-Experiment A type of research design for conducting studies in field or real-life situations where the researcher may be able to manipulate some *independent variables but cannot randomly assign subjects to *control and *experimental groups. The procedures of *quasi-experimentation were developed mainly in the context of *evaluation research projects. See *field experiment, *interrupted time-series design.

For example, you cannot cut off someone's unemployment benefits to see how well he or she could get along without them or to see whether an alternative job-training program would be more *effective for some unemployed persons. But you could try to find volunteers for the new program. You could compare the results for the volunteer group (*experimental group) with those of people in the regular program (*control group). The study is quasi-experimental because you were unable to assign subjects at random to *treatment and control groups.

Questionnaire A group of written questions to which subjects respond. Some restrict the use of the term "questionnaire" to written responses.

Queue Processing See *first in-first out (FIFO).

Quintiles Divisions of the total cases or observations in a study into five groups of equal size. Compare *quantile, *quartile, *decile.

Quota Sample A *stratified *non*random sample, that is, a sample selected by dividing a *population into categories and selecting a certain number (a quota) of subjects from each category. Individual subjects within each category are not selected randomly; they are usually chosen on the basis of convenience. Compare *accidental sampling, *purposive sample, *random sampling, *stratified random sampling, *proportional stratified random sampling.

For example, interviewers might be given the following assignment: "Go out and interview 20 men and 20 women, with half of each 50+ years old." Despite its superficial resemblance to *stratified random sampling, quota sampling is not a reliable method.

Quotient The number that results when one divides one number into another; the answer to a division problem.

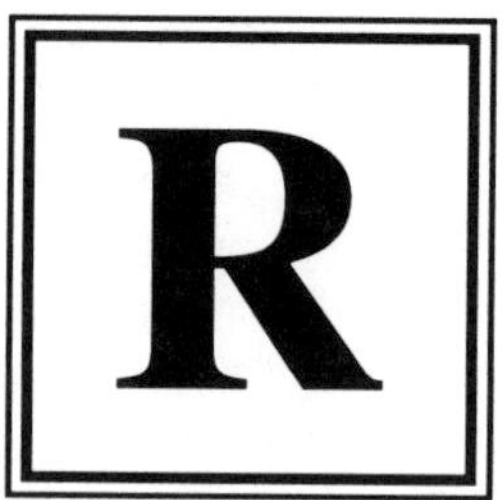

R

r Symbol for a *Pearson's correlation, which is a *bivariate correlation (between two variables). The "r" in Pearson's r originally stood for "regression."

R Symbol for a *multiple correlation, that is, between more than two variables.

r^2 Symbol for a *coefficient of determination between two variables. It tells you how much of the *variability of the *dependent variable is explained by (or accounted for, associated with, or predicted by) the *independent variable. Sometimes written "r-squared."

For example, if the r^2 between students' SAT scores and their grades were .21, that would mean that 21% of the variability in students' grades could be predicted by variability in their SAT scores.

R^2 Symbol for a *coefficient of multiple determination between a *dependent variable and two or more *independent variables. Sometimes written "R-squared."

For example, if the R^2 between average individual income (the dependent variable) and fathers' income, education level, and IQ were .43, that would mean that the effects of fathers' income, educational level, and IQ together explained (or predicted) 43% of the variance in individuals' average incomes.

R_c Symbol for the *canonical correlation.

r_s Symbol for *Spearman's correlation coefficient.

Radical The *root of a number as shown by the radical sign $\sqrt{}$. A number (the "index") to the left of the sign shows the type of root. For example,

$\sqrt[3]{\ }$ means the third (cube) root. If there is no number, the root is a square root.

Random Said of events that are unpredictable because their occurrence is unrelated to their characteristics. The chief importance of randomness in research is that, by using it, researchers increase the probability that their conclusions will be *valid. *Random assignment increases *internal validity. Random sampling increases *external validity.

Random Assignment Putting subjects into *experimental and *control groups in such a way that each individual in each group is assigned entirely by chance. Otherwise put, each subject has an equal probability of being placed in each group. Using random assignment reduces the likelihood of *bias.

Random-Effects Model An *experimental design in which the *levels of the *factors are random in the sense that they are drawn at random from a population of levels rather than fixed by an investigator. Also called "variance components model" and "Model II ANOVA design." Compare *fixed-effects model, *mixed-effects model, *random variable.

The random-effects model is used when there is a large number of categories or levels of a factor. For example, say the head of a survey organization wanted to see whether different kinds ("levels") of telephone interviewers get different response rates. Because there are potentially a very large number of categories (differences in accent, quality of voice, and so on), perhaps as many as there are individual telephone interviewers, a sample is chosen randomly from the population of interviewers, which is also, in this case, a population of levels. On the other hand, if the head of the survey organization were only interested in, say, the difference in response rate between male and female interviewers, she or he would use a *fixed-effects model.

Random Error Another term for *random variation. Also called "unreliability" and *disturbance. See *reliability. "Error" without qualification means random error. *Systematic error is *bias.

Randomized-Blocks Design A *research design in which subjects are matched on a *variable the researcher wishes to control. The subjects are put into groups (blocks) of the same size as the number of *treatments. The members of each block are assigned randomly to different treatment groups. Compare *Latin square.

For example, say we are doing a study of the effectiveness of four methods of teaching statistics. We use 80 subjects and plan to divide them into four treatment groups of 20 students each. Using a randomized-blocks design, we give the subjects a test of their knowledge of statistics. The four who score highest on the test are the first block, the next highest four are the second block, and so on to the twentieth block. The four members of each block are randomly assigned, one to each of the four treatment groups. We use the blocks to equalize the variance within each treatment group by making sure that each has subjects with a similar prior knowledge of statistics.

Random Numbers A sequence of numbers in which the occurrence of any number in the sequence is no guide to the numbers that come next. In the long run, all numbers will appear equally often. Tables of random numbers, found in most statistics texts, are frequently used to select random samples or assign subjects randomly.

Random Sampling Selecting a group of subjects (a *sample) for study from a larger group (*population) so that each individual (or other *unit of analysis) is chosen entirely by chance. When used without qualification (such as *stratified random sampling), random sampling means "simple random sampling." Also sometimes called "equal probability sample," because every member of the population has an equal *probability of being included. A random sample is not the same thing as a haphazard or *accidental sample. Using random sampling reduces the likelihood of *bias. Compare *probability sample, *cluster sample, *quota sample, *stratified random sample.

Random Variable A variable that varies in ways the researcher does not control; a variable whose values are randomly determined. "Random" refers to the way the events, values, or subjects are chosen or occur, not to the variable itself. Men and women are not random, but gender could be a random variable in a research study; the gender of subjects included in the study could be left to chance and not controlled by the researcher.

Random Variation Differences in a variable that are due to chance rather than to one of the other variables being studied. Random variations tend to cancel one another out in the long run. Also called "random error."

For example, say you take two random samples of 100 workers from a local factory. You find that in the first sample 52 are women and 48 men. In the second sample, 49 are women and 51 men. The differences between the sex compositions of the two samples would be due to random variation.

Range A measure of *variability, of the spread or the *dispersion of values, in a series of values. To get the range, you subtract the lowest value or score from the highest.

For example, if the highest score on the political science final were 98 and the lowest 58, the range would be 40 (98 – 58 = 40).

Rank Data Data measured on an *ordinal scale.

Rank Order Scale Another term for an *ordinal scale, that is, one that gives the relative position of a score in a series of scores, such as first in the National League, 18th out of a graduating class of 400, and so on.

Ratio A combination of two numbers that shows their relative size. The relation between the numbers is expressed as a fraction, as a decimal, or simply by separating them with a colon. The ratio of one number to the other is that number divided by the other. The ratio of 12 to 6 (12:6) means 12/6, or 2:1. The statement "the ratio of *X to Y*" means "*X divided by Y.*" Compare *proportion.

For example, say a bird-watcher counted the visits to his backyard feeder by different types of birds; if one afternoon there were 50 visits by nuthatches and 20 by chickadees, the ratio of nuthatches to chickadees could be expressed: 50/20, or 50:20, or 5:2, or 2.5:1.

Rational Number An integer (a whole number) or a fraction composed of integers. Compare *irrational number.

For example, 8,576 and –14 are rational numbers, as are 4/9 and 13/27.

Ratio Scale (or Level of Measurement) A measurement or scale in which any two adjoining values are the same distance apart and in which there is a true zero point. The scale gets its name from the fact that one can make *ratio* statements about variables measured on a ratio scale. See *interval scale, *level of measurement.

For example, height measured in inches is measured on a ratio scale. This means that the size of the difference between being 60 and 61 inches tall is the same as between being 66 and 67 inches tall. And, because there is a true zero point, 70 inches is twice as tall as 35 inches (ratio of 2 to 1). The same kind of ratio statements cannot be made, for example, about measures on an *ordinal scale. The person who is second tallest in a group is probably not twice as tall is the person who is fourth tallest.

Raw Score (or Data or Numbers) Scores, data, or numbers that are in their original state ("raw") and have not been statistically manipulated. Note: The opposite of raw is not, in most cases, "cooked," because cooked implies dishonest manipulation of data. Compare *derived statistics.

For example, if you got 23 out of 25 correct answers on a quiz, 23 would be your raw score. Other ways of reporting that score, such as 92% or third in the class, would have to be calculated and thus would not be "raw."

Realism (a) A philosophical doctrine holding that abstract *concepts really exist and are not, as *nominalism would have it, just names. Compare *holism, *methodological individualism, *latent variable.

(b) A philosophical doctrine holding that the external world really exists, quite apart from our conceptions of it, and that the external world can be fairly directly known by sensory experience. Often contrasted with *idealism. Compare *empiricism. Note that definitions a and b can be close to contradictory.

Real Limits (of a Number) The upper and lower real limits of a number are the points falling between half a measurement unit below and half a unit above the number.

For example, say you are measuring people's height to the nearest inch (in measurement units of an inch). The real limits of someone whose height you record as 70 inches are 69.5 and 70.5; someone whose height falls between 69.5 and 70.5 will be recorded as being 70 inches tall.

R

Reciprocal The reciprocal of a number is that number divided into 1, for example, the reciprocal of 3 is ⅓.

Reciprocal Relation Said of a situation in which *variables can mutually influence one another, that is, can be both *cause and *effect. Compare *recursive.

For example, say you are trying to lose weight and you've taken up running as well as dieting. Running and weight loss could be reciprocal: The more you run, the more you lose; the more you lose, the easier running is; so you run more, which causes you to lose more . . . .

Recode See *coding.

Rectilinear In a straight line. More often called *linear.

Recursive Model A causal *model in which all the causal influences are assumed to work in one direction only, that is, are *asymmetric (and the *error or disturbance terms are not correlated across equations). By contrast, *non*recursive models allow two-way causes. Contrast *reciprocal.

For example, if you were looking at the influence of age and sex on math achievement, your model would probably be recursive because, while age and sex might influence students' math achievement, doing well or poorly in math certainly could not change their age or sex. On the other hand, your model of the relationship between achievement and time spent studying might not be recursive. It could be *reciprocal (or nonrecursive): Studying could boost math achievement, and increased achievement could make it more likely that a student would enjoy studying math.

Recursive Model

A ⟶ B

Nonrecursive Model

A ⇄ B

Reductionism A research procedure or theory that argues that the way to understand something is to reduce it to its smaller, more basic, individual parts—as organisms might be best understood by studying the chemicals of which they are made. Another example would be the view that the behavior of groups can only be understood by studying the behaviors of the individuals who make up the groups. The term "reductionism" is usually pejorative; people who like such procedures more often call them *analysis or *methodological individualism. Compare *holism, *functionalism.

Redundant Predictor A variable in a *regression analysis that provides little or no additional ability to predict the value of the *dependent or *outcome variable. It is redundant because it is highly correlated with one or more other variables. Compare *confound, *intercorrelation, *multicollinearity.

Reexpress To change, or *transform, values measured on one scale to another scale, as one might reexpress speed in miles per hour as speed in kilometers per hour.

Region of Rejection An area in the tail(s) of a *sampling distribution for a *test statistic. It is determined by the *critical value(s) the researcher chooses for rejecting the *null hypothesis. Rejection regions are values of *z* or *t* distributions, not probability values. See the illustration.

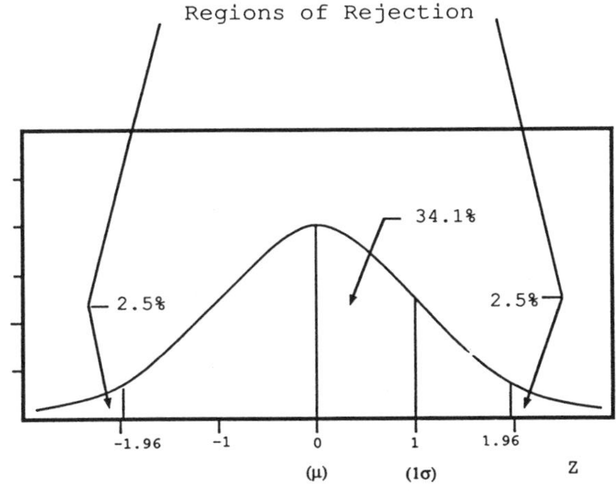

Regions of Rejection (Adapted from Mohr [1990].)

Regression Any of several statistical techniques concerned with predicting some *variables by knowing others. Regression is used to answer such questions as this: "How well can I predict the values of one variable, such as annual income (*Y*), by knowing the values of another variable, such as level of education (*X*)?"

The term "regression" originated in the work of the nineteenth-century researcher Francis Galton. In his studies of the heredity of characteristics such as height, he noted the phenomenon of *statistical regression, or regression toward the mean. Very tall people tend to have children somewhat shorter (closer to the mean) than themselves, and very short people tend to have children somewhat taller (closer to the mean) than they. Put more formally, extreme scores on the *predictor variable (parents' height) are likely to produce less extreme scores on the *criterion variable (children's height). Knowing how much regression toward the mean there is for a particular pair of variables gives you a prediction. If there is very little regression, you can predict quite well. If there is a great deal of regression, you can predict poorly if at all. The "*r*" used to symbolize *Pearson's correlation coefficient originally stood for "regression."

R

Regression Analysis (a) Methods of explaining or predicting the *variability of a *dependent variable using information about one or more *independent variables. Regression analysis attempts to answer the question: "What values in the dependent variable can we expect given certain values of the independent variable(s)?"

(b) Techniques for establishing a *regression equation. The equation indicates the nature and closeness of the relationship between two or more variables, specifically, the extent to which you can predict some by knowing others, the extent to which some are associated with others. The equation is often represented by a *regression line, which is the straight line that comes closest to approximating a distribution of points in a *scatter diagram.

Regression Artifact An artificial result due to *statistical regression or *regression toward the mean. Also called *regression effect.

Suppose a high school gave its students an English proficiency examination. The students with the very lowest scores were then assigned to a new tutorial program to help them prepare for the state-mandated graduation examination. If, after three months of tutoring, the students did better on a retake of the English proficiency examination, their improvement *could* be due to the effects of the program, but part of it could also be due to regression artifacts. At least some of the students probably got their original low scores through *random error (one wasn't feeling well the day of the test, another messed up the answer sheet, a third had her grade mistakenly recorded as a 68 when she had earned an 86, and so on). Without a *control group, there would be no way to tell for sure how much of the improvement was due to regression artifacts and how much could be credited to the tutoring program.

Regression Coefficient A number indicating the values of a *dependent variable associated with the values of an *independent variable or variables. A regression coefficient is part of a *regression equation. A *standardized regression coefficient (one expressed in *z-scores) is symbolized by the Greek letter beta; an unstandardized regression coefficient is symbolized by a lowercase b.

For example, if we were studying the relation between education (independent variable) and annual income (dependent variable) and we found that for every year of education beyond the tenth grade the expected annual income went up by $1,200, the (unstandardized) regression coefficient would be $1,200.

R

Regression Constants In a *regression equation, the *slope(s) and the *intercept. In the typical formulation, $Y = bX + a$; a (the intercept) and b (the slope) are the constants; they are the same regardless of the values of the variables X and Y. "The constant," without specification, usually refers to the intercept.

Note that this usage, while common, is loose by the standards of mathematics, where a "constant" would have neither a variance nor a standard error, as do both the slope and the intercept.

Regression Effect The tendency in a pre-post test design for the posttest scores to regress toward the mean, that is, to be affected by *statistical regression. Also called *regression artifact; see that entry for an example.

Regression Equation An algebraic equation expressing the relationship between two (or more) variables. Also called "prediction equation." Usually written $Y' = a + bX + e$. Y is the *dependent variable; X is the *independent variable; b is the *slope or *regression coefficient; a is the *intercept; and e is the *error term.

For example, in a study of the relationship between income and life expectancy, we might find that (1) people with no income have a life expectancy of 60 years; (2) each additional $10,000 in income, up to $100,000, adds two years to the average life expectancy so that people with incomes of $100,000 or more have a life expectancy of 80 years. This would yield the following regression equation: Life Expectancy = 60 years + 2 times the number of $10,000 units of income. $Y' = 2X + 60$, where Y' equals predicted life expectancy, and X equals number of $10,000 units. (In this highly simplified example, there is no error term.)

Regression Line A graphic representation of a *regression equation. It is the line drawn through the pattern of points on a *scatter diagram that best summarizes the relationship between the *dependent and *independent variables. It is most often computed by using the *ordinary least-squares (OLS) criterion. When the regression line slopes down (from left to right), this indicates a *negative or inverse relationship; when it slopes up (as in the illustration on the previous page), this indicates a *positive or direct relationship.

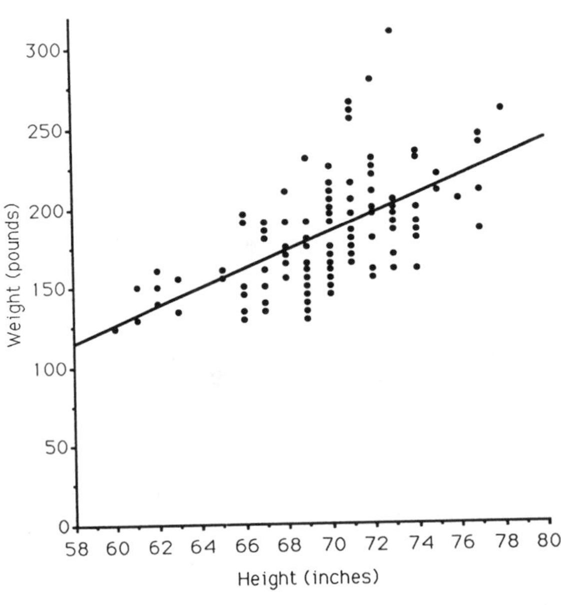

Regression Line

Regression Model Another term for *regression equation. An equation postulating the relationship between a continuous dependent variable, an independent variable or variables, and an *error term.

Regression SS In *regression analysis, the sum of squares that is explained by the *regression equation. It is analogous to the *between sum of squares in *analysis of variance. Symbolized: $SS_{regression}$. See *residual SS.

Regression Toward the Mean A kind of *bias due to the fact that measures of a *dependent variable are never wholly reliable. Another term for *statistical regression. See *regression artifact for an example.

Regress on In *regression analysis, to explain or predict by. To regress *Y* on *X* is to explain or predict *Y* by *X*.

For example, the statement, "We will regress college grade point average (GPA) on SAT scores," means: We will try to explain differences in students' GPAs by differences in their SATs.

Relative Frequency Another term for *proportion, that is, a number calculated by dividing the number of subjects with a certain characteristic by the total number of subjects.

For example, if it rained on average 36.5 days per year, the relative frequency would be 0.1 (36.5/365). To get the percentage of days it rained, you would multiply the relative frequency by 100 ($0.1 \times 100 = 10\%$).

Relative Frequency Distribution The proportion of the total number of cases observed at each score or value. For examples, see *frequency distribution, *probability distribution.

Reliability The consistency or stability of a measure or test from one use to the next. When repeated measurements of the same thing give identical or very similar results, the measurement instrument is said to be reliable. A measure is reliable to the extent that it is free of *random error. Compare *validity.

For example, if you got on your bathroom scale and it read 145 pounds, you got off and on again, and it read 139, repeated the process, and it read 148, your scale would not be very reliable. If, however, in a series of weighings, you got the same answer (say, 145), your scale would be reliable—even if it were not accurate (*valid) and you really weighed 120.

Reliability Coefficient A statistic indicating the *reliability of a scale, test, or other measurement. Reliability coefficients range from 0, when the measure is completely unreliable, to 1.0, when it is perfectly reliable. Reliability coefficients are usually correlations between two administrations, versions, or halves of the same test. See *Cronbach's alpha.

Repeated-Measures Design A research design in which subjects are measured two or more times on the *dependent variable. Rather than using different subjects for each level of treatment, the subjects are given more than one treatment and are measured after each. This means that each subject will be its own *control. See *correlated groups design.

Replacement See *sampling with replacement.

Replication Said of research that tries to reproduce the findings of other investigators so as to increase confidence in (or refute) those findings. Repeating studies with different subjects or in different settings is especially important for *experimental laboratory research, because it helps increase *external validity. Despite the undeniable importance of replication, it is not done as often as it might be, largely because it is not high status work.

For example, if one researcher found that people working in groups exerted less effort than when they worked individually, other researchers would be more likely to believe this finding if it could be replicated, particularly if it could be replicated using different kinds of subjects: women rather than men, adults rather than children, and so on.

R

Representative Said of a *sample that is similar to the *population from which it was drawn. When a sample is representative, it can be used to make *inferences about the population. The most effective way to get a representative sample is to use *random methods to draw it. See also *probability sample.

For example, say you want to survey a sample of students on a college campus to draw conclusions about student opinion. You would have more confidence that your inferences were true of the student body as a whole if the sample strongly resembled the population. Let's say you know that 45% of all the college's students are male and 22% are seniors. You could then look at your sample to see if there is a close match between your sample and these known population *parameters. If the match is close, you can more confidently come to conclusions about the student body—more confidently, at any rate, than if your sample were, say, 80% male and 11% seniors. In that case, your sample would not be representative; it would be *biased because it overrepresents male students and underrepresents seniors.

Representativeness The extent to which a study's results can be generalized to other situations or settings. Another term for *external validity. See *representative.

Research Systematic investigation of a subject aimed at uncovering new information (discovering data) and/or interpreting relations among the subject's parts (theorizing). Research is done in hundreds of ways ranging from lawyers searching among old court cases for legal precedents to physicists smashing atoms to study subatomic particles.

Research Design The science (and art) of planning procedures for conducting studies so as to get the most valid findings. Called "design" for short. When designing a research study, one draws up a set of instructions for gathering evidence and for interpreting it.

*Experiments, *quasi-experiments, *double-blind procedures, and *correlated groups designs are examples of types of research design.

Research Hypothesis Another term for the *alternative hypothesis or scientific hypothesis, that is, the hypothesis that one hopes indirectly to substantiate by rejecting the *null hypothesis. Symbolized H_1 or H_a.

Residual The portion of the score on a *dependent variable *not* explained by *independent variables. The residual is the difference between the value observed and the value predicted by a *model such as a *regression equation or a *path model. It is sometimes assumed that unmeasured *residual variables could account for the unexplained parts of the dependent variable. See *error term.

R

Residualize To *control for or partial out.

Residualized on Said of the variable that was partialed out in a *semipartial correlation.

For example, the semipartial correlation symbolized by $r_{1(2.3)}$ means the correlation between 1 and 2 after 3 was partialed out of 2—or after 2 has been *residualized on* 3.

Residual SS In *regression analysis, the *sum of squares *not* explained by the *regression equation. Analogous to within-group SS in *analysis of variance.

Residual Term Another expression for *error term, that is, the difference between an observed score or value and the score or value predicted by a model.

Residual Variable In a *path analysis, an unmeasured variable; it is assumed to cause the part of the *variance in the *dependent variable that is not explained by the path model.

Resistant Statistics Measures less likely to be influenced by a few unusual, extreme values (*outliers) in a *distribution. Compare the *median (a resistant statistic) and the *mean in the following two distributions. Increasing the last number from 7 (the value in distribution *X*) to 77 (in distribution *Y*) does not affect the median at all; but it more than triples the mean.

	Median	*Mean*
X: 1, 2, 3, 4, 5, 6, 7	4	4
Y: 1, 2, 3, 4, 5, 6, 77	4	14

Respondent A person who answers questions in a survey or an interview.

Rho (a) A symbol for the *correlation coefficient for *population parameters; it corresponds to *Pearson's *r*, which is used for *sample statistics. (b) Symbol for *Spearman's (rank-order) correlation coefficient.

Rise The change in vertical distance between two points on a *regression line; it is used to calculate the *slope. See *run. For a graphic, see *slope.

Robust Said of a statistic that remains useful even when one (or more) of its *assumptions is violated.

For example, the **F* ratio is generally robust to violations of the assumption that *treatment groups have equal *variances.

Root A number that results in a given number when it is raised to a given *power. See *radical.

For example, 4 is the third root of 64, which means that $4^3 = 64$; also $\sqrt[3]{64} = 4$.

Rotated Factor See *factor rotation.

Rounding Expressing numbers in shorter, more convenient units.

For example, 13.834, 58.771, 61.213, and 97.098 could be rounded to 13.8, 58.8, 61.2, and 97.1.

Rounding Error An error made by *rounding numbers before performing operations on them (adding, subtracting, and so on).

The following table shows the number of bowls of soup served in a restaurant as well as the percentage of each kind. "Percent (A)" shows the percentage of each flavor rounded to the nearest whole percent; but, when totaled, this column adds up to 101%, a rounding error. To avoid that error, the restaurant owner would have to round to the nearest thousandth of a percent, as is done in "Percent (B)"—obviously, a silly level of precision in this case.

Bowls of Soup Served, November 16-23

Kind of Soup	*Number*	*Percent (A)*	*Percent (B)*
Bean	46	14	13.855
Vegetable	72	22	21.687
Chicken Noodle	99	30	29.819
Tomato	115	35	34.639
Total	332	101	100.000

Row Marginals The *frequency distribution of a variable shown across the rows of a *cross-tabulation.

For example, in the following table, the numbers printed in bold (under "All") are the row marginals.

Median Income of Full-Time Workers, by Sex and Age in Thousands of Dollars (1987)

	15-19	*20-24*	*25-34*	*35-44*	*45-54*	*55-64*	*65+*	*All*
Men	9.9	14.7	23.8	30.7	32.8	30.9	29.7	**26.7**
Women	9.4	12.9	17.6	19.9	19.1	17.8	19.2	**17.5**

***r*-squared** Another way of expressing "r^2."

***R*-Squared** Another way of expressing "R^2."

R

***r*-to-*Z* Transformation** A way of transforming a *Pearson's *r* correlation coefficient that enables the researcher to compute a *confidence interval and *confidence limits for it. By using an *r*-to-Z transformation, the researcher can determine the *statistical significance of a Pearson's *r*. Note that the "*Z*" is not a **z*-score or standard score. Also called *Fisher's *Z*.

Rule In statistics and mathematics, as in other areas of conduct, a rule is a statement that tells us what to do.

For example, $A = B \times C$ tells us that, to find A, multiply B times C.

Run The change in horizontal distance between two points on a *regression line. To get the *slope, divide the run into the *rise. See *slope for a graphic illustration.

Running Average See *moving average.

Running Median A way of *smoothing a line composed of *medians. The techniques are analogous to those used for *moving averages; and the purpose is the same, to make a trend clearer by reducing the visibility of fluctuations.

S

Sample A group of *subjects selected from a larger group in the hope that studying this smaller group (the sample) will reveal important things about the larger group (the *population).

Sample Distribution A term sometimes used to refer to a *distribution of scores on a *variable in a *sample; an ordered array of the measurements or scores of a *sample of subjects. Not to be confused with a *sampl*ing* distribution.

For example, if the surgeon general were to conduct a study of the birth weights of children, a sample of all the live births in a given time period could be taken; the weights could be recorded and arranged in order, probably from heaviest to lightest, to facilitate study. This ordered arrangement would be the sample distribution and could be used, among other things, to calculate the relative frequencies of different weights.

Sample Point In *set theory, any member of the *sample space. Also called *elementary event.

Sample Space A list of all the possible *samples of a given size that can be drawn from a particular *population. More formally, in *probability theory, a group of *data points (*elementary events) including all possible outcomes of an *experiment. See *underlying distribution.

For example, when talking about the probability of drawing particular cards from a deck, the deck of cards is the sample space. It contains all possible outcomes of any drawing.

Sampling Distribution (of a Statistic) A *theoretical* *frequency distribution of the scores for or values of a *variable (or a *statistic such as a *mean). Any statistic that can be computed on a sample has a sampling distribution.

A sampling distribution is constructed by *assuming* that an infinite number of samples of a given size have been drawn from a particular population and that their distributions have been recorded. *Then* the statistic, such as the mean, is computed for the scores of each of these hypothetical samples; *then* this infinite number of statistics is arranged in a distribution to arrive at the sampling distribution. The sampling distribution is compared with the actual *sample statistic to determine if that statistic is or is not likely to be the way it is due to chance. (Note: Be sure not to confuse the sampl*ing* distribution with a *sample distribution.)

It is hard to overestimate the importance of sampling distributions of statistics. The entire process of *inferential statistics (by which we move from known information about samples to inferences about *populations) depends on sampling distributions. We use sampling distributions to calculate the probability that sample statistics could be due to chance and thus to decide whether something that is true of a sample statistic is also likely to be true of a population parameter.

S

Sampling Error The inaccuracies in inferences about a *population that come about because researchers have taken a *sample rather than studied the entire population. In other words, sampling error is the difference between a population *parameter and a sample *statistic used to estimate that parameter. Sampling error is one kind of *random error. See *sampling variability.

For example, to find out how many students at a particular college cheated in their schoolwork in the past year, you might survey 200 (a sample) of them. Suppose you found that 28% said they had cheated. If your sampling procedure were a good one, 28% would probably be close to what you would have obtained had you surveyed all the students at the college. But your figure is likely to be off, say, as much as 3% one way or the other; that would mean that the true figure is somewhere between 25% and 31%. The sampling error is that plus-or-minus 3%.

Note that there are many other ways, in addition to sampling error, that your figure of 28% could be wrong. Your questions could have been poorly worded or students could have lied about whether or not they cheated, for example.

Sampling Fraction The size of a *sample as a percentage of the *population from which it was drawn; the *ratio of sample size to population size.

For example, a sample of 1,000 of the residents drawn from a town with a total population of 5,000 would yield a sampling fraction of 20%

or one fifth (1,000/5,000). A sample of the same size in a city of a million, however, would result in a sampling fraction of only one tenth of one percent (1,000/1,000,000 = .001 = .1%).

Sampling Frame A list or other record of the *population from which the *sampling units are drawn.

For example, suppose you wanted to select a sample of all the students at a university. If you picked every 25th name listed in the student telephone directory, the directory would be your sampling frame.

Note that a sampling frame might not include all members of the *population of interest (in fact, it almost never does). In the current example, some students do not have telephones. Others enrolled after the directory was published; they are part of the population, but they are not in the sampling frame. Other students have graduated since the directory appeared; they are in the sampling frame but are not part of the population.

Sampling Units Items from a *population selected for inclusion in a *sample. Compare *unit of analysis.

For example, if the population were all the North American cities with populations over 5,000, and the sample were 200 such cities, they would be the sampling units.

Sampling Variability (a) Differences in a *statistic when it is computed on two or more *samples drawn from the same *population. (b) Differences between a statistic computed for a particular sample and that statistic computed for the population. See *sampling error.

Sampling With (or Without) Replacement When drawing a sample from a *population, one can replace or not replace subjects into the *sampling space after each draw. Many statistical procedures *assume* sampling with replacement, and this is the preferred method when possible. For practical reasons, however, most samples actually used in the social and behavioral sciences are drawn without replacement. When the population or sample space is very large, this violation of statistical assumptions is usually not serious.

For example, if you drew cards (sampled) one at a time from a deck and recorded the suit of each, you could replace the card and reshuffle after each draw or not do so. The procedure matters. If you got a diamond on the first draw, replaced it, and reshuffled, your chances of getting a diamond (*with* replacement) would be the same on the second draw as they were on the first (13 out of 52, or 25%). But, *without* replacement after the first draw, there would be one less card in the deck (the diamond). That would reduce your chances of drawing a diamond on the second draw (to 12 out of 51, or 23.5%).

When sampling with replacement, each draw of the cards (event) is *independent of every other draw. When sampling without replacement, each draw is *conditional on the previous draws.

SAS Statistical Analysis System. A widely used *statistical package for data analysis in the social and behavioral sciences. Compare *SPSS, *BMDP.

Scalar (a) Like or pertaining to a *scale. Said of questionnaire items that can be arranged in a definite logical order. See *Guttman scale. (b) The opposite of *vector, as in "scalar multiplication."

Scale A group of related measures of a *variable. The items in a scale are arranged in some order of intensity or importance. A scale differs from an *index in that the items in an index need not be in a particular order, and each item usually has the same weight or importance.

For examples, see the *Bogardus, *Guttman, *Likert, and *Thurstone scales.

Note that many writers do not distinguish between a scale and an index as is done here. It is fairly common to use the terms "scale" and "index" interchangeably to refer to any composite measure or *summated scale.

Scale of Measurement Another term for *level of measurement.

Scaling The process of creating a *scale by putting a group of related items into a logical sequence.

Scatter Diagram See *scatter plot.

Scatter Plot Also called "scatter diagram" and "scattergram." The pattern of points that results from plotting two *variables on a graph. Each point or dot represents one *subject or *unit of analysis and is formed by the intersection of the values of the two variables.

The pattern of the points indicates the strength and direction of the *correlation between the two variables. The more the points tend to cluster around a straight line, the stronger the relation (the higher the correlation). If the line around which the points tend to cluster runs from lower left to upper right, the relation is *positive (or direct); if it runs from upper right to lower left, the relation is *negative (or inverse). If the dots are scattered randomly throughout the grid, there is no relationship between the two variables.

For example, say we went to a busy street corner and asked the first 25 adult males who passed by to tell us their height and weight. If we recorded what they told us on a piece of graph paper, the results might look something like the following.

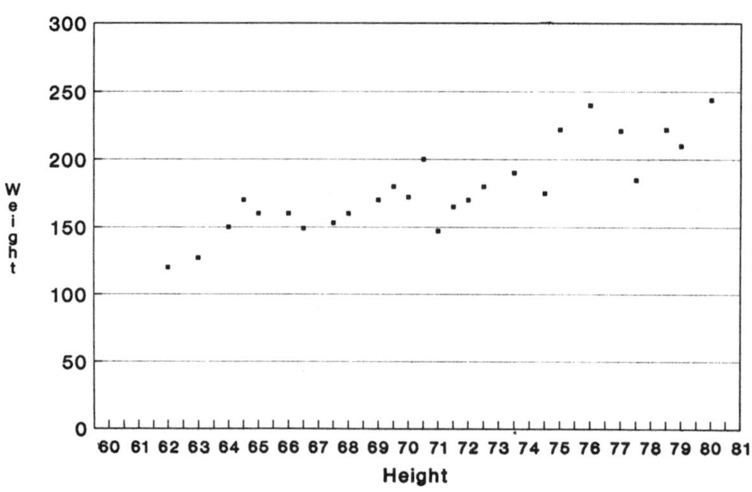

r = .86

Scatter Plot

Scedasticity The degree to which the values of a *dependent variable are scattered or dispersed across the values of an *independent variable. The question that analysis of scedasticity tries to answer is this: As the values of the independent variable change, does the degree of *dispersion in the dependent variable's values remain uniform? See *heteroscedasticity, *homoscedasticity.

Scenario An assumed or imagined sequence of events used to make decisions and contingency plans about future actions or events—often by contrasting two or more scenarios. Compare *decision table, *model.

Schedule See *interview schedule.

Scheffé Test A test of *statistical significance used for *post hoc multiple comparisons after a *regression analysis or an ANOVA. Among its main features are that it is a conservative test (it tends to err on the side of underestimating significance) and that it deals well with unequal *cell sizes.

Schema (plural: schemata) Generally, a diagram, plan, or framework. In cognitive psychology, philosophy of science, and related fields, a system for codifying concepts, experience, and data that organizes the way we perceive, learn, and remember. Compare *paradigm.

Science Most generally, the discovery, creation, accumulation, and refinement of knowledge. There are many controversies about what science is and about which disciplines, specialties within disciplines, and methods are "truly" scientific. See *epistemology, *paradigm.

Scientific Hypothesis Another term for *alternative hypothesis. Also called "research hypothesis." Compare *null hypothesis.

Scientific Significance Another term for *substantive significance. Often contrasted with *statistical significance.

Scientism A term used to belittle or dismiss theories and people who to tend to treat science as a religion or an ideology.

For example, those who believe that science is the highest human value, that it can solve all real problems, and that it is superior to any other form of knowledge or belief are likely to be accused of scientism. Compare *positivism.

Scope Conditions The specifications or limitations on the applicability or *validity of a *theory and its *propositions. Scope conditions indicate the circumstances (such as times, places, kinds of subjects) under which a theory's propositions would hold true.

SD Abbreviation for *standard deviation. Also written: Sd or sd.

SE Acronym for *standard error, often *standard error of the mean.

Secondary Analysis A type of research in which *data collected by others are reanalyzed. In some fields (sociology is one, psychology isn't), secondary analysis may be the most common form of research.

Examples of extensive and widely used data *archives available for secondary analysis include the U.S. Census *Public Use Microdata Samples (PUMS), the *National Election Study (NES) of the Inter-University Consortium for Political and Social Research, and the *General Social Survey (GSS) of the National Opinion Research Center (NORC).

Secondary Source A source that provides nonoriginal ("secondhand") data or information. Compare *primary source.

For example, if you wanted to study the City Council, you could interview its members and attend its meetings, or you could read newspaper articles by a reporter who had interviewed the members and attended their meetings. In the latter case, you would be relying on a secondary source—you would not have obtained the information firsthand.

Second-Order Factor Analysis A method of studying *correlations among factors so as to find factors that lay behind factors. See *factor analysis.

Second-Order Partial Said of a *correlation or *regression coefficient. Second order means that two variables are controlled. See *higher order partials.

Secular Trend A long-term trend or one of indefinite length, usually as opposed to a short-term fluctuation. Compare *time-series data.

Segmented Bar Chart A bar chart in which each of the bars is made up of two or more parts ("segments"). This allows one to use a bar chart for comparisons both of wholes and their constituent parts.

The following example shows the number of deaths per 100,000 attributable to heart disease for selected years for men and women.

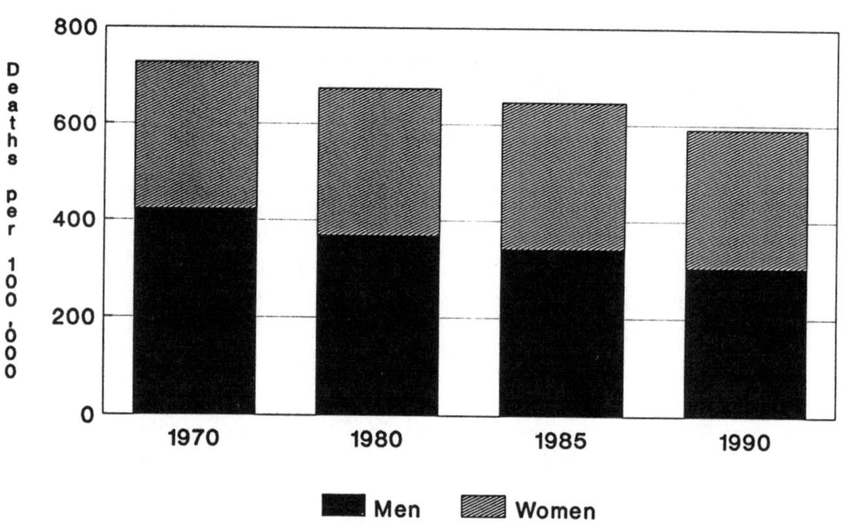

Segmented Bar Chart

Selection Effect See *self-selection bias.

Selection Threat See *self-selection bias.

Self-Fulfilling Prophecy Something that happens because people expect it to happen. (The term was coined by Robert K. Merton.)

For example, suppose account holders believed that Billy-Bob Savings and Loan was about to go bankrupt because depositors would soon be withdrawing all their money. If enough depositors predicted this, it could happen—even if B-B S&L were a financially sound institution.

Self-Selection Bias Also called "selection threat (to validity)" and "self-selection effect." A problem that may arise in the comparison of groups when the groups are formed by individuals who choose to join them and thus are not formed by a researcher assigning subjects to *control and *experimental groups.

For example, comparing the effects on academic achievement of attending two-year colleges versus attending four-year colleges would be difficult because (among other reasons) students who chose to attend two-year colleges might be different in important ways (e.g., goals, income, motivation, aptitude) from those who selected four-year colleges.

S

Semantic Differential Scale A question format in an interview or a survey in which *respondents are asked to locate their attitudes on a scale ranging between opposite positions on a particular issue (described by bipolar adjectives), as in the following. The subject circles a number from 1 to 7 for each scale.

My Boss Is								
fair	1	2	3	4	5	6	7	unfair
passive	1	2	3	4	5	6	7	active
lazy	1	2	3	4	5	6	7	hardworking
efficient	1	2	3	4	5	6	7	inefficient

Semi-Interquartile Range The *interquartile range (IQR) divided by 2. Also called *quartile deviation.

Semilogarithmic Ruling Said of graph paper using *logarithmic ruling on only one *axis (usually the vertical or *y* axis). See *logarithm.

Such graph paper is commonly used for *time-series studies to compare trends for two sets of data.

For example, in the following figure, the population growth of New York City and the United States are graphed on the same piece of paper, something that would be impossible on graph paper with ordinary ruling.

POPULATIONS OF NEW YORK CITY AND THE UNITED STATES

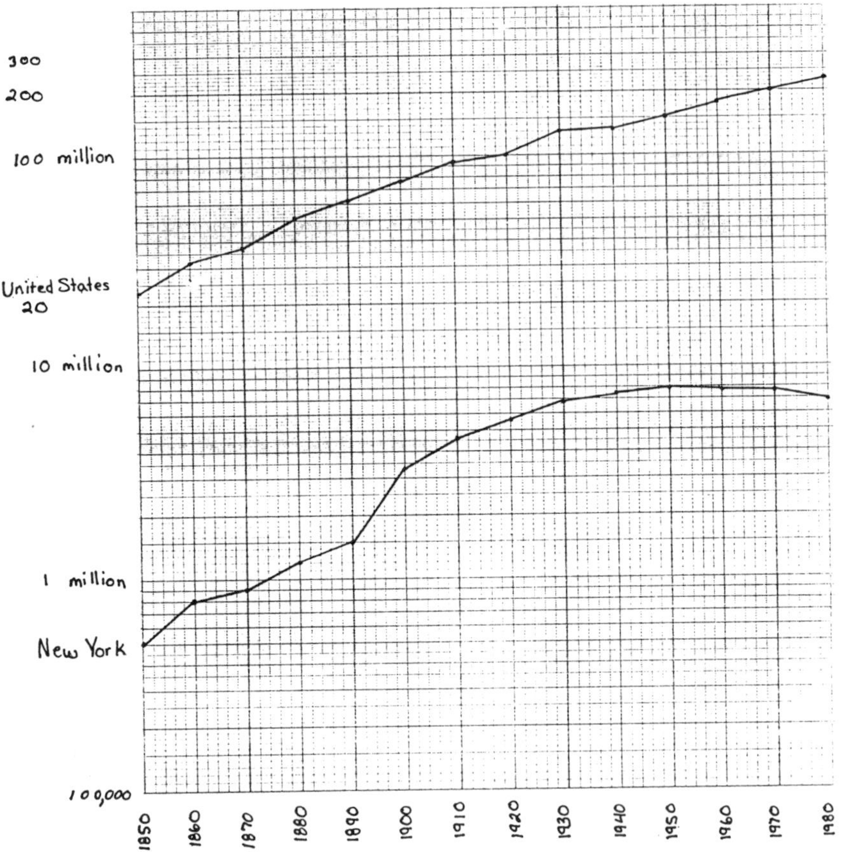

Semilogarithmic Ruling

Semiology The study of signs and their meanings. A branch of linguistics and linguistic philosophy that some theorists believe has great promise as a model of how to study several aspects of human thought and action.

Semipartial Correlation A correlation that partials out (*controls for) a variable, but only from one of the other variables being correlated.

Also called "part correlation." See *partial correlation, which partials out a variable from all other variables.

The formal notation may be of help in grasping this tricky notion. The correlation expressed $r_{1(2.3)}$ means: the correlation between variables 1 and 2 after 3 has been partialed out from 2 but not from 1.

Sequential Analysis A kind of investigation in which researchers decide as they go along (through periodic analyses of the data gathered up to that point) how much more and what kinds of data should be gathered next. Compare *negative case analysis, *post hoc comparison.

Sequential Sampling Observations made until enough data have been gathered to make a decision. This contrasts with the more typical procedure of deciding on the number of observations (or sample size) before beginning the study. Compare *Pascal distribution.

Serial Correlation Another term for *autocorrelation.

SES An acronym for *socioeconomic status.

Set A well-defined group of things. Events, objects, or numbers that are distinguishable from all other events, objects, or numbers on the basis of some specific characteristic or rule.

Examples of sets include all even numbers (those that are exactly divisible by 2); all murders (intentional illegal killings of persons, as opposed to all other forms of death); all female physicians (contrasted with male physicians and/or females who are not physicians). Compare *sample space.

Set-Theoretic Model An application of *set theory to the analysis of data.

Set Theory A branch of logic and mathematics that deals with the characteristics of and relations among *sets.

Sigma (a) The uppercase sigma usually means "sum of" and is thus an indication that the numbers following are to be (or have been) added together. (b) Lowercase sigma is often used to symbolize the *standard deviation of a *population. (c) Lowercase sigma squared means population *variance.

Signal Detection Theory (SDT) The theory that the detection of a signal, such as a sound, depends on sensory input and a decision process about whether and what one has heard. It is interesting for methodology because of the parallels between the decision process of the subject in SDT and of the researcher in *hypothesis testing.

The following matrix shows the possible outcomes in a signal detection experiment. Compare this with the similar illustration of hypothesis testing.

		Subject's Decision About Signal	
		YES	NO
Actual Presence of Signal	YES	Hit	Miss
	NO	False Alarm	Correct Rejection

Significance The degree to which a research finding is meaningful or important. See *practical significance, *substantive significance, *significance testing, *statistical significance.

Significance Level The *probability of making a *Type I Error. The lower the probability, the higher the *statistical significance. Also called *alpha level.

S

Significance Testing Using statistical tests (such as *chi-square, **t* test, or **F* test) to determine how likely it is that observed characteristics of *samples have occurred by chance alone in the *populations from which the samples were selected. If the observed characteristics in the samples are unlikely to be due to chance alone, the characteristics are deemed statistically significant.

Sign Test The simplest and oldest of all *nonparametric statistical tests. So called because the statistic is computed from data in the form of plus and minus (+ and –) signs.

For example, in a two-group experiment, the researcher could simply assign a + to each case where the score in Group A was higher than that in Group B and a – when the reverse was true.

Simple Classical Probability Probabilistic statements about a *sample space whose *elementary events are all equally likely to occur. See simple *random sample.

For example, the sample space of an evenly balanced coin contains the two elementary events "heads" and "tails." Making statements about the likelihood of getting a particular ratio of heads and tails in a given number of tosses would be an exercise in simple classical probability.

Simple Correlation A *correlation between two variables only or a correlation that describes a *linear relationship. Usually used in contrast with a *multiple correlation or with a *nonlinear relation—both of which are more complex than a simple correlation.

Simple Random Sampling See *random sampling.

Simple Regression A form of *regression analysis in which the values of a *dependent variable are attributed to (are a function of) a single *independent variable. Usually contrasted with *multiple regression analysis in which two or more independent variables are used to explain one dependent variable.

Simulation See *computer simulation.

Simultaneous Equations A problem in *regression analysis that occurs when a variable can be both a cause and an effect. Alternatives to *least-squares methods must be used when the direction of causation is unclear or when some variables are believed to be both cause and effect of others. If we thought that X caused Y *and* that Y caused X, to understand the whole, we would need to look at two equations simultaneously, one for how X caused Y and one for how Y caused X. Matrix methods have been developed to handle such problems.

For example, if the number of crimes in a community goes up, the number of police may tend to be increased. But, as the number of police goes up, the number of crimes may tend to decrease. Or, to take a second example, a drop in the level of rainfall can lead to the spread of the desert, which can lead to further declines in rainfall. In both cases, we would need to use simultaneous equations for a regression analysis.

Skewed Distribution A distribution of scores or measures that, when plotted on a graph, produce a nonsymmetrical curve. In a unimodal skewed *frequency distribution, the *mode, *mean, and *median are different. When the skewness of a group of values is zero, their distribution is symmetrical.

A positively (or upward or right) skewed distribution is one in which the infrequent scores are on the high or right side of the *x axis. A left (or downward or negatively skewed) distribution is one in which the rare values are on the low or left side of the x axis. Compare *normal distribution, *kurtosis. One way to sort out which is which is to remember that a skewer is a pointy thing; when the pointy end of the distribution is on the right, it is right skewed, and the converse, for left skewed.

Skewness Said of measures or scores that are bunched on one side of a *central tendency and trail out (become pointy, like a skewer) on the other. The more skewness in a *distribution, the more *variability in the scores. See *skewed distribution for illustrations.

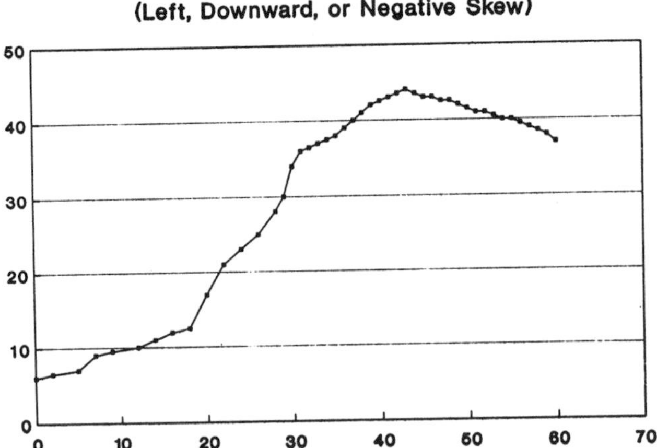

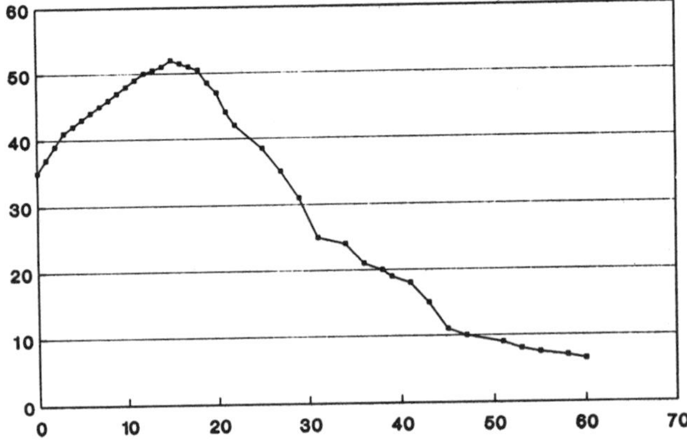

Skewed Distribution

S

Sleeper Effect Originally used in mass communications theory to refer to a delayed reaction to propaganda or other message. More generally, the term can be used to mean any effect that becomes apparent only after the passage of time.

Slope Generally, the rate at which a line or curve rises or falls when covering a given horizontal distance. The most common reference is to the steepness or angle of a *regression line, usually symbolized by the letter *b* in a *regression equation. The slope is calculated by taking any two points on the line and dividing the vertical distance (the "rise") between them by the horizontal distance (the "run") between them.

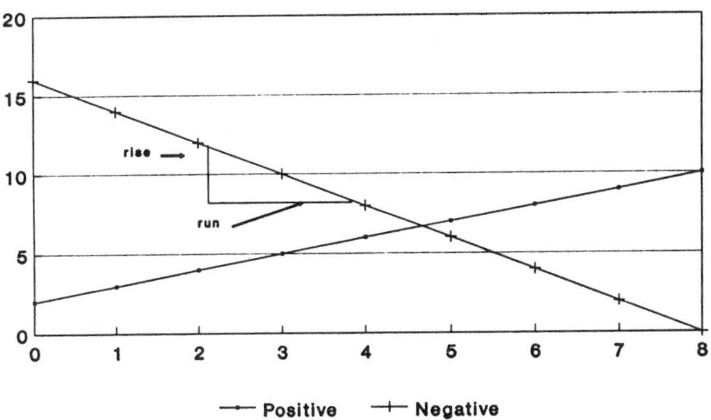

Slope

In a *positive or *direct relationship, the line slopes upward from left to right (see the illustration on the following page). In a *negative or *inverse relation, it goes down from left to right (called negative because the slope "*b*" is a negative number).

Slope Analysis Another term for *regression analysis, so called because it focuses on the angle or slope of a *regression line.

Smoothing Reducing irregularities (*fluctuations) in *time-series data, generally by using a *moving average. This is done to make long-term trends more apparent. See *ARIMA and *moving average for an illustration.

SMSA Acronym for *Standard Metropolitan Statistical Area.

Snowball Sampling A technique for finding research subjects. One subject gives the researcher the name of another subject, who in turn provides the name of a third, and so on. This is an especially useful technique when the researcher wants to survey or interview people with unusual characteristics who are likely to know one another—vegetarians, for example.

Social Capital Productive resources that are a result of individuals' social relations. In a word, "connections."

Social Desirability Bias Bias in the results of interviews or surveys that comes from subjects trying to answer questions as a "good" person "should" rather than in a way that reveals what they actually believe or feel.

For example, if you asked people, "Are you a racist?" most people would probably say "No." Hardly anyone thinks it is acceptable (socially desirable) to admit to being a racist, including people who are racists, at least by some definitions.

Social Indicators *Statistics describing *variables that reflect social conditions, that is, that "indicate" something about the nature and quality of life in a society. The term is used by the U.S. Census Bureau as well as other researchers.

Examples of social indicators include per capita income, average life expectancy, median years of education, and infant mortality rate.

Social Sciences Any of several areas of study that focus on human interaction and culture including sociology, economics, psychology, anthropology, political science, history, and some aspects of geography.

Social Stratification (a) The relatively permanent rankings of social groups (*social classes or strata) in a society. (b) The system of the unequal distribution of the things people in a society value. (c) A subdiscipline of sociology that studies inequalities in social ranks.

S

Socioeconomic Status Any one of several composite measures of social rank usually including income, education, and occupational prestige. Abbreviated: SES. Most SES measures omit power, which, although important, is difficult to measure.

Sociogram Also called "sociograph." A graphic representation of the relations among individuals in a group—constructed on the basis of some *sociometric measure.

For example, the answers to the question, "Who would you most like to work with?" for six people (see the example under *sociometric matrix) could be graphed as follows:

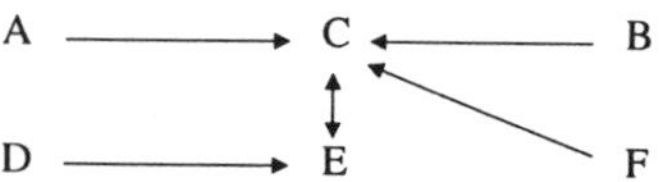

Sociometric Matrix A rectangular arrangement of *sociometric measures. Compare *sociogram.

For example, suppose that a manager asked the six members of one of her production departments two questions: "Which member of your group would you most like to work closely with on a special project over the next year? Which one would you least like to work closely with?" Answers could be useful in planning work assignments.

The results might look like those in the following matrix. 1 = "most like to work with" and −1 = "least like to work with." The matrix can be read vertically (by columns) or horizontally (by rows). Reading horizontally, we see, for example, that A would most like to work with C and least like to work with B. Reading vertically, it becomes clear that A's choices are fairly typical. Most people choose C for "most like to" and most choose B for "least like to"; no one has strong feelings, one way or the other, about A or F, and so on.

	A	*B*	*C*	*D*	*E*	*F*
A	x	−1	1			
B		x	1		−1	
C			x	−1	1	
D		−1		x	1	
E		−1	1		x	
F			1		−1	x

Sociometric Measure Any of several ways to find out about the existence and the strength of relationships among individuals in a group.

For example, grade school students might be given a *questionnaire with items such as these: "Who is your best friend in the class? Who do you play with at recess?" Alternatively, similar *data could be gathered more slowly, but perhaps yielding results of greater *validity, by observing with whom children play at recess, and so on.

Sociometry Any of a number of methods of gathering data on the attractions, repulsions, interactions, communications, and choices of individuals in groups. See *sociogram, *sociometric measure, *sociometric matrix.

Software Instructions, or *programs, that tell a computer how to perform tasks. Software is often contrasted with *hardware, which refers to the physical computer itself.

Word-processing, spreadsheet, and graphics programs are examples of software.

Somers's *d* An *asymmetric *measure of association for variables measured on an *ordinal scale.

Span The difference between the lowest and highest values in a distribution of values. Also called *range.

Spearman-Brown Formula A formula used to predict the approximate gain in the *reliability with which something could be measured if one increased the number of observations.

Spearman's Correlation Coefficient (rho) A statistic that shows the degree of *monotonic relationship between two *variables that are arranged in rank order, that is, that are measured on an *ordinal scale. The abbreviation for Spearman's correlation for a sample is r_S. See *correlation coefficient, *Pearson's correlation coefficient, *Kendall's tau.

For example, suppose you wanted to see if there was a relationship between knowledge of the political system and age (to see if older or younger people were better informed). You could begin by taking a *sample of the adult population and giving them a test of political knowledge. One approach to analyzing the data you collected would be to rank the subjects twice: from youngest to oldest and from worst score on the test to best. You could then use the Spearman statistic to see if there was a relationship between the two rankings.

Specification The act of stating the propositions of a theory or model, of saying (specifying) that a relation exists and indicating under what conditions it will be larger or smaller. See *specification error.

Specification Error A mistake committed when deciding upon (specifying) the *causal model in a *regression analysis. The two most common such errors are (1) leaving an important variable out of the causal model and (2) including an irrelevant variable.

It can be very difficult to tell when such an error has been made because much of the purpose of regression analysis is to decide which variables are important and which are irrelevant. In other words, you have to know which variables are important, and include them in the model, to determine whether they are important. See *paradox of inquiry.

Specification Problem The problem of how to decide (how to specify) which variables to include and which to exclude in a *regression equation. See *specification error.

Split-Half Reliability A way to check the *internal consistency (or *reliability) of an *index by seeing how well the scores on one half of the items *correlate with those on the other half.

For example, suppose you had eight items on a questionnaire that you thought added up to a measure (or index) of racial prejudice. You could check the internal consistency of your index by seeing if respondents answered the odd-numbered questions in the same way as the even-numbered questions. If there was not a strong correlation between the levels of prejudice as measured by the two halves, your index would not be very reliable, probably because it was measuring more than one thing.

Spread Another term for *dispersion, or the *variability of a group of values or scores.

Spreadsheet A *computer program that arranges *data and *formulas in a *matrix of *cells. Originally developed for accounting problems. Lotus 1-2-3 and Quattro are popular brands of spreadsheets.

SPSS An acronym for Statistical Package for the Social Sciences, a widely used brand of computer *software that allows researchers to have computers do most standard statistical analyses of their data. Compare *SAS, *BMDP.

Spurious Relation (or Correlation) (a) A situation in which measures of two or more *variables are statistically related (they *covary) but are not in fact causally linked—usually because the statistical relation is caused by a third variable. When the effects of the third variable are removed, they are said to have been *partialed out. See *confound, *lurking variable.

(b) A spurious correlation, as defined in definition a, is sometimes called an "illusory correlation." In that case, "spurious" is then reserved for the special case in which a correlation is not present in the original observations but is produced by the way the data are handled. Compare *artifact.

For example, (a) if the students in a psychology class who had long hair got higher scores on the midterm than those who had short hair, there would be a correlation between hair length and test scores. Not many people, however, would believe that there was a causal link and that, for example, students who wished to improve their grades should let their hair grow. The real cause might be gender: that is, women (who usually have longer hair) did better on the test. Or that might be a spurious relationship too. The real cause might be class rank: Seniors did better on the test than sophomores and juniors, and, in this class, the women (who also had longer hair) were mostly seniors, whereas the men (with shorter hair) were mostly sophomores and juniors.

SRC Survey Research Center. Located at the University of Michigan, this organization is best known for its *National Election Study (NES). See *archive, *secondary analysis.

SS Sum of squares, that is, the sum of the squared deviations of scores from the *mean. For an illustration, see *sum of squares.

SSE Sum of squared errors. See *error or *residual.

Stack Processing See *first in-last out (FILO).

Standard Deviation A *statistic that shows the *spread or *dispersion of scores in a distribution of scores; in other words, a measure of *dispersion. The more widely the scores are spread out, the larger the standard deviation. The standard deviation is calculated by taking the square root of the *variance. It is symbolized as SD or as an s or as a lowercase sigma. See *sum of squares for an illustration.

For example, say two classes took the same statistics examination. In the first, the scores ranged from 31 to 99; in the second, they ranged from 81 to 92. The standard deviation would be larger for the scores of the first class than the second.

Standard Error Often short for *standard error of the mean or *standard error of estimate. The smaller the standard error, the better the *sample statistic is as an estimate of the *population parameter—at least under most conditions. The standard error is a measure of *sampling error; it refers to error in our estimates due to random fluctuations in our samples. The standard error is the *standard deviation of the *sampling distribution of a statistic.

S

Standard Error of Estimate The "estimate" is a *regression line. The "error" is how much you are off when using the regression line to predict particular scores. The "standard error" is the *standard deviation of those errors from the regression line. The standard error of estimate is thus a measure of the *variability of the errors. It measures the average error over the entire *scatter plot. The lower the standard error of estimate, the higher the degree of linear relationship between the two variables in the regression. The larger the standard error, the less confidence one can put in the estimate. Symbolized: s_{yx} to distinguish it from s (i.e., the standard deviation of the scores—not the error scores).

Standard Error of the Mean A statistic indicating how greatly the *mean score of a single *sample is likely to differ from the mean score of a *population. It is the *standard deviation of a *sampling distribution of the means. The standard error of the mean indicates how much the sample mean differs from the *expected value (which is the mean of the sampling distribution of the means). By so doing, it gives an answer to the question: How good an estimate of the population mean is the sample mean? Compare *sampling error.

Standardization of Data Turning individual observations or data points into *z-scores, or *standard scores. This is sometimes done prior to conducting a *principal components analysis.

Standardized Measure or Scale Any common measure that allows comparisons between things measured on different scales or using different *metrics. The best known is a percentage; others include *percentile ranks, *standard deviations, and *z-scores.

Standardized Regression Coefficient A statistic that provides a way to compare the relative importance of different variables in a *multiple regression analysis. Often symbolized as beta and called the *beta weight or *beta coefficient (not to be confused with the "beta" used to symbolize Type II Error). Also called standard partial regression coefficient (the term "partial" indicates that the effects of other variables have been *held constant). See *regression coefficient, *standard score, *z-score.

Standardized Test A *norm-referenced test such as the Scholastic Aptitude Test (SAT) or the Graduate Record Examination (GRE). As in any norm-referenced test, an individual's grade is a measure of how well he or she did in comparison with a large group of prior test takers; that prior group was used to determine the norm, that is, it is the group upon which the test has been "standardized."

Standard Metropolitan Statistical Area A U.S. census category designating an area made up of a central city of 50,000 or more residents and the region around the city economically tied to it. The term was first used in the 1960 census, when 212 such areas were identified. Compare *census tract.

Standard Normal Deviate Another term for *standard score or *z-score.

Standard Partial Regression Coefficient Another term for *standardized regression coefficient.

Standard Score A measure of relative standing in a group arrived at by transforming raw scores in a way that allows one to compare *raw scores from different *distributions. The most common standard score is the *z-score.

For example, suppose you are a student and you want to compare your scores on the final examinations in each of your five classes. This could be complicated, especially if each of the exams had a different number of questions and each of the classes enrolled a different number of students. You could convert your scores on each of your exams into standard scores. The higher your standard score for each class, the better you did in comparison with other students in that class. The examination with the highest of the five standard scores would be the one on which you did best.

Statistic A number that describes some characteristic of (the "status" of) a *variable or of a group of *data—such as a *mean or a *correlation coefficient.

Strictly speaking, statistics are used to describe *samples and are usually abbreviated or symbolized by English (Roman) letters. *Parameters are equivalent measures for *populations and are abbreviated or symbolized by Greek letters. In common usage, "statistics" is used for both samples and parameters.

Statistical Conclusion Validity The accuracy of conclusions about *covariation made on the basis of statistical evidence. More specifically, inferences about whether it is reasonable to conclude that covariation exists—given a particular *alpha level and given the *variances obtained in the study. See *validity, *statistical significance.

Statistical Control Using statistical techniques to isolate or subtract *variance in the *dependent variable attributable to variables that are not the subject of study. See *control for, *partial out, *ANCOVA.

Statistical Independence A state in which there is no measured relation between two or more *variables. So called because the statistic describing one variable is independent of (has no relationship with) a statistic describing another variable or variables. See *orthogonal relationship.

Statistical Inference Using *probability and information about a *sample to draw conclusions ("inferences") about a *population or about how likely it is that a result could have been obtained by chance. Sometimes called "statistical induction." See *sampling distribution, *external validity, *internal validity.

The same basic statistical concepts are used whether the research is on a representative sample of 1,500 adults surveyed about their attitudes toward political candidates or whether the research is about memory under three different experimental conditions tested on a group of 90 undergraduates. In the latter case, however, the investigators would put much more emphasis on internal than on external validity; that is, they would be more interested in establishing differences among the treatments than in directly generalizing the findings to a broader population.

Statistical Package A type of *software that is a collection of *programs for doing statistical procedures with a computer. *SPSS and *SAS are among the more widely used statistical packages in the social and behavioral sciences.

Statistical Power A gauge of the sensitivity of a *statistical test, that is, its ability to detect effects of a specific size, given the particular *variances and *sample sizes of the study. See also *power of a test.

Statistical Regression A tendency for those who score high on any measure to get somewhat lower scores on a subsequent measure of the same thing—or, conversely, for someone who has scored very low on some measure to get a somewhat higher score the next time the same thing is measured. Also called "regression to the mean" because the second score is likely to move toward or be closer to the mean or average score. Compare *regression, *regression analysis, *regression artifact.

For example, someone who got 150 on one version of an IQ test would be more likely to get a score of 149 or lower than a score of 151 or higher when taking a second version of the test. (This assumes that the *population mean is 100 or, at any rate, less than 150.)

Statistical Significance Said of a value or measure of a variable when it is ("significantly") larger or smaller than would be expected by chance alone. Compare *level of significance, *probability level, *practical significance, *substantive significance.

It is important to remember that statistical significance does not necessarily imply substantive or practical significance. A large sample size very often leads to results that are statistically significant, even when they might be otherwise quite inconsequential.

S

Statistical Test Another term for *test statistic, that is, any of several tests of the statistical significance of findings.

Statistics (a) Numerical summaries of data obtained by measurement and computation. (b) The branch of mathematics dealing with the collection and analysis of numerical data.

Statistics, Descriptive See *descriptive statistics.

Statistics, Inferential See *inferential statistics.

Statistics, Probability Techniques for calculating the likelihood (*probability) that particular events will occur.

Probability statistics are the bridge from *descriptive statistics about *samples to *inferential statistics about *populations. After calculating a descriptive statistic for a sample, one then calculates the probability that this statistic could have been obtained by chance alone. If that probability is low, then one can reasonably infer that what is true of the sample is probably true of the population as well. See *sampling distribution, *statistical inference.

Stem-and-Leaf Display A way of recording the values of a *variable, created by John Tukey, that presents *raw numbers in a visual, *histogramlike display.

For example, if 40 students took a final examination in a course, their scores could be shown as in the following stem-and-leaf display. To represent the scores 56, 57, and 59, you put a 5 in the 10s column and a 6, a 7, and a 9 in the 1s column, and so on with the rest of the scores. The display makes it clear that most students scored in the 80s, not many in the 50s and 60s, and so on. The main advantage of a stem-and-leaf display is that it yields a clear picture of the frequency distribution, but, unlike most graphic representations, it loses none of the numerical data.

Stem-and-Leaf Display of Final Examination Scores

Stem (10s)	*Leaves (1s)* *(Leaf Unit = 1)*
9	22236778
8	11233334444567799
7	4466688
6	35559
5	679

Step Function A graph of a *cumulative distribution function of a *discrete variable.

The graph in the following example shows that 10% percent of the students got Fs. Another 10% got Ds, which, when added to the Fs, is 20%; so the line above D is drawn at the 20% mark. And 20% got Cs, which added to the first two scores is 40%, and so on.

Final Examination Grades (cumulative)

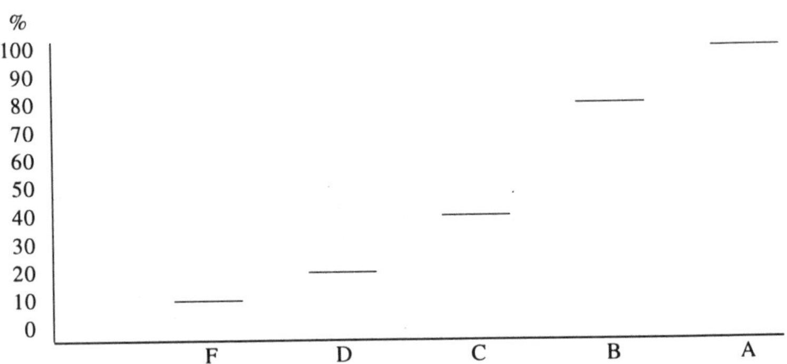

Stepwise Regression A technique for calculating a *regression equation that instructs a computer to find the "best" equation by entering *independent variables in various combinations and orders. Stepwise regression combines the methods of *backward elimination and *forward selection. The variables are in turn subject first to the inclusion criteria of forward selection and then to the exclusion procedures of backward elimination. Variables are selected and eliminated until there are none left that meet the criteria for removal.

Stochastic Said of a *model that is *probabilistic and contains *random elements—as opposed to a *deterministic model. Also used to refer to trial-and-error procedures—in contrast to *algorithmic procedures. (The term is from the Greek for "skillful in guessing" or "aiming at a target," *stoa*.) See *noise.

Stochastic Models Attempts to describe the structure of *systematic and *unsystematic error in a set of observations. Compare *ARIMA.

Stochastic Process When the *probabilities of the occurrence of an event change over time—particularly when the empirical probability approaches the theoretical probability—this is referred to as a stochastic process. See *Markov chain.

Stratified Nonrandom Sample See *quota sample. Compare *stratified random sampling.

Stratified Random Sampling Random or *probability samples drawn from particular categories (or "strata") of the population being studied. The method works best when the individuals within the strata are highly similar to one another and different from individuals in other strata. Indeed, if the strata were not different from one another, there would be no point in stratifying. Stratified random sampling can be proportionate, so that the size of the strata correspond to the size of the groups in the population. It can also be disproportionate, as in the following example.

Suppose a researcher wanted to compare the attitudes of Protestants, Catholics, and Jews in a population in which those three groups were not present in equal numbers. If the researcher drew a *simple random sample, she or he might not get enough cases from one of the groups to make meaningful comparisons. To avoid this problem, the researcher could select random samples of equal size *within* each of the three religious groups (strata).

Stratified Sampling Short for *stratified random sampling.

Stratifying Dividing a *population into groups or "strata" before doing research on it. See *stratified random sampling.

Stratum (plural: strata) A subgroup of a *population. Such groups are used, for example, in *stratified random sampling.

Strength of Association The degree of relationship between two (or more) variables; often the proportion of the *variability in a *dependent variable explained by or accounted for by the *independent variable(s). *Eta squared and *omega squared are two common measures of strength of association. Compare *coefficient of determination, measure of *association.

Structural Coefficients Another term for unstandardized *path coefficients.

Structural Equation An *equation representing the strength and nature of the hypothesized relations among (the "structure" of) sets of *variables in a *theory. See *analysis of covariance structures.

S

Structural Equation Models Models made up of more than one structural equation; thus models that describe causal relations among *latent variables and include coefficients for *endogenous variables. Compare *LISREL.

Structural Functionalism See *functionalism.

Structure Any underlying stable pattern among *variables in a system, such as a social, economic, political, or cognitive system.

Structure Coefficient A ratio of the *zero-order correlation, r, to the multiple *R in a *regression equation. In short, the structure coefficient for a particular *independent variable is its r with the *dependent variable divided by the R for the whole multiple regression equation. The structure coefficient is widely used in *discriminant analysis to determine the nature of the dimensions on which the groups are differentiated. Also called a *loading, because this is how *factor loadings are calculated in a *factor analysis.

Structured Q Sorts See *Q sorts, *Q methodology.

Student's *t* Distributions A family of theoretical *probability distributions used in *hypothesis testing. As with *normal distributions, t distributions are unimodal, symmetrical, and bell shaped. Called Student's t because the author of the article that made the distribution well known (W. S. Gossett) used the pen name "Student."

The t distribution is especially important for interpreting data gathered on small samples when the population *variance is unknown. The larger the sample, the more closely the *t* approximates the normal distribution. For samples greater than 120, they are practically equivalent.

Subject An individual who is studied so as to gather *data for a study. The "individual" is often a person, but it need not be; individual cities, occupations, small businesses, white mice, and so on can also be subjects. Compare *unit of analysis.

Subjective Methods Any approach to the analysis and evaluation of data based on the researcher's feelings or intuitions about the topic being studied. More often than not, the term is used pejoratively and contrasted with scientific methods.

Subjective Phenomenon Something that can only be learned from a *subject; hence something that is dependent upon a subject's perceptions and self-reports and not upon information that can be observed directly by someone other than the subject.

For example, the answer to the question, "Do you like high fiber breakfast cereals?" seeks subjective information. On the other hand, "Do you eat such cereals?" seeks *objective information; there may be ways for a researcher to check the answer if he or she doubts the accuracy of the subject's response.

Subject Matching See *matched pairs.

Subscript A number or letter written below and to the right of a symbol to distinguish it from the same symbol with a different subscript.

For example, the number of cases in group 1 and group 2 might be written N_1 for group 1 and N_2 for group 2.

Subset A *set contained within another set.

For example, if every *element in one set, accounting majors (A), is also an element of another set, human beings (H), then A is a subset of H.

Substantive Hypothesis Like any hypothesis, a substantive hypothesis is a conjecture about the relation between two or more variables. It is called "substantive" because it has not yet been *operationalized and also to distinguish it from the kind of statistical hypothesis used in *hypothesis testing. See *null hypothesis.

For example, " 'Poor' people have fewer 'life chances,' " is a substantive hypothesis. To test it, we would need operational definitions of "poor" and "life chances." Perhaps we would use having an annual income less than half of the median for "poor" and average life expectancy for "life chances." We would then need to put the hypothesis into statistical form, perhaps as follows: The mean life expectancy for poor persons (MLP) is less than the mean life expectancy for nonpoor persons (MLNP), or MLP < MLNP.

Substantive Significance Said of a research finding when it reveals something meaningful about the object of study. Often used in contrast with *statistical significance, which is present when a finding is unlikely to be due to chance alone. Of course, a result that is not statistically significant is usually not substantively significant.

For example, suppose one took large random samples of police officers in California and in New York. Comparing some of the data, one finds that the mean weight of CA officers is 173 pounds, while that of NY officers is 177 pounds. If the sample were large and representative, even this small difference would be unlikely to be due to chance, or *sampling error, alone; it would be statistically significant. But it would be hard to find someone who thought that the 4-pound difference in weight told us anything substantively significant about law enforcement officers in the two states.

Success In *probability experiments, when an event happens as predicted. The term "success" is usually applied arbitrarily to one of two ways a *Bernoulli trial can turn out. "Success" might be drawing a red card; "*failure" would then be drawing a black card.

Sufficient Condition In *causal analysis, a *variable that, by itself, is always enough ("sufficient") to bring about a change in another variable. There are few, if any, sufficient conditions in the social and behavioral sciences. Compare *necessary condition.

Summated Scale An attitude *scale or *index made up of several survey or questionnaire items measuring the same variable. The responses are given numbers in such a way that responses can be added up ("summated").

For example, say we have a five-item attitude index about government responsibility made up of questions in the following form: "The government in Washington should see to it that women and minorities do not experience job discrimination; strongly agree = 4, agree = 3, disagree = 2, strongly disagree = 1." Each respondent's answers can be added up ("summated") to arrive at a single number that measures the positive or negative strength of his or her attitude. On a five-item index using the above numbers, the highest possible score would be 20—strongly agree (4) with all five statements: $4 \times 5 = 20$; the lowest would be 5—strongly disagree (1) with all 5: $1 \times 5 = 5$.

Summative Evaluation *Evaluation research conducted in the latter stages of a program to assess its impact or to determine how well it has met its goals. Often undertaken to help outside policymakers decide whether to continue, expand, reduce, or terminate a program's funding. Compare *formative evaluation.

Sum of Squared Errors In a *regression analysis, what you are trying to minimize when you use the *ordinary least-squares criterion. The *errors in question are the vertical distances of the observed scores from the *regression line (or predicted scores). Also called the sum of squared *residuals.

Sum of Squares The result of adding together the squares of *deviation scores. Often abbreviated "SS." *Analysis of variance is in fact analysis of sums of squares. See *between and *regression sum of squares. Not to be confused (as it often is when doing calculations) with the "square of the sum," that is, all the scores first added together to get a sum, which is then squared.

For example, the following table lists the scores on a test, calculates the *mean, subtracts the mean from each score, squares each of those results, and adds up (sums) these numbers. It is an example of a within-group sum of squares. Computing the sum of squares is often a step on the way to calculating the *variance and the *standard deviation. The variance is found by dividing the sum of squares by the number of scores minus 1 (238 divided by 6 = 39.67 in this example) and the standard deviation is calculated by taking the square root of the variance (which equals 6.3 in this example).

Scores	*Minus Mean*		*Deviation Score*	*Deviation Score Squared*
88	−80	=	8	64
86	−80	=	6	36
84	−80	=	4	16
80	−80	=	0	0
77	−80	=	−3	9
73	−80	=	−7	49
72	−80	=	−8	64
560				**238** (sum of squares)
560/7 = 80 (mean)				

Superscript A number or letter written above and to the right of a symbol to denote its *power.

For example, the 3 in 8^3 is a superscript and means 8 times 8 times 8 (which equals 512).

Suppressor Effect See *suppressor variable.

Suppressor Variable A variable that obscures or conceals (suppresses) a relationship between other variables. It is an *independent variable that is unrelated to the *dependent variable but is correlated with one or more of the other independent variables. Removing the suppressor variable from the study eliminates irrelevant variance and thus raises the correlation between the remaining independent variables and the dependent variable. Compare *confound.

For example, suppose we wanted to test candidates for the job of Forest Ranger. Let's say we're sure that a good Forest Ranger must know quite a lot of botany; we also know that differences in verbal ability will have no effect on the Forest Ranger's job performance. We devise a written botany test to help us pick good Forest Rangers. But, because the test is written, candidates with stronger verbal ability will tend to get higher scores, even if their knowledge of botany is no greater.

In this somewhat fanciful example, verbal ability is the suppressor variable. It gets in the way of studying what we are interested in (knowledge of botany and rangers' job competencies). We could try to *control for or *partial out verbal ability to get rid of its effects, but that is rarely done in practice.

Survey A research *design in which a *sample of subjects is drawn from a *population and studied (usually interviewed) to make inferences about the population. This design is often contrasted with the *true experiment in which subjects are randomly assigned to *conditions or *treatments. See *control group, *experimental group, *random sample, *random assignment.

Survival Analysis A variety of *event history analysis in which there are a limited number of states or conditions. Survival analysis focuses on how long subjects persist in a state ("survive"). It has been used in medical research to study the duration of illnesses, in demography to study life expectancy, in organizational studies to analyze the survival of small businesses, and so on.

Syllogism A pattern of formal *deductive argument that contains a major premise, a minor premise, and a conclusion. If (but only if) the two premises are true, the conclusion necessarily (logically) follows. For example:

Major Premise: All undergraduates like statistics.
Minor Premise: Mary is an undergraduate.
Conclusion: Mary likes statistics.

Symbolic Logic A branch of logic that uses formal symbols, rather than ordinary language, to express its concepts. The purpose is to avoid the ambiguities of ordinary, informal language.

Symmetric Measure A *statistic that has the same value regardless of which *variable is thought of as *dependent and which is *independent. See *asymmetric measure.

*Pearson's *r* and *Kendall's tau are examples of symmetric measures.

Synchronic Said of research focusing on events that occurred at the same time. Usually contrasted with *diachronic. Compare *cross-sectional study.

Synthesis Combining parts (such as *data, *concepts, *theories, and so on) to make a new whole. Sometimes contrasted with *analysis, which involves disassembling wholes to study their parts. In practice, analysis is often a step on the way to synthesis.

For example, suppose we wished to calculate an average (*mean) income figure for citizens of all South American nations. Because nations report aggregate national income figures somewhat differently (some include transfer payments and others not), we might have to *disaggregate the figures. We could then *analyze* the parts that went into making up the whole reported by each nation. After we had analyzed the reports of each nation, we could perhaps figure out a way to synthesize them into a new more general report about all the nations.

Systematic Error Measurement error that is consistent, not random. See *bias. Compare *random error. Also called "invalidity." See *validity, *ARIMA.

For example, say you recorded the temperature at noon every day in your backyard. If your thermometer was wrongly calibrated so that it was always 4 degrees high, the faulty thermometer would produce a systematic error (an upward bias) in your measurements.

Systematic Sample A sample obtained by taking every "*n*th" subject or case from a list containing the total *population (or *sampling frame). The size of the *n* is calculated by dividing the desired sample size into the population size.

For example, if you wanted to draw a systematic sample of 1,000 individuals from a telephone directory containing 100,000 names, you would divide 1,000 into 100,000 to get 100; hence you would select every 100th name from the directory. You would start with a randomly selected number between 1 and 100, say 47, and then select the 147th name, the 247th, the 347th, and so on.

It is always possible to do a simple random sample in cases where one can do a systematic sample (both require a complete list of the population). Because simple random sampling is a more trustworthy method, it is usually more effective than systematic sampling.

Systematic Variance Variance due to a cause that always influences values in one direction. Compare *bias, *cause, *systematic error.

Systems Theory An approach or perspective in several disciplines that emphasizes studying the interrelations of the parts of a whole (the system) more than studying components in isolation from their position in an organization.

Table of Random Numbers See *random numbers.

Target Group The group about which a researcher wishes to draw conclusions; another term for a *population about which one "aims" to make inferences.

Tau See *Kendall's tau.

T

Tautology A statement that is needlessly repetitive; or a statement that involves *circular reasoning.

Tchebechev's Inequality A method for calculating the maximum *probability of a particular score in a *distribution of scores. Although it is important in statistical theory, it has few practical uses because it can be quite imprecise.

***t* Distribution** See *Student's *t* distribution.

Term A part of an *equation. For example, in a *regression equation, the *error term, *e*, is added to the other values in the equation.

Test-Retest Reliability A *correlation between scores on two administrations of a test given to the same subjects. A high correlation indicates high reliability. Subtracting the correlation from 1 $(1 - r)$ gives you an estimate of *random error.

Test Statistics (a) Statistics used to test a finding for *statistical significance—not to describe a *sample or to estimate a *population parameter. The **t* test, *chi-square statistic, and **F* ratio are examples of test statistics. They test hypotheses about sample statistics but provide no information about the samples. (b) Statistics about tests and test items, such as statistical aspects of their *validity and *reliability. See *standardized test.

Tetrachoric Correlation A correlation between two *continuous variables that have been *collapsed to dichotomies. Symbolized: r_{tet}. It gives an estimate of what *Pearson's correlation would have been had the variables not been collapsed.

Before the availability of computers to do the grunt work, r_{tet} was frequently used for quick estimates of Pearson's r. It remains useful today mainly for data containing many gaps and errors, such as imperfect historical records. (To use the r_{tet}, the researcher must assume that the underlying data are bivariately normally distributed.)

Theorem (a) A statement or formula in mathematics or logic deduced from other statements or formulas. (b) An idea accepted or proposed as a clear truth, often as part of a general theory. Compare *assumption, *axiom, *postulate.

Theoretical Probability Distribution See *probability distribution, definition b.

T

Theory A statement or group of statements about how some part of the world works—frequently explaining relations among phenomena. While theory is usually distinguished from practice in ordinary language, Kurt Lewin's oft-quoted phrase nicely captures the belief of most researchers: "There is nothing so practical as a good theory." Compare *hypothesis, *realism.

Theory Trimming In *path analysis, deleting paths whose *coefficients are not *statistically significant.

Threats to Validity Ways of coming to false conclusions. The term was introduced by Campbell and Stanley to refer to the characteristics of various research methods and designs that can lead to spurious or misleading conclusions.

Discussions of threats to validity often lead researchers to recommend using more than one method (see *triangulation). Because different kinds of research designs are open to different kinds of threats, one can reduce the risk of error by using two or more methods.

Thurstone Scaling (a) A method of *scale construction created by L. L. Thurstone in which judges assign weights or degrees of intensity to prospective scale items. The extent to which judges agree determines whether particular items are included in or discarded from the scale. The method is seldom used today, largely because it is slow, expensive, and no more *reliable than *Likert scales. (b) A method, pioneered by Thurstone, of assessing the difficulty of items on a test; it uses paired comparisons between groups taking the test, and it is still widely used.

Time Series A set of measures of a single *variable recorded periodically, over time, such as the annual rain fall in Miami from 1900 to the present.

Time-Series Analysis (a) Analysis of changes in variables over time; *multiple regression is sometimes used for this purpose, but *ARIMA models are more often employed. (b) Any of several statistical procedures used to tell whether a change in *time-series data is due to some variable that occurred at the same time or was due to coincidence. See *interrupted time-series analysis.

Time-Series Data Any data arranged in chronological order.

For example, the annual suicide rate in the United States from 1900 to the present would be time series data, as would the Dow-Jones daily averages for the past 18 months, as would the weekly spelling test scores of a class of sixth graders.

Tobit Analysis A technique in *regression analysis used when the *dependent variable may be either zero or any positive number. For this kind of dependent variable, the *ordinary least-squares criterion cannot be applied. Also known as the "censored regression model."

For example, say the research question is this: How much money will individuals spend on microcomputers this year? The answer will fit into one of two categories: for most individuals, the answer will be zero; for the rest, it will range widely from a few hundred to several thousand dollars.

Tolerance In addition to describing interpersonal relations, tolerance in the social and behavioral sciences also refers to an allowable margin of error in measurement. In some psychological studies, tolerance can mean the ability to withstand some potentially harmful *treatment.

Trait An enduring characteristic; it could be a physical characteristic, such as sex, or a psychological trait, such as shyness. Compare *attitude, which, in comparison with a trait, is learned and always has an external referent.

Trait-Treatment Interaction A *research design using *factorial ANOVA to determine whether there is an *interaction effect between *traits and *treatments, for example, whether a management effectiveness seminar has better results with women or men.

Transformation Changing all the values of a variable by using some mathematical operation. One common example is changing proportions into percents by multiplying them times 100. Another widespread practice is to use a transformation to reduce the complexity of a table reporting large numbers, as when one reports income in thousands of dollars (see example at *row marginals). In that case, the transformation is done by dividing each number by 1,000. See *linear and *nonlinear transformations for more examples.

Transpose A *matrix formed by interchanging the rows and columns (vectors) of another matrix. See *vector for an example.

Treatment In *experiments, a treatment is what researchers do to subjects in the *experimental group but not to those in the *control group. A treatment is thus an *independent variable. See *level, *condition.

Tree Diagram A way of depicting a series of possible events using "branches" to illustrate different outcomes. It is used in *probability calculations and *decision theory. See *decision tree.

For example, the diagram on the following page shows the six possible outcomes, and their *probabilities, of a two-out-of-three set tennis match between A and B. A's record shows that she wins .70 (70%) of the sets she plays; B's set winning rate is 30%. The most likely outcome is that A will win in two sets (.49). The least likely is that B will win the match after having lost a set (.063).

Trend Movement in one direction of the values of a variable over a period of time. See *secular trend and, for an example, *moving average. Compare *fluctuation.

Trend Line A line depicting a *trend. See *moving average and *ARIMA.

Triangulation Using more than one method to study the same thing. The term is loosely borrowed from trigonometry, where it refers to a method for calculating the distance to a point by looking at it from two other points.

For example, if you were interested in people's attitudes toward environmental issues, you could look at patterns of voting behaviors for environmental candidates and issues; or you could interview leaders of the Sierra Club, the Nature Conservancy, and similar groups; or you could conduct a survey of a representative sample of the entire population. Or you could do all three and put the results together, in which case you could say that you had used a research strategy of triangulation.

Trimmed Mean A measure of *central tendency that allows the researcher to deal separately with a *distribution's *outliers. It is a *mean

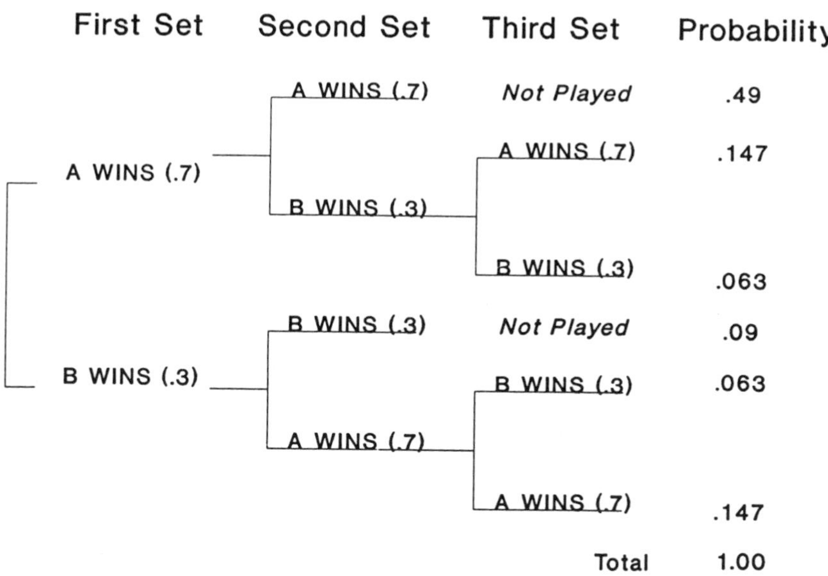

Tree Diagram

computed after the extreme observations have been trimmed off. See *theory trimming.

True Experiment An *experiment. "True" is contrasted with the methods of *quasi experiments and *natural experiments. The key distinction is that, unlike in other research designs, in a true experiment subjects are *randomly assigned to *treatment groups.

***T*-Score** (uppercase T) A way of expressing deviation from a *mean. The mean is scored 50, and one *standard deviation is scored 10. Thus a *T*-Score of 80 equals three standard deviations above the mean; a *T*-Score of 40 is one standard deviation below.

NOTE: Not to be confused with the *t* statistic (lowercase t), which is the basis of a **t* test.

***t* Statistic** The number that is tested in a **t* test, that is, the number that is compared with the *critical region.

***t* Test** A test of the *statistical significance of the results of a comparison between two group averages, or *means, such as the average score on a manual dexterity test of those who have and have not been given a caffeine drink. A *t* test is a *test statistic; *t* tests are also used to test the statistical significance of *correlation coefficients and *regression coefficients.

A *two-tailed *t* test is used to test the significance of a "nondirectional" hypothesis, that is, a hypothesis that says there is a difference between two averages without saying which of the two is bigger. A *one-tailed *t* test is called "directional" because it tests the hypothesis that one of the two group averages is bigger.

Tukey Line A *regression line based on *medians (rather than *means, as in the *least-squares criterion). It is more *resistant to *outliers than the ordinary least-squares regression line.

Tukey's Honestly Significant Difference Test Often abbreviated: Tukey's HSD. After conducting an *analysis of variance of the differences in group means, the researcher knows whether *some* group means are significantly different than the overall mean. To determine *which* means are significantly different, Tukey's HSD Test can be used.

For example, suppose 150 overweight subjects were randomly assigned (30 each) to five different weight-loss programs to see if there were any significant differences among the programs. At the end of 10 weeks, the average weight loss for each group was computed, and an ANOVA **F* ratio showed that the differences among the groups were statistically significant. To determine, however, which groups contributed most to those differences, that is, which programs were better and which worse, individual comparison tests such as Tukey's HSD would have to be conducted. See *omnibus test.

Two-by-Two Design Said of a research design with two *independent variables, each with two values. See **N*-by-*M* design.

The following two-by-two *factorial table shows the percentage of students passing a pass/fail examination given to male and female college sophomores and seniors.

	Percentage Passing Examination	
	Sophomores	*Seniors*
Men	40	62
Women	48	71

Two-Tailed Test of Significance A statistical test in which the *critical region (region of rejection of the *null hypothesis) is divided into two areas at the tails of the *sampling distribution. See *one-tailed test, *Type I Error, and **t* test for an example.

Two-Way ANOVA Two-way *analysis of variance is a way of studying the effects of *two independent variables separately (their *main effects) and together (their *interaction effect).

Type I Error An error made by wrongly rejecting a true *null hypothesis. This might involve incorrectly concluding that two variables are related when they are not or wrongly deciding that a sample statistic exceeds the value that would be expected by chance. Also called *alpha error. See *hypothesis testing.

Type I Error is often considered more serious and more important to avoid than *Type II Error. That is because researchers want to take only a small chance of saying that something is true when it isn't. It may be a more grave mistake to wrongly conclude, for example, that there is a significant difference between the effects Drug X and Drug Y (Type I Error) than it is to say there is no difference between the two when there really is one (Type II Error). One other way to put this slippery concept: It is often better to be wrong by false denial (Type II) than by false affirmation (Type I).

Type II Error An error made by wrongly accepting (or retaining or failing to reject) a false *null hypothesis. Also called *beta error. See *Type I Error.

Type I and Type II errors are inversely related; the smaller the risk of one, the greater the risk of the other. The probability of making a Type I Error can be precisely computed, but the exact probability of a Type II Error is generally unknown.

U

U Symbol for the *disturbance term in a *regression model. In *path analysis, the symbol for unanalyzed effects or unmeasured variables. It is composed both of the effects of *variables not included in the *model and the disturbance or *random error.

Unbalanced Designs Said of *factorial designs when there are unequal numbers of observations for different *factors or when the *cells contain unequal numbers of subjects. Also called "nonorthogonal factorial designs."

Unbiased Estimate A *sample statistic that is free from any systematic bias leading it to over- or underestimate the corresponding *population parameter.

Unbiased Sample Variance A method of computing the sample variance so that it is an *unbiased estimate of the *population variance.

Underidentified Model A *regression model or equation containing too many unknowns to be solved. See *identification problem.

Underlying Distribution The distribution of all possible outcomes of an *event.

For example, if the event is the result (sum) of a roll of two dice, there are 11 possible sums—2, 3, 4 . . . 12—distributed as in the following table. The table shows that there is one way to role a 2, 2 ways to roll a three, 6 ways to role a 7, and so on.

Underlying Distribution of the Sum of a Roll of Two Dice

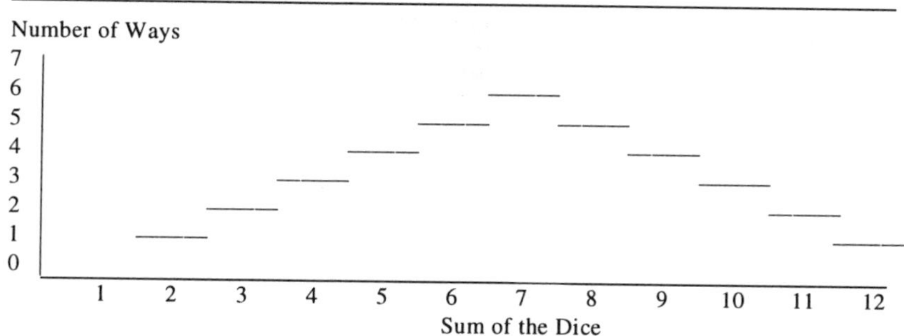

Unimodal Distribution A distribution with only one mode. Compare *bimodal.

Union In *set theory, a *set formed by including all of the *elements of two other sets. Symbolized: $\cup$.

Units of Analysis The persons or things being studied in a research work. Units of analysis in research in the social and behavioral sciences are often individual persons but may be groups, political parties, newspaper editorials, unions, hospitals, schools, monkeys, rats, reaction times, perceptions, and so on. A particular unit of analysis from which data are gathered is called a *case.

Univariate Analysis (a) Studying the distribution of *cases of one variable only—for example, studying the ages of welfare recipients but not considering their gender, ethnicity, and so on. Compare *multivariate analysis. (b) Occasionally used in *multiple regression analysis to mean a problem in which there is only one *dependent variable—a usage that contradicts the more common meaning in definition a.

Universal Constant See *E, definition c.

Universal Set All things to be considered in any one discussion. Usually symbolized by S (uppercase). In *sampling theory, the universal set is the *population.

Universe Another term for *population.

Unstandardized Score A score in the original *metric, one that has not been transformed into a *z-score or other standard score.

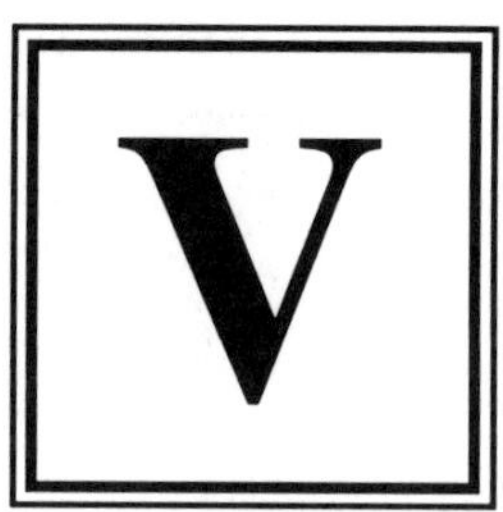

V

Validity A term to describe a measurement instrument or test that measures what it is supposed to measure; the extent to which a measure is free of *systematic error. See *internal, *external, *construct, and *face validity.

For example, say we want to measure individuals' heights. If all we had was a bathroom scale, we could ask our individuals to step on the scale and record the results. Even if the measurements were highly *reliable, that is, consistent from one weighing to the next, they would not be very valid. The weights wouldn't be completely useless, however, because there generally is some *correlation between height and weight. Although we do often have to try to get by with *proxy measures, there is no doubt that a yardstick would be more valid for measuring height than a scale.

Value-Free Said of science when researchers keep their personal values out of the collection and interpretation of evidence. As Max Weber pointed out long ago, value-free means that researchers place the values of science above their other values, not that they have no values. Contrast *value laden.

Value Laden Said of any research or theory that contains (is weighed down by) the values of the researcher or theorist. Often contrasted with *objective and *value-free.

Variability The *spread or *dispersion of scores in a group of scores; the tendency of each score to be unlike the others. More formally, the extent to which scores in a *distribution deviate from a *central tendency of the distribution, such as the *mean. The *standard deviation and the *variance are two of the most commonly used measures of variability.

For example, the following two distributions have the same mean (the total of each is 24, divided by 4 equals a mean of 6), but there is much more variability in *Y* (SD = 4.9) than in *X* (SD = 1.8).

X: 4, 5, 7, 8
Y: 1, 3, 8, 12

Variable Any finding (an attribute or characteristic) that can change, that can *vary,* or that can be expressed as more than one value or in *various* values or categories. The opposite of a variable is a constant.

For example, height: 5'7", 5'8", and so on; or religion: Catholic, Protestant, Jewish, Other; or experimental *treatment: Drug A, Drug B, Drug C. See *categorical, *continuous, *dependent, and *independent variables.

Variance A measure of the spread of scores in a *distribution of scores, that is, a *measure of dispersion. The larger the variance, the further the individual cases are from the *mean. The smaller the variance, the closer the individual scores are to the mean.

Specifically, the *population variance is the mean of the sum of the squared deviations from the mean score. The sample variance is computed by dividing the sum of squared deviations by the number in the sample minus 1. (See *sum of squares for an example.) Taking the square root of the variance gives you the *standard deviation.

Variance, Explained In *regression analysis, the variance in the *dependent variable that is associated with or accounted for by the independent variables. *R^2 is a common measure of the variance explained.

Variance Components Analysis Another term for *random effects model or *Model II ANOVA.

Variance of Estimate A measure of the degree of *variability of the points around a *regression line or surface. The square root of the variance of estimate is the *standard error of the estimate, that is, the standard deviation of the *residuals. The variance of estimate is also called the *mean square residual (MSR).

Variate (a) Another term for *variable. (b) Another term for *random variable. (c) Any specific value of a *variable, as 37 would be a variate of the variable "age." See *multivariate analysis, *univariate analysis, *covariate.

Variation Commonly used to mean the extent of the "variety" in a *variable, such as the spread of values in a *distribution of the values for a particular variable. It is also often used to refer loosely to any *measure of dispersion.

More formally, but less commonly, the "variation" is a step on the way to calculating other measures of dispersion, such as the *variance and the *standard deviation. This variation is the total of the squared deviations from the mean score (i.e., the *sum of squares). Because adding up all the squared deviations from the mean can produce a huge sum, the number is divided by the number of cases (minus 1 for a sample) to get the variance. One often takes the square root of the variance to get the standard deviation.

Variation, Coefficient of A measure used to compare the dispersion or variation in groups of scores. It is appropriate only for scores measured on a ratio scale. To obtain the coefficient of variation, one divides the *distribution's *standard deviation by its *mean. Compare *Gini coefficient.

Varimax A method of *orthogonal rotation of the axes in a *factor analysis.

Vector A column (or a row) of a *matrix, or a matrix with only one column or one row. A vector is a set of ordered values. Any particular value (e.g., 7 in the following example) is called an "element" of the vector. The number of elements in the vector is its "dimension," which in the example is 5; that is, there are 5 elements in vector ***b***.

$$\text{column vector } \boldsymbol{b} = \begin{pmatrix} 3 \\ 7 \\ 9 \\ 4 \\ 8 \end{pmatrix} \qquad \text{row vector } \boldsymbol{b}' = [3\ 7\ 9\ 4\ 8]$$

$\boldsymbol{b}'$ is the *transpose of ***b***.

Venn Diagram A type of graph using circles to represent variables (composed of sets of points) and their relationships. The rectangle represents the *universal set (*population) and the circles inside the rectangle are sets (variables). *Union and *intersection are represented by the circles' overlap.

Verstehen A German word meaning "understanding." It was used by Max Weber and Wilhelm Dilthey to refer to a method of interpreting social interaction that involves putting oneself in the place of another. Broadly, today, any method using empathic means of gaining insight into the motives or behavior of another, such as role-playing.

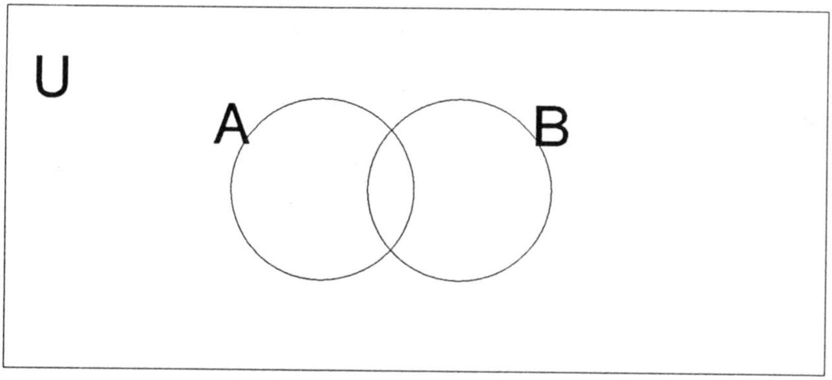

The rectangle U represents the "universe" of all the adults in a particular city. The circle A stands for all of the registered Republicans, and the circle B stands for the city's adult African Americans. The overlap of A and B indicates those African Americans who are registered members of the Republican Party.

Venn Diagram

Vital Statistics In reporting to the U.S. government, statistics about births, deaths, marriages, and divorces—so called because they have to do with life (*la vita*). Also used more loosely to include information about health and diseases.

W Symbol for the *Wilcoxon test of statistical significance and for *Kendall's coefficient of concordance.

Wave In a *panel or longitudinal study, when the same subjects are interviewed more than once, each session is called a wave.

Weighted Average (or Mean) A procedure for combining the means of two or more groups of different sizes; it takes the sizes of the groups into account when computing the overall or grand mean.

For example, say 239 students in Economics 201 took the midterm and you know the average grade of each of three groups: economics majors, economics minors, and others, as summarized in the following table. But you want to know the grand mean of all 239 students. You cannot just add up the three groups' mean grades and divide by three (which would give you an average of 83.2). So many more majors than minors and others took the test that you have to give their mean more weight to get the true overall average. To do so, for each group you multiply the mean (column B) by the number of people in the group (column A), add up the results, and divide by the total number of students who took the test: 21,228.4/239 = 88.8.

Group	*A* *Number*	*B* *Mean Grade*	*C* *A × B*
Majors	168	93.2	15,657.6
Minors	51	78.8	4,018.8
Others	20	77.6	1,552.0
Total	239		21,228.4

Weighted Data (a) Any information given different weights in calculations, as when the final examination counts twice as much as (is weighted double) the midterm. (b) Data whose values have been adjusted to reflect differences in the number of *population units that each *case represents. See disproportionate *stratified sampling, *weighted mean.

For example, suppose we want to generalize about the attitudes of all 75-year-olds. We have a *sample of 100 men and 100 women, all in their 75th year. We might want to give the women's attitudes more weight, because there are many more 75-year-old women than men and the goal is to generalize to the attitudes of all 75-year-olds.

Wilcoxon Test A *nonparametric test of *statistical significance for use with two *correlated samples, such as the same subjects on a before-and-after measure.

Wilks's Lambda A widely used *test statistic for equality of group means in *MANOVA and in other multivariate tests.

Within-Group Differences See *between-group differences.

Within-Subjects Design A before-and-after study. A research design that *pretests and *posttests within the same group of subjects, that is, uses no *control group. Compare *between-subjects design, *repeated measures design.

Within-Subjects Variable (or Factor) An *independent variable or factor for which each subject is measured at more than one *level or *condition. Compare *between-subjects variable. See *counterbalancing for an example.

***x* Axis** The horizontal axis on a graph. Also called *abscissa.

***X*-Bar** An uppercase *X* with a line over the top of it ($\bar{X}$); this is an often used symbol for the *mean of a *sample. The mean score for a *population is usually symbolized by the Greek letter, mu.

***X* Variable** The *independent variable (or cause), so called because, when graphed, it is plotted on the **x* axis (also called the abscissa or horizontal axis).

Y′ The predicted value of *Y* in a *regression equation. Also *Y* hat, $\hat{Y}$.

Yates's Correction (for Continuity) An adjustment in the computation of the *chi-square statistic to improve its accuracy for 2 × 2 tables, especially those with small cell values. "Continuity" refers to the fact that the correction is made because one is using a continuous distribution (chi square) to estimate a discrete distribution.

Yates's continuity correction is less widely used than it once was, largely because it apparently does not improve the estimate as much as once believed. Compare *Fisher's exact test.

***y* Axis** The vertical axis on a graph. Also called the *ordinate.

***Y* Intercept** The point where a *regression line intersects the **y* axis. Sometimes referred to simply as the *intercept. In a *regression equation, it is usually symbolized by the letter *a*.

Yule's Q A measure of the *covariation between two nominal variables measured on a two-point (dichotomous) scale.

***Y* Variable** The *dependent variable (or effect), so called because, when graphed, it is plotted on the **y* axis (also called the ordinate or vertical axis).

Y

Z

Z Uppercase Z, see *Fisher's Z. Lowercase z, see **z*-score.

Zero-Order Correlation A correlation between two *variables in which no additional variables have been *controlled for (or held constant or partialed out). A first-order correlation is one in which one variable has been controlled for; a second-order correlation controls for two; and so on. Zero-order associations are the opposite of those found by *multivariate analysis.

Zero-Sum Game Any game (or, more broadly, social situation) in which one player (or social actor) can gain *only* at the expense of another and in which one player gains exactly as much as another loses.

For example, if you and I were to play poker for money, it would be a zero-sum game; the only way you could win money would be for me to lose it, and vice versa. The term "zero sum" comes from the fact that, if you add my losses to your winnings, the result, or sum, is zero. Certain forms of social interaction (such as poker) are clearly zero-sum games; others (such as donating blood) may benefit both the giver and the receiver; and for others (such as affirmative action), the extent to which they are zero-sum situations is open to debate.

***z*-Score** (lowercase z) The most commonly used *standard score. In *z*-score notation, the mean is 0 and a standard deviation is 1. Thus a *z*-score of 1.25 is one and one-quarter standard deviations above the mean; a *z*-score of –2.0 is 2 standard deviations below the mean. *z*-scores are especially useful for comparing performance on several measures, each with a different mean and standard deviation.

For example, say you took two midterm exams. On the first, you got 90 right, on the second, 60. If you knew the *means and *standard deviations, you could compute *z*-scores for each of your exams to see the one on which one you did better. The procedure is to take your score, subtract from it the mean of all the scores, and divide the result by the standard deviation (in symbols $z = X - M/\text{Sd}$), where X is your score, M is the mean, and Sd is the standard deviation. Following are some figures to illustrate how comparisons can be made. In this example, you did better (ranked higher in the class) on your second midterm. Your score of 60 was 2 standard deviations above the mean; your 90 was only 1 Sd above.

First Midterm	*Second Midterm*
X = 90	X = 60
M = 80	M = 42
Sd = 10	Sd = 9
(90 – 80)/10 = 10/10 = 1	(60 – 42)/9 = 18/9 = 2

Suggestions for Further Reading

Readers wishing to consult statistics and methodology texts to supplement the information available in this dictionary have *many* works from which to choose. The following brief list focuses on books that are especially clearly written, and/or widely cited "classical" accounts, and/or representative of some of the many disciplines in which these methods are used.

The books are grouped by level of difficulty. The more elementary works, in group I, are basic enough that most readers can get through them on their own. Group II contains more advanced volumes that, while usually starting with the basics, move quickly to more difficult topics and pursue them in greater depth. Group III lists other dictionaries that contain methodological and statistical terms.

Special mention should be made of the Sage series "Quantitative Applications in the Social Sciences." Works in this series introduce readers to quite advanced topics in booklets of about 96 pages. By focusing on general concepts rather than proofs and derivations of formulas, the authors deal with their subjects at an advanced level without requiring the reader to have more than basic statistical knowledge.

I. Elementary Methodology and Statistics

Babbie, Earl. (1989). *The practice of social research* (5th ed.). Belmont, CA: Wadsworth.

Borg, Walter R., & Gall, Meredith D. (1983). *Educational research: An introduction* (4th ed.). New York: Longman.

Bowen, Bruce D., & Weisberg, Herbert F. (1980). *An introduction to data analysis.* San Francisco: Freeman.

Craft, John L. (1990). *Statistics and data analysis for social workers* (2nd ed.). Itasca, IL: F. E. Peacock.

Haskins, Loren, & Jeffrey, Kirk. (1990). *Understanding quantitative history*. Cambridge: MIT Press.

Jaeger, Richard M. (1990). *Statistics: A spectator sport* (2nd ed.). Newbury Park, CA: Sage.

Judd, Charles M., Smith, Eliot R., & Kidder, Louise R. (1991). *Research methods in social relations* (6th ed.). Fort Worth, TX: Holt, Rinehart & Winston.

McCall, Robert B. (1986). *Fundamental statistics for behavioral sciences* (4th ed.). New York: Harcourt Brace Jovanovich.

Slavin, Robert E. (1984). *Research methods in education: A practical guide*. Englewood Cliffs, NJ: Prentice-Hall.

II. More Advanced Methodology and Statistics

Blalock, Hubert M. (1979). *Social statistics* (rev. ed.). New York: McGraw-Hill.

Bohrnstedt, George W., & Knoke, David. (1988). *Statistics for social data analysis* (2nd ed.). Itasca, IL: F. E. Peacock.

Cook, Thomas D., & Campbell, Donald T. (1979). *Quasi-experimentation: Design and analysis for field settings*. Boston: Houghton Mifflin.

Edwards, Allen L. (1972). *Experimental design in psychological research* (4th ed.). New York: Holt, Rinehart & Winston.

Fisher, Ronald A. (1970). *Statistical methods for research workers* (14th ed.). New York: Hafner.

Fisher, Ronald A. (1971). *The design of experiments* (9th ed.). New York: Hafner.

Hays, William L. (1988). *Statistics* (4th ed.). Fort Worth, TX: Holt, Rinehart & Winston.

Keppel, Geoffrey, & Zedeck, Sheldon. (1989). *Data analysis for research designs*. New York: Freeman.

Kerlinger, Fred N. (1986). *Foundations of behavioral research* (3rd ed.). Fort Worth, TX: Holt, Rinehart & Winston.

Miller, Delbert C. (1991). *Handbook of research design and social measurement* (5th ed.). Newbury Park, CA: Sage.

Nunnally, J. (1978). *Psychometric theory* (2nd ed.). New York: McGraw-Hill.

Pedhazur, Elazar J. (1982). *Multiple regression in behavioral research: Explanation and prediction* (2nd ed.). Fort Worth, TX: Holt, Rinehart & Winston.

Tufte, Edward R. (1983). *The visual display of quantitative information*. Cheshire, CN: Graphic Press.

Tukey, John W. (1977). *Exploratory data analysis*. Reading, MA: Addison-Wesley.

III. Other Dictionaries and Reference Works

Andrews, Frank M., et al. (1981). *A guide for selecting statistical techniques for analyzing social science data* (2nd ed.). Ann Arbor, MI: Institute for Social Research.

Chaplin, J. P. (1985). *Dictionary of psychology* (2nd ed.). New York: Dell.

Daintith, J., & Nelson, R. D. (1989). *Dictionary of mathematics*. London: Penguin.

Darcy, L., & Boston, L. (1988). *Dictionary of computer terms* (3rd ed.). New York: Webster's New World.

Karush, William. (1989). *Dictionary of mathematics*. New York: Webster's New World.

Kendall, Maurice G., & Buckland, William R. (1982). *A dictionary of statistical terms* (4th ed.). London: Longman.

Scriven, Michael. (1991). *Evaluation thesaurus* (4th ed.). Newbury Park, CA: Sage.

Theodorson, George A., & Theodorson, Achilles G. (1969). *Modern dictionary of sociology*. New York: Crowell.

About the Author

W. Paul Vogt teaches the Sociology of Education and Research Methodology in the Department of Educational Administration and Policy Studies at the State University of New York at Albany, where he is Associate Professor. His articles have appeared in the *Journal of the History of the Behavioral Sciences, Revue Française de Sociologie, Review of Education, Knowledge and Society, History and Theory,* and other periodicals.